THE ECONOMY IN MIND

THE ECONOMY
IN MIND

Warren T. Brookes

Foreword by George Gilder

UNIVERSE BOOKS
New York

To our friend Ophelia

The writing of this book was sponsored by the Manhattan Institute for Policy Research.

Published in the United States of America in 1982
by Universe Books
381 Park Avenue South, New York, N.Y. 10016

82 83 84 85 86/10 9 8 7 6 5 4 3 2 1

Printed in the United States

Library of Congress Cataloging in Publicatic)ata

Brookes, Warren T.
   The economy in mind.
   Includes index.
   1. Supply-side economics. I. Title,
HB241.B76   1982   330.12'2   82-8335
ISBN 0-87663-413-7   AACR2

Contents

Foreword by George Gilder   7

Preface   11

1 The Unlimited Economy in Mind   17
The Energy of Mind vs. the Entropy of Matter 28

2 The Individual as Capital   37
The Need for New Blood 39 / A Tale of Two Cities 43 /
Coming Labor Shortages 46

3 What Is Progressive about Taxation?   50
The Laffer Curve 53 / The Mellon Tax Cuts 55 / The JFK
Tax Cuts 56 / The Capital-Gains Tax Experience 59 / The
Tax Wedge 63 / The Mounting Case for Fundamental Tax
Reform 68 / Real Wealth Cannot Be Redistributed 70 / The
Challenge of Ideological Myths 76

4 Inflation and the Crisis in Confidence   79
The Failure of Keynesianism 83 / The Death of the
Phillips Curve 83 / The Easy-Money Myth 86 / Inflation and
the Falling Dollar 88 / Behind the Gold Panic 93 / The
Golden-Oil Standard 95 / Inflation and the Money
Credit-Explosion 99 / Can We Ever Restore Sound Money?
103 / Inflation as a Moral Issue 105

5 Ideas vs. the Babel of Bureaucracy   107
The Seduction of Serfdom 116 / The Great GNP Con
Game 118 / The Dilution of Democracy 120 / Competition
in Government 123 / Can We Deregulate Washington? 124

6 The Ecology of the Free Market   129
Is Uncle Sam Becoming Aunt Liz? 129 / Auto Industry
Woes Started in Washington 133 / The Rental Housing
Crisis 135 / The Natural-Gas Fiasco 139 / But What About
Safety Regulations? 145 / OSHA Follies 146 / Technology
and Danger 148 / The Free Market in Jeopardy 151

7 Social Spending, Subsidies, and the Pursuit of Poverty 157
Rising Tide vs. Canal Locks 160 / The Compassion Trap
162 / The Message from Miami 164 / The Need for Real Jobs
166 / The Marginal Tax of Welfare 167 / Disincentives,
Disabilities, and Social Security 169 / Breaking the Subsidy
Mentality 172 / Protectionism 177

8 Massachusetts on the Laffer Curve 180
A Tale of Two States 184 / New Hampshire Cries All the
Way to the Bank 186 / Taxes vs. Employment 187 / Taxes
and Services 188 / Welfare State vs. Economic Growth and
Income 190 / Massachusetts's Federal Dependency 191 / The
Tax-Limitation Debate of 1978 192 / Proposition 13
Awakens Massachusetts Voters 193 / Proposition 2½ and the
Massachusetts Budget 197 / After Proposition 2½ 198 /
Climbing Down the Laffer Curve and up the Growth
Curve 200

9 Goodness and the GNP 203
Christianity and Capitalism 208 / God and the Welfare
State 210 / Capitalism and Healing Poverty 214 /
Government as God 218 / The Profit Motive Is Not Enough
220 / The Compassionate Capitalist 223 / Theology vs.
Entropy 224

Notes and Sources 227

Index 236

Foreword

Warren Brookes is the nation's best columnist on economics and society largely because he is the best educated. Not at Harvard, where in 1952 he graduated in economics and endured a memorable course on the corporation from John Kenneth Galbraith, but at Kimberly Clark, W. R. Grace, and Kenyon and Eckhardt, Inc. During a 20-year career in business he helped launch food and paper products, worked a technological revolution in the meat packing industry, and learned economics on the supply side.

Many economists are atheists who replace a belief in God with a belief in a strange metaphysical realm called *the economy*, imagined to transcend the mere doings and decisions of businessmen and consumers and to exist on a more elevated plane of abstractions. Economics becomes a realm of impalpable and often unintelligible concepts—such as M 2, aggregate demand, investment multipliers, Gini coefficients, and GNPs—accessible chiefly through faith in a revelation of numbers.

Although Brookes is a master of statistics, having employed them to good effect in both his business and journalistic careers, he is not so superstitious as to allow statistics to master him, or to confound his keen sense of practical reality. While a shrewd analyst of economic concepts, he never lets them distract him from the grit and serendipity, the inspiration and sweat, the papermaking and meat packing which constitute the substance of economic life.

From this vantage of simple facts, Brookes is able to expose fallacies in many of the abstract ideas which govern current economic analysis. He shows that even the hallowed statistics of capital formation and investment—the aggregations of expenditures on plant and equipment as a measure of the growth of productive assets in an economy—are often deeply misleading. Real productive capital, as he explains in practical detail, is less physical and arithmetical than metaphysical and conceptual; value has its roots in a society's values, more than in its so-called resources. Similarly, he demonstrates that even many so-called natural resources are in fact the product of industrial artifice; it was the internal combustion engine, for example, that gave value to oil, rather than the other way around. It was the semiconductor industry that made a treasure of the silicon in sand. And though the world of material resources is finite, as Brookes stresses, the resources of mind are essentially unlimited.

Equally misleading, Brookes says, is the widespread notion of money and aggregate demand as driving forces of economic growth. Years in business, on the supply side, have shown him that demand is chiefly a result of the resourceful and laborious operations of suppliers.

One of his achievements in business exemplifies the point. Working for Cryovac, by then a subsidiary of W. R. Grace, he came to believe that his company's product—a saran-type plastic packaging for frozen poultry—could also be used for fresh red meat. Meat could be efficiently processed into appropriate cuts and boxed at the slaughterhouse or packing plant rather than transported in whole carcasses and cut by retail butchers. A rationalization of meat packing and distribution that would permit huge efficiencies, this change was demanded by virtually no one but Brookes and a visionary product engineer at Cryovac. Least of all was it demanded by the established butchering and meat packing industries. Brookes and his co-workers had to reeducate the entire industry, and after a long period of slow progress, they succeeded. But as usual the demand came after the supply of the new product, not before.

Moreover, as Brookes observed, the crucial capital in this change was not money or machinery, or plant, or any other of the physical elements conventionally catalogued as investment. The crucial capital was a new idea, and no matter what funds were lavished on "reindustrializing" the previous system—whether for newer and more modern trucks, bigger storage space, more modern freezing and aging facilities—it could not compete with the capital saving and transforming concept from Cryovac.

Both from this experience and from observing the Massachusetts high technology firms, which are growing fastest and creating the most jobs—while showing very low levels of measured capital formation—Brookes now concludes that economists on both the right and the left are seriously misdiagnosing our so-called capital shortage. Low measured "capital" formation, he believes, may in part have become an index of capital-saving industrial progress as we move into the age of knowledge industries.

Confined to his home in the mid-1970s, he wrote a series of newspaper columns and dispatched them to the publisher of the *Boston Herald-American.* Their publication on successive Sundays evoked an unusually strong response and launched Brookes on an entirely new career as Boston's most influential newspaper columnist. After his key role in conceiving and promoting the tax-cutting Proposition 2½ movement, drastically reducing property taxes in Massachusetts, he became an important national figure. His column is now published two times weekly in some forty cities through both Hearst and the Heritage Features Syndicate and is reprinted frequently in a number of conservative magazines. The column is also read and quoted regularly in influential circles from *The Wall Street Journal* editorial page to the White House.

I have never met Warren Brookes, but his columns provided me a continual fount of inspiration and information, cited far more than any other source in *Wealth and Poverty*. When the ultimate history of the supply-side movement in America is written, Warren Brookes will be seen as playing a key role. But his ideas transcend the technicalities of economics to embrace a vision of the world, reaching from chemistry and cybernetics, practical engineering and marketing, on to the largest matters of political economy and even theology.

The Economy in Mind is a wise and luminous work by a major thinker.

George Gilder
Tyringham, Mass.
21 June 1982

Preface

This book is the work not of an economist but of a journalist. Given the present public esteem for economists, this may prove to be a modest asset.

As Martin Feldstein (one of the few economists who has been consistently right during the last decade) admits, "The economics profession has discovered a new humility as the economy's performance has worsened."

The dreadful failures, both in the United States and in Great Britain, of the more extreme redistributionist notions of Keynesian economics have proved a bitter vindication for its critics. Yet it is no satisfaction to have been right about the faulty economic policies our nation has followed. Had our own arguments and hypotheses been more thoroughly and carefully developed and more gracefully presented, we all need not have traversed the flawed course that we did. It is not essential to learn only by suffering, though we continue to do so.

With the nation now turning, however hesitantly, away from the socialist-populist notions of the 1970s, it is necessary for all economists, and for journalists who write about economics, to remain exceedingly humble even if some of us occasionally seem to be on the right side of the public debate for a change. The past year (1981–82) proves that Murphy's Law still lives in mortal experience. There is no utopia in matter, no perfection in imperfection, and, so far, no repeal of the Second Law of Thermodynamics. Even the most orderly economic plans can produce unexpected disorder.

Above all, we need to learn more of why the things we did in the 1970s worked out so badly, instead of simply taking satisfaction (or being pained) that they did. The most important search of human existence is always teleological and ontological–finding primary causes, instead of thrashing around with superficial effects.

It is not enough to gloat, "You see, the Keynesians were wrong; redistribution doesn't work; stimulation only produces inflation; government doesn't know how to manage the economy." We all need to understand better, and more profoundly, the underlying laws (both metaphysical and mathematical) of economic experience, so that we can cease this endless bickering over particular policies and get on with the evolutionary development of more successful designs, rather than indulge in reactionary swings to the right or left.

The underlying premise of this book is that most, if not all, of the economic mistakes we have made (and continue to make) over the last generation have resulted from a fundamental misconception about the real nature of substance or wealth, and that what is needed to generate sound economic policy is to gain a more correct understanding of what wealth really is and (perhaps more important) what it is not.

Since economic thought first became formalized over two centuries ago, there have been essentially two different views about wealth. One view, first defined by Adam Smith and Jean-Baptiste Say, is that wealth is primarily metaphysical, the result of ideas, imagination, innovation, and individual creativity, and is therefore, relatively speaking, unlimited, susceptible to great growth and development. The other, espoused by Thomas Malthus and Karl Marx, contends that wealth is essentially and primarily physical, and therefore ultimately finite. The modern presentation of this view argues that since usable energy is steadily diminishing into entropy, all wealth is really *cost* to be shared more equitably.

For the first group, it is only natural that their preoccupation is with the supply side of economic activity and the creation and generation of new wealth and productivity. Thus, their approach to economics tends to emphasize the individual, or "micro," aspects of economic policy and favors maximum economic freedom. After all, if wealth truly is metaphysical, the result more of mind than matter, "the wealth of nations" has to be seen as the direct result of the creative activity of individuals and the degree to which that activity is either liberated or restricted by governmental, trade, or societal structures and strictures.

For the second group, it is inevitable that their preoccupation is with the demand or distribution side of the economic process. If one believes that wealth is primarily a function of material resources, and is therefore limited (or declining), it is only natural that one would see the role of economic policy as the just and collective conservation, distribution, and redistribution of these limited resources until the end is reached. Marx's "From each according to his abilities, to each according to his needs" was perhaps the first demand-side economic statement, the taxing of supply for the fulfillment of demand, the transfer of physical wealth from one group to another, the "just" reallocation of fixed substance in a "zero-sum" economy.

It is not hard to determine where this book comes out on this issue. Its thesis is clear and, I hope, consistent: The primary and essential character of wealth is metaphysical, not physical, and is the direct result of the creativity of mind, not the availability of raw materials—the sum product of individual efforts, not the manipulated static resources of collective nations or governments or lands.

Ultimately, a human being is wealthy not because of what he has but because of what he knows. What he has, he can lose through disaster, obsolescence, taxation, or theft. What he knows, he can never lose unless he loses life itself. Thus, his real wealth is a characteristic of his thinking, not a measured amount on a bank ledger. In fact, our accounting systems are notoriously and increasingly inadequate in their measurement of the real wealth (and potential) of our economy.

For example, when America was drawn into World War II, its economy was weak, its unemployment was massively high at 17%, and its physical resources were immediately endangered by the loss of access to tin, rubber, and a host of other physical materials essential to a war machine. Yet the nation built, in an incredibly short time, the most sophisticated and productive economic apparatus in history to that point. Where it lacked material resources, it invented new ones. Where it lacked equipment and plant, it quickly built them. Where it lacked experience and understanding in warfare planning, it found them in the people's unified mental will to resist.

America went into World War II as one of the most depressed economies in the world and came out of it as the dominant world economic force. It had found within its metaphysical resources—namely its free people—the imagination, drive, talent, energies, ideas, and determination to overcome, to build, and to strengthen. The thinking of its people provided the capital it needed to win.

As we now move progressively into this so-called age of limits, and face the immense challenge of reindustrialization, it is increasingly clear that the need is not nearly so much for more physical plant but for more ideas, more invention, more mental energy, and more creativity than ever before. The most obvious physical resources of our nation and our planet seem to have been skimmed away, and we are now being asked to think that we have finally arrived at the Malthusian limits of economic growth.

Fortunately, most of America's economic growth is no longer coming from traditional sources, steel, autos, minerals, petroleum, or even chemicals (some of which are in serious decline). It is coming increasingly from high technology, from significant breakthroughs in cybernetics, genetics, life sciences, and a host of as yet only fractionally explored realms of human imagination. We are now, in many parts of our national economy, generating rapid growth and unaccounted new wealth, even as the actual use of raw materials and energy is declining. The necessity of conservation is producing the inventions that fulfill it.

The nation's massive computer and data-processing industry has been built, quite literally, on the creative use of previously useless silicon from sand. Biogenetics now promises plants that fertilize themselves and grains that need no pesticides. Solar-power development, still in its infancy, offers renewable energy for the millenniums, while the potential of fusion seems as vast as the oceans themselves, from which we have only begun to mine the rich resources of a new "mind-based" economy.

We are proving, at an increasing rate, that our wealth is not a function of the matter we can measure but of the ideas and inventions we cannot presently imagine and our accounting systems cannot measure. Elaborate equations chalked up on blackboards are each year becoming new companies with payrolls and new products with vast new markets.

Yet even in the face of this metaphysical explosion, much of the dominant economic thought over the past two decades has been steadily more Malthusian and Marxist, centered on the notion of the limited and even declining physical character of wealth, and preoccupied with government manipulation of distribution and demand and the allocation of scarcity. While the real economy has been growing daily more metaphysical, our economists and our accounting systems, it seems, have grown steadily more materialistic in their perspective.

Out of this increasingly finite and material view of substance (it seems to me) have come so many of the horrendous mistakes we have made in economic policy, from inflation (itself a product of the fallacy that money is wealth instead of merely a medium of exchange) to taxation and transfer as a means of redistributing wealth (as if real wealth could ever be found in government fiat money) to the crushing burden of statism and regulation that have so stifled the whole creative wealth-generating process.

It is the premise of this book that it is time for a nation which has proved repeatedly the essentially metaphysical and unlimited character of its real substance to give up those economic misconceptions and to trade in an economy based on material limits for the potentially unlimited economy of mind. The route to doing this lies, as it always has, in maximizing individual freedom and minimizing the oppressive human domination, both organizational and governmental, that always arises from a materialistic perspective. Adam Smith has more relevance to today's economy than he did to the 18th century.

Above all, we need to develop a more mature sense of *compassion*. A significant share of the economic tragedies of the past two decades arose not only from a false sense of true substance, but from a superficial, even maudlin perspective on what constitutes true compassion in the economic as well as the social sense.

Two of the most compassionate and humane political figures of the past decade were John Lindsay, former mayor of New York, and Frank Sargent, former governor of Massachusetts. Yet their policies and administrations wreaked financial havoc on their respective constituencies, leaving both New York City and Massachusetts on the brink of bankruptcy and their people vastly overtaxed and in serious economic distress with above-average unemployment and below-average growth in jobs and income. In hindsight, their policies must be judged as anything but compassionate. Had both men been tougher at restraining spending and taxation, the people they governed and especially the poor would have been infinitely better off, even though the superficial media would probably have labeled them as "lacking in compassion."

Jimmy Carter was and is an immensely compassionate man. Under his administration social spending grew at the fastest rate in U.S. history and to its highest levels. So did inflation and the tax burden. As a result there were 4 million more people living below the poverty line at the end of his term than at the beginning, the worst antipoverty performance for the economy since the Great Depression. There turned out to be nothing "compassionate" about 13% inflation.

President Ford had an opportunity in 1974 and 1975 to decontrol the price of oil and gas. He failed to seize it because he was afraid of being "uncompassionate" about the heating costs for Americans. Yet hardly any economist, left or right, would not admit that, had he decontrolled then, the price of oil and gas would be 20%–30% lower than it is today (1982) and everyone from consumers to auto workers, and especially the poor and elderly, would be better off.

In one economic policy after another, we find that what seemed initially to be the compassionate approach turned out with the 20–20 vision of hindsight to have been anything but, and what often seemed uncompassionate frequently promoted the greatest good.

If we are ever to develop our full economic potential, and to lift the terrible burden of poverty from all mankind, it is essential that we stop the poisonous and often childishly pejorative assaults (such as we have seen these past two or three years) on the alleged lack of compassion or human motivations of leaders from either the left or the right. There is little evidence, at least in this country, that the politics of envy and class warfare have ever fed and clothed many folks, or given them jobs and real opportunity. We need to begin in a rational and reasonable way to determine just what true compassion in the economic sense really is, and what it is not.

This book could not have been written without the enormous help, both direct and indirect, of too many to mention here. But a few credits are absolutely essential: To Milton Friedman, for his gracious willingness through some very long telephone conversations to help me learn more about economic logic and discipline than from all the economic course content during my Harvard undergraduate days. To Colin Campbell of Dartmouth, who was a constant source of encouragement. To Irving Kristol for his brilliant essays in *The Wall Street Journal* and for *The Public Interest* quarterly which he founded. To R. Buckminster Fuller, whose *Operating Handbook for Spaceship Earth* in the 1960s crystallized for me the metaphysical character of wealth. To Martin Feldstein of the National Bureau of Economic Research for his enlightenment and courageous debunking of economic illusions of both the right and the left. To *The Wall Street Journal*'s editorial page and to Robert Bartley, who first gave broad exposure to the thinking of Arthur Laffer, Robert Mundell, Jude Wanniski, Jack Kemp, Paul Craig Roberts, Roy Jastram, Lewis Lehrman, Julian Simon, Lindley Clark, James Ring Adams, David Ranson, and many, many others.

It is only fair to add that without the *Boston Herald American* and especially its former publisher Robert Bergenheim and my first editor Ken Thompson, I could never have had the opportunity to write and freely express views that, in the liberal climate of Massachusetts, were, to put it mildly, considered wildly reactionary.

This book would never have come into existence had it not been for the generous appreciation of my columns by George Gilder, the gifted author of *Wealth and Poverty*, which has provided a philosophical underpinning for today's supply-side economics.

Nothing I have done would ever have been done without the compassionate support of my wife Jane. In a life together as close as we have enjoyed, there can be no pride of authorship and no adequate gratitude rendered.

Most of all, this book is an expression of profound gratitude that I have lived in America, with all its incumbent rights, privileges, blessings, and responsibilities—a special place, some of us believe, where freedom of religion and freedom of enterprise have combined to an extraordinary degree to give us a higher and better sense of economy and well-being than even the best secular political and economic system alone could have generated.

1

The Unlimited Economy
in Mind

*My own picture of humanity today finds us just about to step out from amongst
the pieces of our just one-second-ago broken eggshell. Our innocent,
trial-and-error-sustaining nutriment is exhausted. We are faced with an entirely
new relationship to the universe. We are going to have to spread our wings of
intellect and fly or perish; that is, we must dare immediately to fly by the
generalized principles governing the universe and not by the ground rules of
yesterday's superstitious and erroneously conditioned reflexes. . . .*

*Possibly it was this intellectual augmentation of humanity's survival and success
through the metaphysical perception of generalized principles which may be
objectively employed, that Christ was trying to teach in the obscurely told story of
the loaves and the fishes.*

—R. Buckminster Fuller

On the 50th anniversary of our nation's Independence, 4 July 1826, Thomas
Jefferson, hero of modern liberalism, and John Adams, the great conservative, passed away. Their nearly simultaneous departure followed more than a
decade of warm and profound correspondence, in which these two former
antagonists exchanged their views on a broad range of topics.

As Adams wrote to Jefferson on 1 September 1816, "You and I ought not to
die before we have explained ourselves to each other." What they "explained" to each other in that exchange was their mutual dedication to
individual liberty and their common distrust of overweening government at
home and abroad as the greatest enemy to freedom and to economic
prosperity.

In his first letter of the exchange, Jefferson told Adams, "[Your letter]
carries me back to the times when, beset with difficulties and dangers, we
were fellow laborers in the same cause, struggling for what is most valuable to
man: his right of self-government.

"Laboring always at the same oar," he continued, "with some wave ever ahead threatening to overwhelm us, and yet, passing harmless under our bark, we knew not how, we rode through the storm with heart and hand, and made a happy port."

Now in the third century of its Independence, the United States is once again riding through a storm that may prove more violent than any we have yet faced, a storm that threatens to sweep away our "right of self-government" and our economic freedom.

Despite the so-called Reagan Revolution a vast army of unelected bureaucrats, thick volumes of unlegislated laws and regulations, and confiscatory taxes still threatens to destroy the richness, variety, and vitality of our private economy, while some members of the intellectual establishment scorn both the market and economic growth as viable in "an age of limits."

Internationally, we confront totalitarian Marxist nations which cannot long tolerate juxtaposition or active trade with free democracies and which can survive their own bankrupt economic policies only through military expansionism.

So we are a nation whose freedom and independence are on the firing line, from without and within. How well we respond to this challenge really depends on how much we genuinely cherish our freedom and whether we are prepared to make real sacrifices to preserve it—and, in turn, that depends on the degree to which we equate liberty with economic progress and well-being.

Despite the 1980 elections and President Reagan's early congressional victories, the signs are hardly reassuring. Most troubling of all are the insistent efforts of the predominantly left-liberal "new class" in media and academia to undermine this revived commitment to economic liberty and the market system, and the effectiveness with which they have already painted it with the broad brush of class warfare and the politics of envy.

Even newspapers that ought to know better use the pejorative and classist epithet "trickle-down" to describe even the fairest of broad-based tax-cut proposals—and to suggest that the most classical use of investment incentives and monetary restraint is in some way radical or unconventional.

Although Marxism has fully discredited itself everywhere, its hopeless illusions still seem to mesmerize most of the U.S. media. The economic lines of battle are drawn as never before between those who continue to favor a demand-oriented and redistributionist approach to economic policy, and those who want to shift our policies back to the supply side—between those who favor stimulating and controlling demand with heavy government spending and regulation, and those who want to stimulate more supply through more incentives and a freer market, and who see economic *growth* as the solution to our problems.

In the final analysis, this debate between supply-side and demand-side economics boils down to a question of which is more important to us, liberty or security.

If we believe (as most demand-siders do) that the world economy is substantially a zero-sum game, and that wealth is physical and therefore finite, then collective security will be our primary goal, and the sacrifice of individual liberty will be the inevitable price. But we shouldn't be surprised if, as Thomas Jefferson warned, the trade turns out to be a very poor one, providing neither comfort nor security. Certainly the last decade has made that clear.

If, on the other hand, we are convinced that wealth and substance are essentially metaphysical (and therefore potentially unlimited) and individually generated, we will see liberty as the prerequisite for economic growth, prosperity, and ultimately real security—and economic rights and freedoms as indivisible from civil liberties.

It seems no coincidence that Adam Smith released *The Wealth of Nations* at about the same time that this nation proclaimed its independence from Britain. Freedom and wealth are mutually compatible and complementary, and ideas are pervasively universal in their influence on men and nations. Smith's theoretical challenge to turn loose the production of wealth, by lifting from England and Europe the restrictive bonds of highly regulated mercantilism (with its almost fascist emphasis on licensure, tariffs, guilds, and customs) found its natural metaphysical response in the American colonists' demand to be free of the Crown's economic tyranny. The premise of Smith and the colonists was that real wealth and human prosperity were ultimately the product of individuals, not of the state; and the nation, or group of nations, that provided the most individual freedom would ultimately generate the most prosperity, the most real wealth for all.

Unfortunately, for the past 10–15 years, U.S. economic policies have been dominated by the Keynesian notion that it is demand and government that run the economy, not supply and the market; and that government, through its fiscal and regulatory policies, can manage the economy by raising or lowering the level of demand, at will. Reinforcing these policies has been the idea that the distribution of wealth is more important than the production of it, that the way to stimulate economic growth is to tax money out of savings and investment and redistribute it into consumption and demand. Not surprisingly, such policies have resulted in a soaring of consumer demand (by inflating money income) and a drastic slowing down of supply (investment and productivity), with the inevitable consequence of raging inflation.

As we reap the harvest of this demand-side approach, we face the uniquely grotesque combination of high unemployment and high interest rates— slamming on the credit brakes trying to cure inflation with interest rates that can be described only as usury.

Fortunately, not all economists have fallen for the Keynesian demand-side illusions. Far from it. The 1980 election, in fact, represented a rejection of such policies and a reaffirmation of highly traditional, classic supply-side, pro-growth economic ideas that had their roots in Say's Law (supply generates its own demand) and Adam Smith's paean to free markets and individual incentives, *The Wealth of Nations*, both products of the 18th century.

These neotraditional supply-siders argue that trying to manage the economy solely through government manipulation of money demand is a little like trying to run a Diesel tractor with power in only one track. They argue that since inflation, in the last analysis, is too much money chasing too few goods, it is at least as important to increase the output of goods supply as it is to reduce the flow of money demand. And since tight money alone only cuts demand (while it also reduces supply through recession), its inevitable result is terrible economic pain without any real purpose, a concentric circle of accelerating despair.

In 1979, a famous U.S. Keynesian economist was passing through customs at Kennedy Airport when the customs officer, noting his name and occupation, said to him: "I don't know whether I should let you back in, Professor, considering what you economists have done to this country." That customs officer may not have understood all the nuances of the supply-side/demand-side debate, but he knew back in 1979 that something terribly important had gone wrong with the American economy during the last decade or so; and he was ready for some *common sense*—another word for supply-side economics. He knew by then that the demand-side track had become a dead-end siding.

The best proof of this was that in 1979 and 1980, the United States was the only major industrial nation in the free world whose productivity and standard of living were actually declining, as the average real wage of workers was falling by 3%–5% each year.

This decade-long erosion in real wages clearly signaled that something had to be fundamentally wrong with the economic thinking that was guiding the nation. After all, the whole purpose of economics is to increase income and productivity, not diminish it. The very word "economy" describes and defines "productivity," since both terms encompass that process by which human beings use their intelligence, inventiveness, and investment to produce progressively more value with progressively less effort and fewer materials—to do more with less.

Thus, as presented in 1981, the supply-side program for healing the economic mess was a combination of reducing money demand through restraint in government spending and the money supply, and increasing goods supply, or productivity, through massive reductions in taxes and regulations on both individuals and business. In other words, the new administration proposed to heal inflation by real economic growth taking place in a freer market and with sound money—a formula that was successful long before Keynesian policies were adopted.

It is no accident that the United States, until the late 1960s, was the world's strongest and fastest-growing economy. Though with notable imperfections, it led the world in individual freedom and in rewards for productivity, invention, and investment.

But in the last decade or so, that has changed dramatically; and contrary to belief, it started well before OPEC and the so-called energy crunch, with the increasing domination of the marketplace both legally and logistically by the heavy hand of government regulation and fiscal policies and the ever-tightening brakes of "taxflation." That has been done not so much by the substitution of one economic policy for another, but rather by trading in true economy, per se, for government—exchanging productivity and supply for demand and redistribution.

That is what Keynesian economics is really all about. It provides a rationale for government to stimulate or retard economic activity through the manipulation of aggregate demand, through policies designed to siphon money out of savings (investment) and pump it directly into consumption through heavy deficit spending and transfer-payment programs. It's a rationale that politicians and their close friends, the bankers, find irresistible.

Since the government, in and of itself, produces no wealth or supply, the inevitable result of such policies must always be to depress (through taxation and inflation) real supply, while it stimulates demand and consumption, thus producing diminishing productivity, unemployment, and rising inflation at the same time, something we now call "stagflation."

Social Security is a classic example. Few people realize that the original rationale for this program in the Depression (and within the Roosevelt Brain Trust) was not so much compassion for the elderly as it was the specific Keynesian purpose of pulling money out of savings and pumping it directly into consumer demand as a means of stimulating a then stagnant and deflated economy. Forty-five years later it was still doing the same thing on a grand scale, but for a hugely inflated economy. It worked so well that in 1981 it was siphoning off more than $150 billion a year from productive payrolls and savings (thus depressing investment and productivity) and pumping it right back into consumer demand, spending, and, therefore, inflation. Social Security taxes in 1981 were nearly 50% larger than the nation's total personal savings. They had been *equal* in 1975.

Furthermore, Social Security has also directly led to the huge drop in one of the most productive segments of the U.S. work force, ages 50 to 65, where, because of early retirement and growing disability pensions, participation dropped from 90% in 1965 to 74% in 1980. Retirees are now growing in number nearly three times as fast as young workers are entering the labor force. This has forced still higher taxes on payrolls (and productivity) and still lower rates of savings and investment, promoting inflation. Inflation, in turn, has led to more and more cries to subsidize demand still further by imposing price controls over energy, rents, and housing—and increasing benefits to pay for them.

The so-called energy crisis was very largely the result of such demand-oriented policies. It is no accident that the decline of U.S. domestic production of oil began in 1971—the same year we first imposed price controls on domestic crude oil. Our refusal to lift those controls in 1974–75 directly stimulated demand, depressed supply, thwarted conservation, and ultimately led to even higher prices when decontrol finally was forced upon us in 1980–81. After full decontrol in January 1981, the demand for oil imports quickly fell 23%, and prices started back down by as much as $6–$8 a barrel, even as domestic supply and production increased for the first time, and a worldwide glut developed.

Unfortunately, the statists, who have dominated economic thought in the

United States, told us that the only solution to these problems lay in still more controls over wages and prices—that is, the rationing of demand, not the production of supply or the operation of the market.

Deep beneath the surface of this debate over demand-side vs. supply-side economics is a basic struggle between those who now believe that an aggressive pursuit of growth and wealth is no longer a viable option for a resource-scarce world and those who still cherish and believe in the so-called American Dream of ever-upward mobility.

Back in May 1979, Speaker of the House Thomas P. "Tip" O'Neill told the graduating class at Providence College that we must "learn to live with limits" and accept "scarcity and shortages as facts of life." In 1981, liberal economist Robert Lekachman warned us that "the era of growth is over, and the era of limits is upon us"; and he called for a "credible agenda" to include total government management and allocation of credit, investment, and natural resources in what he described as "a democratically planned policy," in which wages and prices would be permanently controlled.

This debate was joined symmetrically at the very moment of the 1981 presidential transition:

> The rapid depletion of irreplaceable minerals, the erosion of topsoil, the destruction of beauty, the blight of pollution, the demands of increasing billions of people all combine to create problems which are easy to predict and observe, but difficult to resolve.
>
> —Jimmy Carter
> Farewell Address
> 16 January 1981

> It is time for us to realize that we are too great a nation to limit ourselves to small dreams. We're not as some would have us believe doomed to inevitable decline. We have every right to dream heroic dreams.
>
> —Ronald Reagan
> Inaugural Address
> 20 January 1981

The flight to freedom of the 52 American hostages, commencing minutes after President Reagan finished his address, seemed a perfect metaphor for the inaugural itself. After a four-year litany of limitation, 226 million Americans finally were liberated—at least from the dismal dirges of President Carter's modern Malthusianism—and asked to dream heroic dreams.

Curiously, pessimism was not Mr. Carter's natural demeanor. He came to office exuding confidence and competence. He seemed unafraid and un-daunted by the challenges that faced him. His attitude seemed characteristi-cally American in its buoyancy. But the seeds of his destruction were contained in the large coterie of limits-to-growth ideologues with which he staffed his administration. Ironically, their policies, born and bred in the think tanks and academies of an economically declining Northeast, shaped both the substance and the rhetoric of the first president from the new Sunbelt, where economic growth is almost a religion in itself.

So President Carter's smiling walk down Pennsylvania Avenue on his inaugural day gradually gave way to the melancholy metaphors of his "national malaise" speech of July 1979, when, for the first time, the American mood shifted from its normal 2-to-1 "optimistic about the future" to nearly 2-to-1 "pessimistic about the future" (CBS-N.Y. Times polls). It was that pessimism that Americans ultimately rejected at the polls.

Long before the 1980 election, the distinguished British-born journalist Henry Fairlie told a dinner party of startled sophisticates, "No matter who wins this election, by 1984 America will be surging with new life. It will have recovered its confidence and creativity, economically, politically, and culturally." Fairlie had apparently sensed what most of the intellectual establishment hadn't. The American people were already in the process of reaffirming their faith in the potential of the individual human spirit for creativity and growth.

In that sense, the 1980 election, far from being devoid of issues, turned out to be a profoundly metaphysical debate between the more spiritual, or theistic, view of the world and the more humanistic and materialistic view of it; between those who sense that the spiritual is the dominant force and those who see the physical as the primary limiting factor; between those who feel that the real energy of the universe is mental and, therefore, infinite and those who believe with equal passion that energy is material, finite, and running out; between those who believe that an economy should be an expansively unfolding creative idea and those who look upon it largely as a zero-sum game.

This was at its roots a religious debate. After all, to believe in a wholly materialistic universe, governed by chance, necessity, and implacable physical laws, is, by definition, to accept entropy, mortality, and despair—and by inversion, to disbelieve in immortality, hope, future, and God.

Out of such a nihilistic view must arise a profound desire for collective security against a hostile environment. To such a mentality the notions of faith, individuality, freedom, confidence, and even incentives are regarded merely as psychological factors instead of substantive spiritual and economic forces. After all, if wealth and substance are really finite, why bother with incentives? Why strive to grow?

Given the dominance of this intensely materialistic scientific determinism in academia as well as the media, is it not surprising, in a land largely built by religious refugees, Jew and Christian, Protestant and Catholic, that religion itself should finally rear its head and plunge full blown into the political arena? What we are talking about, however, is something far more profound than the sometimes petty puritanism and rural religiosity which at times have seemed to dominate recent elections.

We are dealing, no less, with the basic conflict between two entirely different concepts of man and his universe, concepts that affect every aspect of our social and economic lives, one determinedly physical and finite and the other profoundly metaphysical and infinite; the one (collective socialism) rooted in fearful concern about visible resources, the other (market capitalism) springing from faith in spiritual reality. Or, as George Gilder has written in *Wealth and Poverty*, "Capitalist production entails faith—in one's neighbors, in one's society and in the compensatory logic of the cosmos. Search and you shall find, give and you shall be given unto; supply creates its own demand. It is this sequential logic that essentially distinguishes the free from the socialist economy." Above all, he warns, "When faith dies, so does enterprise." St. Paul puts it more profoundly: "We walk by faith, not by sight."

For more than a decade now, America has been moving away from its historic approach of walking by faith and has been attempting vainly to walk by sight—that is, to chart a precisely econometric course toward the elusive grail of material security and safety, using the life nets of collective government, steered by the lifeboat mentality of environmental extremism that measures our wealth with physical callipers—by what we can *see* rather than by what we can *know*. Not surprisingly, productivity and enterprise have deadened even as security has diminished.

Just as Adam Smith's expansive *Wealth of Nations*, which spawned the American dream, was nurtured in the rich spiritual soil of the Anglo-Scottish enlightenment of Locke and Burke, with its profoundly metaphysical (and, therefore, infinite) view of mankind and the world, so today's distributionist and age-of-limits economic thinking has sprung full-blown from the largely atheistic, scientific determinism of the 20th century, with its deeply physical (and therefore finite) view of the world, and has found its rationale in the dialectical materialism of Marx.

Yet even Karl Marx, who so despised individuality and spirituality as economic or political perspectives, nevertheless understood their extraordinary potential for the generation of wealth and productivity:

> The bourgeoisie has been the first to show what man's activity can bring about. It has accomplished wonders far surpassing Egyptian pyramids, Roman aqueducts and Gothic cathedrals . . . the bourgeoisie, during its rule of scarce one hundred years, has created more massive and more colossal productive forces than have all the preceding generations together.

Unfortunately, while Marx acknowledged (and his contemporary followers still acknowledge) the power of free-market incentives, their preoccupation with an intensely material view of the world led them to the conclusion that such incentives would only lead to the unfair distribution of a finite resource base. To this day, those on the left, including the most noble civil libertarians and traditional liberals who otherwise support political and social freedom, argue that the free marketplace cannot cope with the equitable distribution of what they regard as limited material wealth.

While they reject the totalitarianism of Marxist states, they succumb to Malthusian views of limits to growth. In this sense, they fail to understand that the intellectual and spiritual forces that seem to produce wealth relatively easily in a free-market setting are, themselves, the real wealth of the universe—the unlimited substance which sustains us. These are what R. Buckminister Fuller refers to as "the metaphysical component of wealth"— the ideas, inventions, and technology that have enabled us to go right on expanding real wealth, even as the so-called physical resources seem to the superficial materialist to be narrowing.

It is this essentially spiritual view of the world's economy that really separates the supply-siders who believe in growth as a fundamental economic mandate and the demand-siders who think in terms of redistribution. The more materialistic one's perspective on the world, the more inevitably economics itself becomes a science of rearranging and allocating demand and wealth, and the more likely one is to accept the prognoses and prescriptions of Marx and Malthus. After all, if there really is only so much to go around, it should at least be distributed fairly.

Conversely, to believe in supply-side economics is by definition to reject this construct of a strictly matter-based economy, and especially to reject the materialistic premise of environmental extremists that the Second Law of Thermodynamics is leading humanity quickly toward an entropy watershed in which the planet itself rebels against its inhabitants and their economic values.

The central message of nearly all religious prophets throughout history has been to look beyond these limited presentations of the physical senses into the ultimate potential of the mind and spirit. The common denominator of faith was and is the willingness to recognize that our real wealth comes not from finite natural resources or uncertain material conditions, but from the triumph of the metaphysical over the physical, of attitudes over appearances. Or in St. Paul's words, "Through faith we understand that the worlds were framed by the word of God, so that things which are seen were not made of things which do appear."

The history of our nation, for all of its myriad faults and shortcomings, is the unfolding of the progressive triumph of the free human spirit and intelligence over limitation and lack. True, we have been blessed with abundant natural resources. But other nations and continents have had even more. Yet they prospered much less.

The prosperity that has unfolded around the Western world is, to no small extent, the direct result of the outpouring of American technology and the overflowing wealth of ideas that have fueled not only our own growth, but so many of the economic miracles of Japan and Germany, not to mention the prosperity of some Third World nations.

As Professor John W. Kendrick of George Washington University wrote in the American Enterprise Institute's Economist, "Actually much of the high growth of productivity abroad has been due to catching up with U.S. levels of technology." His econometric analysis of the sources of our productivity gains and losses over the last two decades attributes most of the net gain to "advances in knowledge," which is shorthand for technological breakthrough. Only a small fraction has come from capital investment in present plant and equipment.

It is Kendrick's thesis, in fact, that as our economy moves more and more into the realm of high technology, capital investment will have less and less relationship to economic growth or productivity, since so many of the technological breakthroughs of the 1970s and '80s are effectively reducing the amount of capital needed to produce economic value itself.

Kendrick's analyses grew out of the seminal work of Edward F. Denison at the Brookings Institution which shows the immense degree to which differences in productivity among even the most developed nations arise not so much from capital investment or economies of scale as from fundamental differences in the level of technological knowledge. Denison found that almost half of the productivity differentials that the United States has enjoyed over its main competitors has been a function of technological knowledge and research and development advances.

For example, of the 44% productivity advantage the U.S. enjoyed over Great Britain in 1976, nearly 30 points of that arose from technological factors and other aspects of the knowledge gap, which give U.S. industry its real lead over the rest of the world. Similarly, of the 49 point advantage the U.S. enjoyed over Japan in 1976, 26 points (more than half) derived from the technology gap.

So, even as economists and policy makers in Washington are concentrating on ways to increase capital investment in new plant and equipment, the thing that is most responsible for keeping the United States competitive in the world market has relatively little to do with physical assets and almost everything to do with metaphysical assets—invention and technological breakthroughs. It is an interesting and significant fact that the state of Massachusetts in 1981 had one of the lowest levels of new capital formation in the nation and one of the highest rates of economic growth. Its high-technology industries involve relatively modest plants but an enormous investment in individuals (engineers and scientists) and in their ideas, which are providing the greatest breakthroughs in our economy today.

In 1955 a company I worked for installed a computer to handle payroll and billings. It cost $150,000 a year in rentals, took up 900 square feet in floor space, and required eight full-time people just to keep it going. In 1981 a Massachusetts company produced a computer that sold for less than $15,000, does four times as much work, is about the size of a small desk, and requires only one person to operate.

Back in 1970 an electronic desk calculator cost $280 and weighed nearly 20 pounds. In 1980 one could buy a hand calculator that does the same work more quickly for less than $20, and it weighs only four ounces.

In its infancy in the 1940s, television was a tiny screen in a huge box. Today it is a big screen with a much smaller box of longer-lasting and more efficient parts.

In the 1930s, the average radio was a large box with a separate speaker and a small sound. Today it is a three-inch rectangular cube held in the palm of one's hand, with enough volume to make dogs scream in terror, and it uses a fraction of the energy it once required.

Twenty-five years ago it took 15 pounds of feed and 14 weeks to raise a 2½-pound frying chicken. Today it takes 5 pounds of feed and 7 weeks to raise the same size bird for market.

These examples help to explain why most economists spell America's economic future in two words: high technology—that is, the technology not of more complex material structures but of better mental expression. In Cambridge, Massachusetts, for example, Polaroid now employs more than 12,000 people, largely because of the creative inspiration of one man, Edwin Land, whose ideas and inventions have brought great economic progress and jobs to the state, not to mention satisfying products to hundreds of millions of people around the world, and permanent wealth for many. He did this by transforming low-cost metal, paper, chemicals, and plastics into tremendously valuable and useful photographic products. All through the genius of his ideas.

In much the same way, most of U.S. economic growth in the 1970s and 1980s came not out of the mines or mills or assembly lines but off the chalkboards of the universities, as high technology replaced old-fashioned durable goods as the nation's economic leader.

Despite the fact that America's automobile and steel industries have steadily lost out to imports, despite the destruction of American textiles and leathers by Taiwan, South Korea, and Spain, and despite slowing productivity compared to the rest of the free world, U.S. manufacturing exports have actually been soaring. Prior to the recession of 1980, our economy was providing work for the highest percentage of our population in history, nearly 60%—far higher than in any other Western nation.

The single most important reason for this was the boom (both domestically and internationally) in the products of American high technology, from computers to communications equipment, from genetics to cybernetics. High technology has offered positive solutions to the world's most pressing economic problems, such as:

- Inflation—The real costs of most high-technology products have actually been *declining* steadily.
- Productivity—High-technology products are fundamental to increasing it.
- Energy use—Most high-technology products require very low inputs of energy to produce or use them, and are intimately associated with energy conservation.
- Environment—Most high-technology industries are noninvasive, that is, they do not pollute, and they make heavy use of plentiful resources (such as silicon from sand).
- Capital costs—Most of all, high-technology industries are not capital intensive but labor intensive, requiring, on average, less than half the

level of capital formation (plant and equipment) per worker as heavy durable-goods industries such as autos and steel.

Both the glory and the potential danger of the high-technology boom is that the real capital for these industries is not in factories and machines but in creative and inventive people and their ideas; not in money but in mind-wealth. The future of our country, with its apparently narrowing base of the more obvious material resources, lies more than ever before in building up this metaphysical capital through high technology in its broadest sense and the sponsorship of the invention it implies.

Consider Japan, whose 114 million people are now crowded on less than 144,000 square miles of some of the lowest-resource territory in the world. Yet with a population density 15 times that of the United States and 11 times that of the world as a whole, Japan is now the world's leading manufacturing exporter, the third-richest nation, and the fastest-growing economy in terms of productivity.

When we compare Japan, with its per capita GNP of more than $9,000 a year from a population density of 900 per square mile, with Zaire, one of the richest resource countries of Africa, with its per capita output of less than $120 from a population density of only 30, we realize that even in this age of resource scarcity, a nation's wealth still has far more to do with people than with territory.

As F. A. Hayek put it so well:

Only since industrial freedom opened the path to the free use of new knowledge, only since everything could be tried—if somebody could be found to back it at his own risk—and, it should be added, as often as not from outside the authorities officially entrusted with the cultivation of learning, has science made the great strides which in the last hundred and fifty years have changed the face of the world. The result of this growth surpassed all expectations. Wherever the barriers to the free exercise of human ingenuity were removed, man became rapidly able to satisfy ever-widening ranges of desires.

The Energy of Mind vs. the Entropy of Matter

Ironically, in the face of this actual experience of the progressive unfolding of mental wealth, one of the more persistent arguments of our time is the doomsday prophecy that America's economic future is now limited. The basic premise of this doleful scenario is that America became rich because of our rich material resources, particularly oil. Now that our oil seems to be running out, it is time for Americans to begin scaling down our economic expectations. These ideas were summed up in a special section dealing with "The Energy Crisis" prepared by the editors of *The Christian Science Monitor* on 28 June 1976: "The United States' dominant position in the world today is largely due to the historical fact that the potential of oil as a cheap energy source was realized during the nation's industrially formative years and the country has been blessed with large domestic reserves." With these reserves now seeming to decline, the *Monitor* goes on to propose that "Americans, as a people, rethink many of their national and personal priorities. It is clear that the consumptive lifestyle which has developed in the U.S. in the last quarter-century cannot continue indefinitely."

In short, we are told that Americans must begin to scale down their standard of material livelihood and hold down their economic growth because their material resources are limited. Not only do such concepts not square with America's basic mental posture as the land of unlimited individual opportunity, but they do not readily agree with historical or economic reality.

In an article in the June 1980 issue of *Science* magazine (and also in his book, *The Ultimate Resource*), Julian Simon of the University of Illinois has taken on the no-growth prophets with an overwhelming mass of statistical evidence: "Bad news about population growth, natural resources, and the environment that is based on flimsy evidence, or no evidence at all, is published widely in the face of contradictory evidence." He refutes these assumptions: "Statement: The food situation is worsening in less-developed countries. Fact: World per capita food production has been increasing roughly 1% yearly for the last 40 years. . . . Statement: The danger of famine is increasing. Fact: Since World War II there has been a dramatic decline in famines. . . . Statement: Urban sprawl is paving over the U.S. including prime agricultural land. Fact: All the land used for urban areas, plus roadways, totals less than 3% of the U.S. Each year 1.25 million acres are converted to efficient cropland, while only 0.9 million acres are converted to urban and transportation use."

Simon's most telling critique deals with our supposedly diminishing resources of energy and minerals—a routine charge that flies directly in the face of historical fact. Data prepared by the National Commission on Materials Policy show that the known reserves of virtually every major mineral and energy form are larger today than they were in 1950, despite accelerating use. Or, as the National Commission on Supplies and Shortages concluded in 1976, "The geologic, economic, and demographic evidence indicates that no physical lack of resources will seriously strain our economic growth for the next quarter century and probably for generations thereafter."

Why? As Professor Simon points out, "Because we find new lodes, invent better production methods, and discover new substitutes, the ultimate constraint upon our capacity to enjoy unlimited raw materials at acceptable prices is *knowledge* . . . And the source of knowledge is the human mind."

Simon, like Buckminster Fuller, is arguing that the continuous unfolding of human knowledge and intelligence is the principal cause of our becoming equipped to do progressively more with progressively less, that is, to turn otherwise useless matter into useful life-sustaining value—in short, to practice *economy*.

In this sense, economics itself is anti-entropy, the constantly evolving process of imposing order, utility, and value on otherwise orderless, useless, and valueless matter. The danger, of course, is that even as our economic and metaphysical processes generate wealth where none was before, we are easily mesmerized into believing that the wealth is in the objects and products we have created instead of in the thought process and ideas behind them. We transfer the focus of our mental accounting process from the metaphysical to the physical. We fail to remember, for instance, that it was the internal combustion engine that gave oil its present value, and not the other way around.

It is this largely unaccounted metaphysical component of wealth that is the real reason why in the last 70 years alone we have gone from less than 1% of humanity being able to survive at any reasonable level of health and comfort to nearly half of humanity now surviving at a standard of living positively unimagined at the beginning of this century. As Fuller points out, "This utterly unpredicted success occurred within only two-thirds of a century despite continually decreasing metallic resources per each world person."

In fact, economic analyses show that, contrary to the doomsdayers, the real prices of virtually all major natural resources, both in terms of constant hours of effort and general commodity price levels, have steadily *decreased* for as long as there are reliable statistical records, or more than two centuries. Economic history, in other words, puts the lie to these limits-of-growth notions.

As Simon argues, "The fall in the costs of natural resources decade after decade, century after century, should shake us free from the idea that scarcity must increase *sometime*. There is no convincing economic reason why these trends toward a better life, and toward lower prices for raw materials (including food and energy) should not continue indefinitely . . . there are no meaningful limits to the continuation of the process."

Why then are we subjected to so many gloomsday prophecies of limited resource scarcity? Aside from the obvious ideological biases of the sources of these predictions, the primary reason seems to be the adoption of the *engineering* approach of inventorying natural resources rather than the use of historical *economic* analysis.

"With the engineering method," Simon says, "you forecast the status of a natural resource by estimating the presently-known quantity of the resource on or in the earth; predict the future rate of use . . . and subtract the successive estimates of use from the physical inventory."

The problem with this method, of course, is that no one really *knows* what the present inventory is for any resource, nor can we possibly predict either the discovery of unexpected new lodes of these resources or the substitution factor—that is, the arrival of altogether new products to displace old ones.

As scientists H. E. Goeller and A. M. Weinberg argued in the *American Economic Review*:

We now state the principle of "infinite" substitutability. With three notable exceptions—phosphorus, a few trace elements for agriculture, and energy-producing fossil fuels (CH₂)—society can subsist on inexhaustible or near inexhaustible minerals with relatively little loss of living standard. Society would then be based largely on glass, plastic, wood, cement, iron, aluminum, and magnesium.

Dynamic economic analysis, as opposed to static engineering inventories, makes a convincing case for this rosy prediction; and it has been used with great effect to refute one scarcity scenario after another with the actual historical perspective of steadily rising resource availability at steadily lowering costs. George Gilder notes that "such [doomsday] views are suitable for analysis not in the universities (where they often prevail) but on the [psychiatrist's] couch."

Unfortunately, under the sanction and direction of President Carter, such views found their way off the academic couch and well into the mainstream of American political and pseudoscientific thought through the publication, in the summer of 1980, of the much-touted *Global 2000* report. It was prepared very largely by bureaucrats within federal agencies whose organizational power stake lies not in abundance but in scarcity, and whose summary forecast was predictably gloomy:

> If present trends continue, the world in 2000 will be more crowded, more polluted, less stable ecologically, and more vulnerable to disruption than the world we live in now. Serious stresses involving population, resources, and environment are clearly visible ahead. Despite greater material output, the world's people will be poorer in many ways than they are today.

> For hundreds of millions of the desperately poor, the outlook for food and other necessities of life will be no better. For many it will be worse. Barring revolutionary advances in technology, life for most people on earth will be more precarious in 2000 than it is now.

The problem of course was that *Global 2000* (like so many of its predecessors) presented a viewpoint supported by semiscientific conjecture but deeply marred by historical and statistical reality.

Herman Kahn and Ernest Schneider of the Hudson Institute called the report "Globaloney":

> The insistence of "Global 2000" that the world is headed straight for disaster is intrinsically implausible. Gross World Product and Gross World Product per capita have been *growing* inexorably almost every year for at least a century. Life expectancy, the best single available indicator of human life and welfare, continues to lengthen almost everywhere, year after year. Pollution levels in the developed world are being reduced: as the rest of the world becomes more affluent, this pattern will probably be repeated. Even more basic, of course, is the peaking of world population growth which occurred in the 1960s. Given

these facts, it seems passing strange that the doomsdayism of "Global 2000" is playing to rave reviews.

Julian Simon was even more specific and blunt in debunking the essential contentions of the report, many of which are still prominently accepted as conventional wisdom in the public consciousness and media. In noting that *Global 2000* predicted that "the world fish harvest is expected to rise little, if at all, by the year 2000," he cited the statistical evidence that in the past 20 years the catch has more than doubled, with increases almost every year— hardly a case for stagnation. As for "Globaloney's" thesis that per capita food production would increase by only 15% from 1970 to 2000, Simon argued, "over the less than 30 years from 1950 to 1977, per capita food production rose by around 30%. Why project *half* that rate of increase for an even longer period of time?" Why, indeed.

Probably the most invidious and pervasive gloom of *Global 2000* concerns the Department of Agriculture's repeated assertion that "each year the nation loses 3 million acres of farmland" to urban development and transportation (highways, etc.). Curiously, H. Thomas Frey, of the USDA's own Economic Research Service, found that from 1969 to 1974 the total shift of land from agriculture to urban-plus-transport was only 0.9 million acres per year, less than one third as much as *Global 2000* had contended. In 1978 the Economic Research Service put out a study which showed that new cropland was being created by draining swamps and irrigating deserts at the rate of 1.3 million acres per year. So 400,000 acres *more* of new agricultural land are now being added than old land is actually being lost each year to urban development. These facts support the contention of geographer John Fraser Hart that "urban encroachment on rural land is not a serious problem in the United States." They also verify the statement by Frey that "we are in no danger of running out of farmland."

Because of the hysteria generated in the media by *Global 2000*, Americans are routinely subjected to headlined articles about "America's vanishing farmland." While U.S. farmers struggle to market surpluses caused by excess crop production, local officials pass unnecessary new laws to protect us from these nonexistent dangers. In July 1980 Governor James B. Thompson of Illinois issued an executive order to "protect prime agricultural land," which, he said, has steadily declined [in Illinois] at an average rate of approximately 100,000 acres per year." Professor Simon quickly reminded the governor that the U.S. Census of Agriculture shows that between 1974 and 1978 the land actually harvested in Illinois rose from 21,517,665 acres to 22,826,463 acres, an average annual *increase* of 262,000 acres.

The most serious economic challenge facing U.S. agriculture today is keeping excessive productivity from so glutting the market that it wipes out farm income. The fact that less than 3% of the American population who are farmers now feed not only the most food-consuming national populace on earth but also 20% of the rest of the world as well, does not seem to deter the Globaloney-makers. Entropist Jeremy Rifkin concludes his appointed round of dismal despair:

As more and more energy is expended in American agriculture, the entropy of the overall environment increases. The accumulating disorder in the form of pollution and soil erosion increases the overall cost for both society and the agricultural sector. . . . The final victim of the process is the consumer at the checkout line at the neighborhood supermarket, who is forced to pay higher prices every week for the food—energy—needed to sustain life.

The truth, though, is that these American consumer "victims," about whom Rifkin and others worry so much, continue to pay the lowest cost for finished food goods of any nation on earth, and receive the highest level of nutrition. Even in a so-called deep recession, they experience a level of abundance in the marketplace about which most nations, and especially those with planned economies, can only dream.

Now, if it is true, as many argue, that America's position of economic power and its broad distribution of wealth really were solely the result of our vast but now supposedly diminishing material resources, how can we explain the extraordinary backwardness of the USSR, which sits on even more natural resources than ours? Why is it, for example, that the Soviet Union, with greater agricultural potential, must import our wheat? Why is it that Brazil, with some of the richest natural resources in the world, has a standard of living only an eighth of ours? The answer, of course, is that wealth is only partly dependent on material resources. It is far more dependent on the ideas that give those material resources value.

The oil we now regard as so precious was utterly worthless to the American Indians, who did not even know it was there, and only a little more valuable to the white men who first discovered it but had few uses for it. What ultimately gave oil its value were the technological inventions of those who found ways to use it, to make it serve us, to increase our freedom, our mobility, and our standard of living. More than 300 billion barrels of oil lay useless and valueless under the Persian Gulf for eons until a developing Western civilization gave oil its temporary value. Does it not seem likely that the same inventive forces of human imagination will one day take that value away from oil even before it runs out and give it to some other resource, say, to hydrogen or tritium or some other element?

Similarly, uranium was worthless until Einstein (working alone, and removed from economic necessity) comprehended more of the real nature of the material universe, and thus potentially released all of us from bondage to old and limited ideas of energy. From *Spaceship Earth*: "Abraham Lincoln's concept of 'right triumphing over might' was realized when Einstein as metaphysical intellect wrote the equation of physical universe $E = Mc^2$ and thus comprehended it. Thus the metaphysical took the measure of, and mastered the physical."

In the last analysis, real wealth is (and always has been) productivity—the ability, as Buckminster Fuller puts it, "to cope with the forward days of our lives"—that is, to provide the goods and services that further free mankind from bondage to drudgery and unrelenting toil. In turn, this ability to cope derives from ideas and the inventive capacity to take inanimate materials and transform them into useful inventions and products—to make the planet productive.

"Wealth is the progressive mastery of matter by mind," says Fuller, and in his equation, even supposedly "rich" natural resources take on the qualities of wealth only as the result of human invention and ideas. And since ideas are unlimited, so, Fuller argues, is real wealth. From this perspective both the capitalist and socialist ideologies are wrong because they continue to approach the material world from the standpoint of limitation—of not enough to go around—of thinking that matter itself is wealth, that material energy is the only energy, and that because of entropy, wealth itself is inevitably disappearing, not being generated.

The result is that the world has too long been dominated by the "pirate mentality," the race for control by nations and enterprises over specific and seemingly finite material resources—"a constant Malthusian-Darwin-you-or-me-to-the-death-struggle," all on the assumption that some kind of economic Armageddon was just always around the corner. Yet this Armageddon, or Doomsday, which has regularly been predicted as imminent for centuries, has not come because it does not have to and shouldn't. The discoveries of Einstein and subsequent physical scientists have released us partially from the cruel physical laws that declare that our universe is running down and our energy running out. We are protected by the laws of conservation, as Fuller points out:

> Energy is not only conserved but it is also finite. It is a closed system. The universe is a mammoth perpetual motion process. We then see that the part of our wealth which is physical energy is conserved. It cannot be exhausted, cannot be spent, which means exhausted. We realize that the word "spending" is now scientifically meaningless and is therefore obsolete.

To this promising view, critics may correctly argue that Fuller is considering only the First Law of Thermodynamics (conservation) and conveniently ignoring the Second Law, which states that even though total energy is conserved, it is continually moving from a usable state to an unusable state (entropy). From Jeremy Rifkin:

> For example, if we burn a piece of coal, the energy remains but is transformed into sulfur dioxide and other gases that then spread out into space. While no energy has been lost in the process, we know that we can never reburn that piece of coal and get the same work out of it.

The problem, however, with this extreme fixation with the Second Law is one of perspective. The universe may indeed be a closed system according to the laws of thermodynamics, but the earth itself is not.

To a fascinating degree, today's environmentalists have adopted the scientific equivalent of the 19th-century millenarians, and have become the 20th-century "billenarians," worried about the extinction of the cosmos and vainly trying to sell that worry as a paradigm for earth's immediate future. Even as the millenarians lost their credibility in the 19th century, it now seems likely that the billenarians will lose theirs in this era, as they continue to ignore the anti-entropic rush of human thought from the purely physical to the increasingly mental and metaphysical, a rush which, thus far at least, has far outdistanced the so-called narrowing resource base. It is still creating new wealth and capacity at a rapid pace, even as it pauses to clean up the environment.

To many, the history of the Western Judeo-Christian world has been marked by this slow but progressive triumph of the spiritual and metaphysical over the physical and finite. The Bible itself is a central message of anti-entropy, the pursuit of an economy that exists in spirit and mind transcending the boundaries and limits of matter. Jeremy Rifkin gives tacit notice to this:

> It should be emphasized that the Entropy Law deals only with the physical world where everything is finite and where all living things must run their course and eventually cease to be. . . . It is mute, however, when it comes to the vertical world of spiritual transcendence. The spiritual plane is not governed by the ironclad dictates of the Entropy Law. The spirit is a nonmaterial dimension where there are no boundaries and no fixed limits to attend to. The relationship of the physical to the spiritual world is the relationship of a small part to the larger unbound whole within which it unfolds.

At the same time, even within the physical construct of the Second Law of Thermodynamics, experience shows that the most important energy is not physical but mental, and that if the physical or energy part of our wealth may seem to diminish, the metaphysical or know-how part of our wealth can only increase. Even when we make mistakes we learn more; and the more we learn, the more we understand and the wealthier we become. We are always being taught through clearer ideas how to do more with less.

This process, which Fuller calls "synergy," is nothing more than a restatement of the old postulate that the whole is greater than the sum of its parts, that a complete idea is more valuable and powerful than its individual components. Man is obviously more than $4.98 worth of chemicals. A computer is clearly more than a few hundred pounds of metal, plastic, silicon, and wire. A car is far more than 3,000 pounds of metal, rubber, and plastic. Synergy, then, is the description of the process by which whole concepts or ideas transform otherwise useless material parts into valuable products or services. The wealth, or value, is produced not by the matter but by the ideas that transform it. The ultimate extension of this synergistic process is that as the *idea* of any product becomes better understood, the less matter is needed and the more real wealth is created.

The promise of synergy is that as we increase our metaphysical capital—our know-how, our understanding of the world around us—our economic wealth can only grow, it can never decline. The danger Fuller sees is that "because our wealth is continually multiplying in vast degree unbeknownst and unacknowledged formally by human society, our economic accounting systems are still unrealistically identifying wealth as matter," and therefore ignoring our real potential. Some economists now question, for example, whether the level of capital investment any longer bears any relationship to economic growth—and whether we are even measuring economic growth adequately in present accounting models. These models leave us wholly ignorant of vast changes in real economic development.

Such ignorance not only leads to individual limitation and hoarding but also promotes the establishment of the very governmental and bureaucratic structures, controls, and regulations that could stifle the economic and technological progress of which we are truly capable. The ballyhooed energy crisis was a vivid illustration. As soon as price controls were lifted we experienced a world oil glut. Proponents of a still more dangerous notion called "reindustrialization" argue that we should pour vast capital funds into old industries that technology is now rendering obsolete, instead of encouraging the process that replaces them with new breakthroughs.

It would also seem that a nation which can put a man on the moon can, through the same inventive process, the same devotion to the technological mastery of material limitations, break down the presently assumed limitations on our material energy resources—either by discovering whole new reserves of current fuels or by breaking new ground into entirely new sources of energy not even now understood, and (as is now happening) through the exigencies of the market learning how to use far less energy to more effect.

In recent times, the apparent decline in uranium supplies prompted the development of the breeder reactor, which produces new fuel about as fast as it uses up old. We may not ever decide to use it, but it demonstrates our synergistic capacities, and may well become, with more effective safeguards, a future energy resource. No one yet knows the full potential of solar energy, or of genetic engineering, or of fusion, since all these fields are still relatively early in their development. But in each area our horizons are expanding, not contracting. Biotechnology all by itself provides a glimpse at renewable resources within earth's open system.

Our economic future is not now and never has been tied to the physical assets we now see, but to the vast untapped potential of creative thinking—the metaphysical process which can show us entirely new reserves and new and easier ways of doing things, extending value and increasing wealth without depleting our planet. The only impediment to this is a fearful or limited concept of the real source of our wealth, a lack of faith in our ability as free individuals and institutions to generate whatever we need and to allow new ideas to unfold and new processes and resources to develop—in short, to continue to explore the unlimited economy that exists in mind.

2

The Individual as Capital

The main fuel to speed our progress is our stock of knowledge, and the brake is our lack of imagination. The ultimate resource is people—skilled, spirited, and hopeful people who will exert their wills and imaginations for their own benefit, and so, inevitably, for the benefit of us all. . . . In short, our cornucopia is the human mind and heart, and not a Santa Claus natural environment. So has it been in the past, and therefore so is it likely to be in the future.

—*Julian Simon*

A 1980 cartoon showed two native American Indians standing astride Plymouth Rock, skeptically eyeing the approaching *Mayflower*, loaded with Pilgrims. One of them was saying, "There goes the neighborhood," and the other, "Just more unemployment and welfare, and besides, they talk funny."

The cartoon was an ironic reminder that of the 230 million Americans, fewer than 1 million can trace their original roots to this land. The other 99.6% of us are rooted in other lands and are the offspring or descendants of immigrants. It was also a commentary, by inversion, on an economic reality: While the Indians themselves were brutalized by their arrival, this nation's great economy was entirely built by immigrants.

When the Pilgrims landed, there were fewer than 300,000 native American Indians living on 3.5 million square miles—or less than one individual eking out the barest subsistence from each 10 square miles, with a life expectancy of about 30 years. Today, there are more than 600 Americans on every 10 square miles of our country, living at a level of affluence undreamed of in most of the rest of the world, and with a life expectancy of 73 years.

Yet, given today's media-hyped specter of limited energy resources and inflation, it is not surprising that Americans took a somewhat mixed view of the arrival, in 1980, of 100,000 Cuban refugees on Florida's shores. On the one hand, we were inspired by their courage, and proud that they reached out to America; on the other hand, we wondered if they would take our jobs or consume too many of our tax dollars and use up our resources.

Americans do well to remember, however, that this nation's greatest economic growth took place from 1880 to 1930, when we took in 37 million immigrants who, with their offspring, accounted for fully 60% of our huge population growth in that period. It must be apparent that not all of these 37 million were the ideal, that among them were the usual number of "undesirables." Yet, without this huge influx, America could never have achieved its economic supremacy.

Here again is a useful reminder that the wealth of any nation is not in the ground, but in its people, and in the qualities, ideas, energies, hopes, and dreams they express. The best modern proof of this lies in the more than 600,000 Cuban Americans who have emigrated to our shores since 1958, most of them settling in Florida. Prior to the 1980 boat armadas, this huge influx had done far more for Florida's economy than against it. While Florida's population has grown three times as fast as the nation, its personal income and jobs have consistently grown twice as fast as the nation, and its unemployment rate actually fell sharply throughout the 1960s, the period of the greatest influx of Cuban immigrants. The average Cuban in Cuba still produces less than $1,000 a year in gross product, yet the average Cuban in Florida produces more than $10,000—ten times as much.

What is more important, the percentage of Florida's population on welfare actually declined between 1970 and 1980 by 18%, even as it grew by 31% in the nation and by over 75% in Massachusetts. In 1980, only 2.7% of Florida's vastly inflated population received Aid to Families with Dependent Children (AFDC), compared with 4.7% of the nation and 6.3% of the population of Massachusetts. Also, less than 5% of the Cuban-American population in Florida were on welfare and less than 7% were unemployed, compared with 24% of urban blacks who were on welfare and 16% who were receiving unemployment benefits.

The infusion of more than half a million Cubans into the Florida economy has been one of the reasons why Florida has now outstripped (in total gross state product) many northern urban states like Massachusetts, which it used to trail before the Cuban migrations began. In short, the Cubans brought their wealth with them, despite the fact that they came without the English language and with only the clothes on their backs.

Less than 30% of our annual population growth in 1980 came from immigration, compared with nearly 50% from 1900 to 1930. The Florida experience suggests that the nation as a whole may well be suffering more from restricted immigration than benefiting from it. Is it a coincidence that three of the world's richest nations, Canada, Australia, and the United States were all built by immigrants?

Thomas Edison was once asked whether he thought invention had more to do with the peculiar American character than with the nation's political and economic system. He replied that he had noticed that most of our invention and innovation had been the work of immigrants who, for some reason, found in the American system the right environment for their creativity to flourish.

TABLE 2-1

IMMIGRANTS — THEIR COSTS AND CONTRIBUTIONS

(per family for 1975)

Year of Immigra-tion	Public* Assistance	SOCIAL COSTS				CONTRIBUTIONS		
		Social Security	Medical Assistance†	Public Education	Total Costs	Family Earnings	Taxes Paid	Net Contributions‡
1974	$532	$ 3	$ 61	$ 820	$1,416	$ 9,192	$2,666	$1,250
1973	361	49	35	755	1,200	11,387	3,302	2,102
1972	536	127	66	781	1,510	10,610	3,077	1,567
1971	496	5	16	716	1,233	10,826	3,140	1,907
1970	518	34	64	1,042	1,659	10,383	3,011	1,352
1965-69	646	152	75	1,068	1,941	12,247	3,552	1,611
1960-64	575	326	109	1,237	2,247	14,014	4,064	1,817
1950-59	515	424	96	1,237	2,292	13,542	3,927	1,635
All natives	$498	$735	$187	$ 859	$2,279	$11,037	$3,201	$ 922

SOURCE: Survey of Income and Education, Bureau of Census. Analysis by Julian Simon, University of Illinois, 15 September 1980, for U.S. Select Commission on Immigration.

* Includes welfare AFDC, SSI, unemployment compensation, food stamps.
† Includes Medicaid and Medicare.
‡ Subtract "Total Costs" from "Taxes Paid."

The Need for New Blood

There are economists who believe that what this country now needs to restore its productive and innovative spirit and vitality is more immigration, not less. That was the conclusion of a University of Illinois study for the Select Commission on Immigration and Refugee Policy, chaired by the Reverend Theodore Hesburgh of Notre Dame University. The basic finding of that study was that "immigrants contribute more to the public coffers [in taxes] than they take from them [in public aid]." The conclusions were drawn from an analysis of the comprehensive U.S. Census Survey of Income and Education (SIE) done in 1976 (see Table 2-1), which gives detailed data on a sample of 158,500 U.S. households, broken down by population categories, natives and immigrants:

- From the time of entry, until about 12 years later, immigrants use substantially fewer public services (largely due to less use of Social Security, because of youth) than do native families.
- After about two to six years, immigrant families come to pay as much in taxes as do native families, and after that they pay substantially more, because they earn more.
- The net balance of these two forces is positive in every year for natives; that is, immigrants contribute substantially more to the public coffers than they take from them.
- The results generally square with findings of previous research. The pattern of immigrants quickly contributing more in taxes than they receive in services is also found in Israel and in Canada.

For example, during 1975, the families who had arrived in the United States in 1974, on average, used about $532 worth of public assistance (unemployment compensation, welfare, food stamps), only 7% more than the national average for native families of $498. But because immigrant families are younger, they used fewer other social services (Social Security, medical assistance, public education) than the established native families; so their total social services costs were actually $863 less than the average native family.

At the same time, they paid in taxes some $2,666 (much of it for Social Security), or about $1,250 more than they took out in social benefits. This was a $328 better balance than the balance for the native families, which was $922.

As a result, these newly arrived 1974 immigrants made a net contribution of $328 per family to the economy of native American families. This contribution rises substantially over the next few years.

On average, then, native Americans in 1975 *gained* about $700 per family in net contribution to their own economy from the immigrant families who came here between 1950 and 1974. In practically every year studied the immigrants outperformed the native population, using fewer government services and contributing more taxes and private productivity.

One does not have to look very hard at these figures to realize that the fastest way to pump new life into the U.S. economy may well be to open the gates still wider to immigrants and to carefully screened refugees. It is clear that they quickly demonstrate their appreciation of the unique opportunities of the American system by producing more for the economy than they take from it.

This analysis debunks the theory of capital dilution that has plagued economic thinkers from Malthus to the 1972 Club of Rome Study, *The Limits to Growth*—namely, that the more people, the lower the per capita income, all else being equal.

If wealth is, as we have postulated, essentially metaphysical (the product of invention and knowledge), then the more people given freedom, the faster wealth should grow, not diminish. That is what the facts suggest.

Sounds good, perhaps, but does it really work that way? The answer according to the research of Simon Kuznets (one of the world's leading economic demographers) is a definite yes. As Kuznets (Table 2-2) found, during the 20th century in the essentially democratic Western countries, there was absolutely no loss of economic growth to population growth. Indeed, two of the countries with the fastest population growth, the United States and Canada, also enjoyed very rapid rates of economic growth, per capita.

Lest we ascribe this wholly to their untapped resource frontiers, we need only consider the experience of already resource-limited countries such as Germany and Italy with even higher rates of output growth.

While the Kuznets studies may not prove that rapid population growth in itself produces more economic growth, they certainly show that population growth does not decrease economic growth. The long-term demographic studies of Kuznets, combined with the work on productivity by economists

TABLE 2-2

POPULATION GROWTH AND OUTPUT GROWTH
OVER HALF A CENTURY IN CONTEMPORARY
MORE-DEVELOPED COUNTRIES

		Population growth rate per decade	Output per capita growth rate per decade
France	1896 to 1963-66	3.5	18.6
U.K.	1920-24 to 1963-67	4.8	16.9
Belgium	1900-04 to 1963-67	5.3	14.3
Italy	1890-99 to 1963-67	6.9	22.9
Switzerland	1910 to 1963-67	8.8	16.1
Germany	1910-13 to 1963-67	10.4	20.5
Netherlands	1900-09 to 1963-67	14.2	15.1
U.S.	1910-14 to 1963-67	14.2	18.4
Australia	1900-04 to 1963-67	18.8	13.1
Canada	1920-24 to 1963-67	19.4	20.9

SOURCE: Simon Kuznets, *Economic Growth of Nations* (Princeton University Press, 1971), pp. 11-14.

Denison, Kendrick, and Solow, prove that, in the long run, the most important economic impact of population size and growth is the effect of additional people "upon the stock of useful knowledge." The work of Solow and Fellner, in particular, shows that in the United States the rate of individual productivity growth actually increased as population growth quickened, and then decreased (during the last half of the 1970s) as the population growth leveled off.

Furthermore, there is now pretty general agreement that one of the greatest potential limitations on U.S. economic growth in the 1980s is the rapid slowdown in the annual work-force growth rate. It has fallen from nearly 3% per year to less than 1.5%, as population growth has correspondingly fallen sharply from 1.3% per year to less than 0.9%. The economic significance of this slower population growth shows in Kuznet's analysis of 21 non-Communist countries, including Japan from the early 1950s to 1964. The countries with the mid-range of population growth (1% per year) actually had nearly 50% faster rates of per capita productivity growth than the countries with less than one third the average population growth rate. Furthermore, even those countries with double-the-average population growth rates maintained very acceptable overall economic growth rates, while countries with low population growth suffered.

What this demonstrates is that the combination of relative economic freedom and easy access to knowledge and learning characteristic of non-Communist countries can turn population growth into an economic asset rather than a liability. The reason why the standard of living of Sweden or the United States is so much higher than that of Mali or India is that in the Western countries there is a much greater stock of technological know-how and much less superstition that would otherwise prevent using such knowledge effectively.

The key to knowledge is freedom, because while Kuznet's work demonstrates the metaphysical-wealth case in the Western democracies, it does not support it in the Communist-bloc countries of the East or in the nations of the Third World. At the heart of the thesis that "individuals are capital" is the premise that the economic value of this capital is in direct proportion to the degree of freedom with which it can be developed. It seems no accident that the freest nations are also the richest, even where education and social services may be relatively less developed. Hong Kong and Singapore come quickly to mind.

Conversely, the wealth of any nation seems to suffer almost in exact proportion to the denial of freedom to all or any significant proportion of its citizens. There is no better illustration of this than right within the United States. The spectacular economic rise of the New South since the birth of civil rights and desegregation, compared to the general stagnation and poverty that persisted in the Old South both before and after the Civil War, supports the conclusion that it is no accident that the burgeoning of the Sunbelt has coincided with its release from the bondage of segregation. The tumbling of racial barriers has signaled the economic rebirth of the whole region.

Yet in spite of this powerful economic evidence in favor of universal freedom, and even as the nation continues to wrestle with the complex and thorny problems raised by *Bakke* and busing, by affirmative action and quotas, many Americans still ask the troubling question, "Is integration worth the price? Can we afford civil rights?"

Liberal whites who warmly supported the struggles of Martin Luther King, Jr., nevertheless wonder, "Can we quickly open up economic opportunity for black Americans without, at the same time, limiting economic opportunity for many whites? Isn't it necessary to hold back whites to let blacks catch up?" Or, putting it even more bluntly, "Doesn't the legitimate economic progress of black Americans have to come at the expense of whites?"

Superficially, the current debate is over the *methods* being used to promote black economic integration. The whole idea of quotas seems repellent to even the most liberal of reformers. But the debate goes far deeper than that. At the bottom line lies raw economic fear—the concern, particularly among lower- and middle-income whites, that blacks will take their jobs. This pervasive fear, which is sometimes oversimplistically labeled only as racism, has made the issue raised by the *Bakke* case the most sensitive in modern domestic politics, not to mention the main reason for an alarming revival of the Ku Klux Klan. Yet this fear has no real foundation, either in economic theory or in practical and historical reality, as we have seen.

While most economists, as well, recoil at the notion of quotas, they also reject the concept that the economic progress of one group must be at the expense of another. In fact, the history of the South, old and new, is proof that it is not possible to systematically deprive one group of human beings of their economic freedom and growth without drastically limiting the total growth of the entire region, and that more freedom always means more economic growth.

A Tale of Two Cities

Nowhere is this lesson more vividly illustrated than in the 30-year comparative history of two of the Old South's largest cities, Atlanta and Birmingham.

In 1940, these two cities, though identical in size, were a study in contrasts. Atlanta was a somewhat somnolent trade center for the rural South, with a metropolitan population of 442,294 (24% black) and no industrial economy to speak of. Birmingham, by contrast, was the industrial capital of the Southeast, home of the southern steel industry and a railroad center, with a population of 407,851 (44% black) and grand prospects for the future.

Thirty years later, in 1970, their roles had been reversed; Atlanta was one of the fastest-growing metropolitan areas in the nation. With a total population of 1.6 million (22% black), it was indisputably the economic and social capital of the New South, soon-to-be urban home of the nation's thirty-ninth president, the eighteenth largest city in the country, and the home of the South's most economically advanced black community with a distinguished black mayor. Birmingham meanwhile had fallen far behind the rest of the Sunbelt economy, both in jobs and population growth and in family income. It also had fallen to forty-eighth place in the nation, with a metropolitan population (once identical to Atlanta's) that by 1970 was less than half Atlanta's present size, and an economy fully 60% smaller in wealth and output.

What had happened? Undoubtedly, many, many things. But, the most striking single difference in the development of these two cities was in their approach to the opening up of economic opportunity for blacks. More than any other southern city, Atlanta led the New South into the civil rights era, while Birmingham was dragged into it kicking and screaming all the way. While Atlanta was the first major southern city to integrate its shopping centers—and its job mart—Birmingham became in the 1950s and 1960s a national symbol of dogged resistance to all forms of integration.

Today Atlanta stands as a remarkable testament to the economic principle that a city's wealth is the sum of the development of all of its citizens. Small wonder that Jimmy Carter once said, "The best thing that ever happened to Georgia was the civil rights movement." The glittering skyscrapers that now line Peachtree Street are a visual statement of that belief.

But the economic miracle that is Atlanta today commenced long before Jimmy Carter even thought about Georgia politics. It started in the 1940s with the articulate and insistent voice of a great liberal newspaper editor named Ralph McGill, who systematically began to prick the conscience of Atlanta's "establishment" with his columns and editorials in the *Atlanta Constitution*. Over a period of nearly 30 years, McGill admonished his white Atlanta audience that the future of their city depended on its willingness to open social, political, and economic opportunity to the 50% of its inner-city residents who were black.

McGill warned Atlanta businessmen that segregation was limiting the city's ability to grow by excluding nearly half of its residents from effective contribution and participation in its economy. Above all, he stressed that Atlanta could not expect its share of the big influx of northern capital investment that was coming, unless it began to throw off the arcane racial segregation policies of the prior 70 years. McGill was instrumental in getting the city to elect and reelect a brilliant, moderate mayor, Ivan Allen, who slowly convinced the Atlanta business community that opening up Atlanta's economic marketplace to blacks would be to the advantage of the entire city.

Long before the ugly confrontations in Montgomery and Selma, and the eruptions in Mississippi and South Carolina, Atlanta quietly commenced and steadily furthered the progress of voluntary desegregation of its economy. Even as Birmingham was fighting the battle in the streets with bullhorns and bullwhips, Atlanta was getting ready to become the economic capital of the South.

The results of these two contrasting attitudes were obvious, and startling. They are summed up in Table 2-3, which shows that despite Atlanta's lack of major physical and industrial resources (as compared with Birmingham's), it left Birmingham behind in an economic cloud of dust. While Atlanta's population boomed (261%), Birmingham's barely kept pace with its birth rate (88%).

The primary reason for this population boom was jobs. Opening the Atlanta job market to blacks did not deprive whites of jobs. Atlanta's job growth was nearly three times that of Birmingham.

A skeptic might say that the growth of Atlanta's job market came only from those northern businesses which came in to exploit cheap labor, and that the availability of cheap black labor would only bring down income levels. Not so. Between 1950 and 1970 Atlanta's average family income grew faster than that of almost any other American city, except Washington, D.C. While Atlanta and Birmingham had identical pre-World War II income levels for families, by 1970 Atlanta was 25% above Birmingham, and as of 1979 was competing favorably with most northern cities.

What makes this income performance even more impressive is that it came when Atlanta's black population was also growing faster than that of any other major southern city and over seven times as fast as Birmingham's. So, even though the northern "invasion" brought new white population growth to Atlanta, the city's metropolitan area in 1970 was still 22% black, compared with 24% 30 years before.

Between 1940 and 1970 Birmingham's black population dropped from 42% to 29%. One might expect that such a drop would mean a higher average income level for the city as a whole, as lower-paid blacks comprised a smaller and smaller share of the city's population. But just the opposite took place. During the period when Birmingham lost a significant share of its black population, its family-income growth actually fell far behind the rest of the South. By holding back all those years on black economic progress, Birmingham only punished its own total economy, both black and white.

TABLE 2-3

A MODERN TALE OF TWO CITIES

Population (000)—Metro Area			
	1940	1970	% Change
Atlanta	442.3	1,598.0	261%
Birmingham	407.9	767.4	88%

Jobs (000)—Metro Area			
Atlanta	178.5	668.4	274%
Birmingham	139.6	278.2	99%

Black Population (000)—Metro Area			
Atlanta	104.6 (24%)	348.4 (22%)	233%
Birmingham	169.8 (42%)	221.0 (29%)	31%

Average Family Income			
	1950	1970	
Atlanta	$2,477	$10,310	316%
Birmingham	2,426	8,222	239%

SOURCES: U.S. Department of Commerce; U.S. Bureau of the Census.

Conversely, in Atlanta remarkable economic progress for whites has coincided with excellent economic progress for blacks. More than in any other city in America, blacks figure prominently in Atlanta, not only in its political scene, but in its financial and business circles as well. Around Atlanta there are affluent, mostly black suburban communities, where luxury housing abounds, a testament to the fact that blacks are moving up economically in Atlanta faster than any other community in the nation. Blacks would rightly argue that they are not yet getting enough of a share of Atlanta's economy, nor has integration gone far enough. But the progress over three decades has been solid.

Economists will argue too that there were many other factors in Atlanta's economic miracle and in Birmingham's relative decline in position. And, indeed, there were. Integration was only one element in the "mix," and perhaps not the most important one. But we still cannot ignore two simple economic facts: First, there is no evidence that voluntary integration hurt the economic progress of Atlanta; and second, there is no evidence that holding back racial economic and social integration benefited Birmingham.

The lesson seems clear: While Americans may dispute some of the more heavy-handed methods being used to force economic and social integration, they should at the same time reject as economically specious, the notion that the economic growth and opportunity of one group need come at the expense of another.

The economic progress of America's black and other minority populations is something not to be feared but welcomed. If it comes by free and voluntary cooperation, it will mean real progress for all. After all, productivity, technological development, imagination, and know-how are not the private province of the already established elite, or only from those with advanced educational degrees.

The best proof of the widespread base of individual metaphysical capital, Julian Simon argues, is that "there have been so many more discoveries in the past century than in previous centuries, when there were fewer people alive," and he postulates what proponents of zero-population growth must regard as the ultimate heresy, that if we only had *more people*, productivity and technological breakthrough would be even greater!

Our national economic growth will indeed be limited if we fear and so deliberately limit population growth, or in other ways hinder the freedom of our "individual capital" to develop itself. We cannot protect our own economic position or future by limiting the access of others.

Coming Labor Shortages?

We are already seeing a particular challenge in the nation's high-technology industries where severe labor shortages are now developing not only among skilled engineers and scientists, but also in rank-and-file technical and production workers. Since each trained senior engineer generates 12 to 16 direct high-technology industry jobs, and another 16 to 18 jobs that service them, it is clear that the primary limiting factor to the growth of this labor-intensive sector is not financial capital but individual capital—trained, skilled people, well motivated, and rewarded with incentives. Unfortunately, with the combination of explosive growth in this field and a rapid buildup in defense spending, the human capital for technological growth is already in very tight supply.

There are economists who believe that in the late 1980s America's most crucial shortage will not be physical energy sources (such as oil) but human energy (labor). Indeed, so severe is the labor crunch that is predicted, it could have major economic and social consequences for more than a generation.

If the population-trend data of the Census Bureau is right, America is entering a period when, barring fundamental changes in our retirement programs or our immigration policies, the growth in the nation's domestic labor force will actually be decreasing each year for perhaps seven to 12 years. Instead of having to find new jobs for a growing number of work-age Americans each year, the economy will have to find ways either to increase productivity or to import new workers from abroad.

To understand why this is, consider the dramatic pace at which the age composition of our population is changing. During the period 1970–76 the nation's labor force exploded as the postwar baby-boom children came of employment age. During that period, the labor pool grew at 2.5% to 3% per year, not only because of the baby boom but because female participation in the labor market was growing rapidly as well. As a result, the nation was being called upon to increase its jobs by 3%–4% a year just to keep unemployment from rising too rapidly.

TABLE 2-4

POPULATION AND WORK-FORCE TRENDS

POPULATION AGE GROUP	1970 1975	1975 1980	1980 1985	1985 1990 (Projected)
14-17	+6.4%	-6.1%	-10%	-11.3%
18-21	+12.1%	+4.2%	-10%	-6.0%
18-55	+9.0%	+8.4%	+6.7%	+5.4%
65 & over	+11.6%	+12.7%	+8.0%	+9.2%
Work force	+12.0%	+13.1%	+7.0%	+6.0%
Average annual work force growth	2.3%	2.5%	1.3%	+1.2%

SOURCES: U.S. Bureau of the Census; U.S. Bureau of Labor Statistics.

All that is now about to change dramatically. While the teenage job market was booming, the nation's birth rate was plummeting, with sub-work-age population declining every year. By 1980 this declining birth rate was beginning to show up in the leveling off of new entrants into the 16-to-19-year-old work-force group, which is now experiencing its first decline since World War II.

Meanwhile, the nation's work force is being sapped at the other end by a retirement-age group that is growing almost three times as fast as the population as a whole, and each year at a higher rate. During the next 15 years not only will more people be leaving the work force at the tail end, but fewer and fewer will be joining it at the front. And now that female work participation is close to male levels, women will not easily make up the slack.

The unmistakable conclusion of this trend is that throughout the 1980s, and particularly in the early 1990s, America will be experiencing labor tightness of historic magnitude. We could actually be seeing work-force growth of as little as 1% annually, and the economic and social implications are immense:

- The inflationary pressures will be very great as the nation attempts to maintain substantial economic growth with a very tight labor market.
- The pressure to automate will increase, and unions will likely cease to fight it as their own bargaining power grows and forces automation on their own terms.
- Conversely, as the labor market tightens, unions could have more trouble convincing opulent workers of their necessity in this labor-sellers' market.
- The growing level of automation may make structural unemployment problems worse for some poorly educated minorities.
- There will be intense pressure to raise the Social Security retirement age to 68 or 70, as a smaller workforce tries to support a larger retirement community.
- The demand for capital investments in productivity improvement will

be greater than this nation can now handle, and the tax laws will have to be revised to meet it.

- The federal government is likely to take a more and more benign attitude toward illegal aliens, since their willing hands will be desirable in a nation with a tight domestic labor force of its own. Immigration quotas may even be raised.
- Teenage unemployment for both blacks and whites will be significantly reduced, both by population trends and by the tightening of the labor market; but the pressure on public education to improve literacy and mathematical skills for a more automated environment will be intense.
- Women will have less trouble gaining access to higher-skill jobs and more parity with males.

Although all this may seem far away, it is not. In fact, even in the midst of high unemployment the nation is already experiencing acute shortages of skilled workers in many industries and markets. There is now a significant migration of both blacks and whites to the Sunbelt to fill new and burgeoning job markets. But the big crunch is coming from about 1984 forward, when each successive graduating class will be 2% to 3% smaller than the previous one, while retirement losses in the work force will be growing at 5%–6% per year.

If President Reagan and Congress are depending on annual growth rates of 3%–5% in real GNP to balance the federal budget and hoping to reduce inflation permanently to manageable levels, they are going to have to stimulate capital formation, both human and in physical plant, through tax incentives.

In 1980 the United States was still last in free world savings and investment growth. This, combined with a tightening labor market, could send inflation skyrocketing again, and the balance of payments into more serious deficits than ever, if labor costs soar and output levels off.

So swiftly is this fundamental change in labor supply coming, that Congress was much too slow in 1981 in enacting a significant tax reform to stimulate capital investment, productivity, and savings, and freeing more of our individual capital to multiply its productivity through technological development.

Above all, we need to stop the more extreme zero-population-growth approach of looking upon individuals and their offspring as environmental liabilities, instead of the capital which they assuredly are in a free society.

The only way economic progress can ever really be stopped is by destroying freedom—by throttling the creative process in the mire of benevolent tyrannies, of well-meaning bureaucratic regulators, planners, and politicians who are still dealing in what Buckminster Fuller refers to as "pirate theories of not enough to go around." Fuller argues that "because science now finds there can be ample for all," the only impediment to widespread sufficiency is what he calls "sovereign fences" which hedge about individual creativity and promote both national and class warfare to the detriment of all.

Metaphysics along with science and technology has made both Marxism and Malthusian premises obsolete and irrelevant. It has destroyed the zero-sum game which dominates the politics of envy and redistribution. It has made the protectionism of mercantilism pointless, a quaint relic of the fargone past. It demands an economy without oppressive limits.

Yet today, at least as many of those sovereign fences that prevent the fulfillment of Fuller's dream of infinitely expanding metaphysical wealth can be found within nations as well as among them. Even as our physical limits to growth have been receding, we have been erecting more and more artificial fences, including punitive marginal-taxation rates, inflation, regulation, and bureaucracy, all of which prevent the legitimate individual evolution and development essential to reversing the entropy of overorganized and overgoverned economies.

3

What Is Progressive about Taxation?

You cannot bring about prosperity by discouraging thrift. You cannot strengthen the weak by weakening the strong. You cannot help the wage earner by pulling down the wage payer. You cannot help the poor by destroying the rich.

—Abraham Lincoln

If it is true, as we have postulated, that in this increasingly high-technology economy, the individual is the real capital, then anything that limits individual initiative, opportunity, and development will automatically limit the economic wealth potential of the nation. Certainly high on the list of such possible limits must be taxation, which, when stripped of the rhetoric that surrounds it, is a price or penalty that is imposed on individual effort and enterprise. The higher the price, the lower the development of our nation's economic potential.

There is no better example of this "penalty" than that great central plank of Western liberalism, the graduated income tax—the notion that taxes can be regarded as progressive if they fall more heavily on higher incomes than on lower; while "tax reform" is invariably regarded as meaning higher tax rates for the few and lower tax rates for the many—until the few disappear or stop producing. It is the kind of merchandising the devil himself would admire, because it gets us to accept as "progressive" and "good" that which we would otherwise understand as harmful.

It would be hard to imagine a more self-contradictory term than "progressive taxation." The dictionary defines the fundamental meaning of the word "tax" as "to deplete, to erode, to wear out, to exhaust."

Justice Marshall wrote in *McCulloch* v. *Maryland* in 1819, "The power to tax involves the power to destroy." Literally translated, then, "progressive taxation" is "progressive destruction" or "progressive depletion." Can there really be anything progressive about destruction?

Progress is, after all, the gradual release from lack and limitation. Throughout history, mankind has enjoyed the greatest progress in those nations with the greatest and most consistent *overall* economic growth. "It is the rising tide that lifts all ships," John Kennedy observed; and while some ships always seem to rise higher than others, it is a statistical fact that the greatest triumphs over poverty have been in those nations with the greatest overall economic development.

In turn, the key to economic progress is productivity, since no nation can ever have more than it produces. Productivity is the basic economic reason why some nations are rich and others poor. The 9.5 million people of Cuba, for example, produced a subsidized GNP of only $10 billion in 1980, while the 5.7 million people of Massachusetts produced more than $60 billion in gross state product, six times as much with 40% fewer people. Is it any wonder that the average Cuban's per capita income was less than $600 while the average Massachusetts resident's was over $9,000?

Obviously, the total wealth of the nation depends directly on the willingness and ability of its people to produce, and anything that inhibits this willingness or ability limits progress. Yet that is precisely the effect of the progressive income tax, which is, in reality, a penalty for productivity. Consider what would happen to total output if each weekday's work were taxed at progressive rates, 10% on Monday, up to 90% on Friday. Would people work as hard on Friday as on Monday?

In the graduated income-tax system, the important thing is not the "average" rate of taxation on *all* one's income, but the "marginal rate" of taxation on the last dollars one earns—that is, the tax bracket on the highest dollars of earnings. This determines how much one will get for extra effort, or *additional* labor and investment, and is crucial to economic growth rates and incentives.

So long as 90% of a nation's population are earning at fairly low levels, and paying at moderate marginal tax levels (10%–15%), a progressive tax has relatively little impact on overall economic growth. But as this working population is pushed by inflation into higher and higher tax brackets (30%–40%), the effect of this "tax on progress" becomes "progressively destructive."

In 1960 fewer than 4% of Americans were paying at the 30% marginal tax rate or above. But in 1980, as a result primarily of inflation, over 40% of all Americans were paying marginal tax rates of 30% and higher on their incomes. By 1985, this figure will approach 60% of the people, unless drastic revisions are made in the nation's tax laws.

For example, in 1980 the $20,000-income earners paid a top marginal tax rate of 28% on an income whose gross buying power was actually no greater than the $10,000 income on which they had paid 17% just ten years before. As a result, individual real income after taxes and inflation was 8% lower, as federal taxes had risen 2.3 times as fast as prices, 2.8 times as fast as output, and 3.6 times as fast as productivity, the source of real income. No surprise that productivity declined precipitously when top marginal tax rates were increased over 50% in a single decade even as gross real wages declined. In the 1950s, productivity grew, on average, over 3% per year; in the 1960s, by 2.5%; and in the 1970s, about 1.5%.

TABLE 3-1

PERCENTAGE OF TAXPAYERS PAYING AT VARIOUS
MARGINAL TAX RATES OR HIGHER

	20%	30%	40%
1960	8.7	2.9	0.5
1970	12.9	5.4	1.6
1976	31.0	18.0	5.2
1978	41.4	26.5	8.6
1981	62.0	34.0	16.0

SOURCE: U.S. Treasury.

That is why middle-class America has now discovered that the dream of upward mobility has been replaced by a frustrating taxflation treadmill, forcing families to expend more and more total working hours just to break even. What they may not realize is that this frustration is precisely what the man who invented the progressive income tax had in mind.

In 1980, during his stirring speech to the Democratic national convention, Senator Edward M. Kennedy mocked Ronald Reagan for claiming, "The progressive income tax was spawned by Karl Marx, and declared by him to be the prime essential of a socialist state—the method prescribed for taxing the middle class out of existence." Kennedy suggested that "Mr. Reagan has confused Karl Marx with Theodore Roosevelt," and columnist Richard Strout asked, "Can America really elect a man as president who believed that the graduated income tax was invented by Karl Marx? Why does Reagan say such things?"

If Kennedy or Strout had bothered to go back and read Marx and Engels's *Communist Manifesto* of 1848, they would have found (among the ten important measures by which the proletariat would seize power from the hated middle class) the following item: "A heavy progressive or graduated income tax."

Now Marx was much too astute to think that such a tax would be sound economics. He knew, as every student of Economics I should know, that the inevitable effect of progressive marginal tax rates would always be to punish total productivity and output. Marx also understood that steeply progressive tax rates would never hurt the already rich, who would always find ways to escape them, either by physically moving, or through sheltering their wealth in the "underground" economy, or through legislated loopholes. But Marx also knew that the greatest threat to socialism was not from the rich, who are few in number, but from the upward aspirations and mobility of the vast middle class, whose legitimate desire is to join the upper class.

George McGovern discovered the depth of this aspiration when in 1972 he proposed a $1,000 "demogrant" to every family with an income below $17,000—to be financed by taxing more heavily citizens earning more than $17,000. Even though three quarters of the citizenry in 1972 earned less than $17,000, the proposal caused McGovern to nosedive sharply in the polls. McGovern said later, "I just didn't realize how many Americans there

CHART 3-A

THE LAFFER CURVE

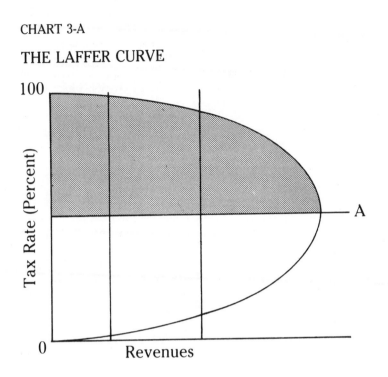

are who are making less than $17,000 a year, who someday hope to be making more than $17,000."

It is precisely that unegalitarian aspiration that Marx wanted to crush, and the steeply progressive income tax was just the tool to do it with.

That tool has nothing to do with raising more tax revenues, or even with the average "effective" tax. It is simply a punishment mechanism. Indeed, the fastest way to *reduce* the collection of tax revenues, particularly from the rich, is to go on raising marginal tax rates. At 100%, no one would work, or invest, or start new businesses, or create new jobs. Conversely, the fastest way to get rich people to pay more taxes has always been to reduce high marginal tax rates and encourage them to invest their money in productive enterprise, instead of in leisure.

The Laffer Curve

Over the past few years the press and the establishment economists have heaped more than a little scorn on Professor Arthur B. Laffer and his famous curve—the thesis of which is that lower marginal tax rates will usually produce higher revenue growth. Yet in Laffer's defense is the fact that over the past two decades, every time the U.S. capital-gains tax was raised, tax revenues fell off, and every time it was reduced, tax revenues began to rise again.

There is, of course, nothing new either about this experience, or, for that matter, about the Laffer Curve itself. It is simply a restatement of what everyone learns about "demand elasticity" in his first course in economics. For every product there is a curve of demand elasticity, which defines how consumers react at varying levels of price. As prices rise, demand (i.e., sales) falls off, and vice versa, depending on the nature of the product. Every department store merchandiser understands price elasticity. When sales and revenues are off, one doesn't raise prices, one lowers them. Lower prices generate higher sales, more traffic, and, up to a point, more real profits.

Arthur Laffer has taken this age-old economic principle and applied it to tax rates. He suggests that there are two tax rates at which one will collect no revenues, 100% and 0%. In between there is a curve that, theoretically, should look like Chart 3-A. As tax rates are raised from 0%, revenues will continue to rise until, when they get too high (Point A), people will begin to find ways to avoid paying them by reduced economic activity, sheltering or hiding income, or barter. At that point, higher tax rates will produce less and less revenue growth as the curve bends back on itself. There is really no fundamental disagreement with this hypothesis. The argument comes over the precise shape of the curve and how it can be used as a predictive instrument of economic policy-making.

The idea of taxation as a "price" of working, having an elasticity curve is nothing new. In *Taxation: The People's Business*, Andrew W. Mellon wrote in 1926:

> An income tax is the price which the government charges for the privilege of having taxable income. If the price is too low, the government's revenue is not large enough: If the price is too high the taxpayer, through the many means available, avoids a taxable income, and the government gets less out of a high tax than it would get out of a lower one. What the proper figure is between these two extremes is not determinable with absolute accuracy. It is the opinion of some authorities on taxation that this figure is below 15%. None of them places it as high as 25%.

He argued that when tax rates get above 25% they begin to become self-defeating and should be reduced to gain more total revenues.

The great liberal economist John Maynard Keynes restated Mellon's basic thesis in 1933, when he told the struggling governments of Europe and America that in the midst of a depression they should not try to balance their budgets by raising taxes, and that lowering taxes then might be a better route to prosperity and budget balancing.

> Nor should the argument seem strange that taxation may be so high as to defeat its object, and that, given sufficient time to gather the fruits, a reduction of taxation will run a better chance than an increase of

balancing the budget. For to take the opposite view today is to resemble a manufacturer who, running at a loss, decides to raise his price and when his declining sales increase the loss, wrapping himself in the rectitude of plain arithmetic, decides that prudence requires him to raise the prices still more—and who, when at last his account is balanced with nought on both sides, is still found righteously declaring that it would have been the act of a gambler to reduce the price when you were already making a loss.

The Mellon Tax Cuts

Mellon practiced what he and Keynes preached. Between 1921 and 1925 he got Harding, Coolidge, and Congress to cut the tax rates four times, by a grand total of 66%, from a top range of 4%–73% to a final range of 1.5%–25%.

Despite the enormity of these cuts, the actual revenues to the Treasury from the income tax actually rose every year except in 1923 (when there was a recession). More important, all of the revenue gains came from the income groups earning above $50,000 a year, whose total payments to the Treasury, at vastly reduced tax rates, rose by more than 60%, even as the revenues paid by the income brackets below $20,000 dropped by more than 70%.

So, even though Mellon earned a place in history as an apostle for the rich, the actual effect of his tax-cut program was to make the rich pay a much bigger share of the tax burden, as the percentage of taxes paid by the $100,000-and-over income-earners rose from 28.8 in 1921, to 48.8 in 1925, while the lowest group (below $10,000) actually watched their share of the tax burden decline from 22.5% to 4.5%. This made the Mellon tax cut the most "progressive" in history, and the "progressive effects" didn't stop in 1925. By 1928, under this same vastly reduced structure, the $100,000-and-over income group (less than 1% of all taxpayers) were paying 61% of all the federal income taxes. That compares with only 15% of total federal income-tax revenues that this same group accounted for in 1981. (In other words, after Mellon got through, the U.S. tax structure was three times as progressive in effect as it is today.)

It totally vindicated a commonsense editorial by, of all institutions, The New York Times, which in 1923 still understood rational supply-side economic theory when it observed that Secretary Mellon "wants in reality to get more money out of [the rich] than they are now paying. But he proposes to do it by making their rate of taxation lower." Although the Times admitted that such a notion "seems a ridiculous proposition to those whose thoughts are all of aiming sharp arrows of taxation at wealth," it pointed out that the rich invariably find ways "to relieve themselves" by "escaping the heavy taxes placed on them." The result, the Times noted, is that instead of hurting the rich, these high taxes "are all the while striking at the poor. The true way to help the latter is to make it possible for the [rich] to put more money into enterprise and industry, and less into tax-exempt securities."

That is why, ironically, the higher the marginal tax rates laid on the rich, the less progressive the tax system becomes. More and more wealth is moved out of the tax system, leaving the rest of the people to carry more of the burden.

Consider that in 1925 we had the most "progressive" federal tax burden in modern history, with the overwhelming majority of the public (those earning less than $10,000) paying only 4.5% of the tax burden, while the richest (.02%) in our society paid nearly half of all the taxes. Yet the top marginal tax rate in 1925 was only 25%.

Then, during World War II, the Democrats introduced the most steeply progressive tax rates in our history, ranging from 20% at the bottom to 91% at the top. After 20 years with these high rates, what happened? The richest, the over-$100,000 salary group (which still made up less than .05% of all taxpayers), were paying only 5% of the tax burden, while the lowest-income taxpayers were shouldering 48% of the burden. So between 1925 and 1963, even as the top marginal tax rates were raised by 264%, the share of the tax burden paid by the richest group had dropped by 90%, while for the poorest group it had risen 971%. The Democrats had only succeeded in massively redistributing the tax burden from the rich to the poor. (See Table 3-2.)

This should forever disabuse us of the notion that a steeply graduated income-tax system is progressive. That is one of the great hoaxes of "democratic" socialism—alias Marxism—designed to make the masses feel better, even as they are being taken to the cleaners.

The JFK Tax Cuts

It was Chancellor Ludwig Erhard of the German Federal Republic who first impressed this idea on President John F. Kennedy. When Kennedy visited Germany in 1961, Erhard told him to avoid the British high-tax model, to stop punishing wealth creation, and to cut America's egregiously high wartime tax rates.

That is precisely what Kennedy did—over the stiff opposition of many liberals in his own administration, who wanted to make the nation's tax structure even more punitive and progressive. In December 1962, in a speech to the Economic Club of New York, President Kennedy warned the nation that because of a sluggish economy, high unemployment, and an already unbalanced budget, he wanted to cut taxes to increase revenues:

> Our true choice is not between tax reduction, on the one hand, and the avoidance of large federal deficits on the other. It is increasingly clear that no matter what party is in power, so long as our national security needs keep rising, an economy hampered by restrictive tax rates will never produce enough revenue to balance the budget—just as it will never produce enough jobs or enough profits.

In 1961 and 1962 President Kennedy put forth a massive tax-cut program for individuals and business. For individuals he proposed a two-year plan to cut

TABLE 3-2

TAX CUTS MAKE THE SYSTEM MORE PROGRESSIVE

Tax revenues paid by income class	1921-25 Mellon cuts (millions of dollars)			1963-65 Kennedy cuts (billions of dollars)		
	1921	1925	% Change	1963	1966	% Change
Under 10,000	$161.6	$ 33.6	−79%	$23.2	$20.7	−11%
10,000-20,000	92.9	47.5	−49%	12.9	18.3	+41%
20,000-50,000	146.8	147.8	——	6.7	8.7	+30%
50,000 & over	317.9	506.6	+59%	5.4	8.5	+57%
All classes	719.4	734.6	+2%	48.2	56.1	+16%
Tax rate range	4%-73%	1.5%-25%	−66%	20%-91%	14%-70%	−23%
Share of taxes paid						
Under 10,000	22%	4%	−82%	48%	37%	−23%
10,000-50,000	33%	27%	−18%	41%	48%	+17%
50,000 & over	44%	69%	+57%	11%	15%	+36%

SOURCES: IRS data; U.S. Tax Foundation.

income-tax rates across the board by about 23%—from 91% to 70% at the top and from 20% down to 14% at the bottom. For businesses he proposed substantial investment tax credits to stimulate new plant and equipment purchases and to improve the nation's sluggish economy. In making these proposals he did not worry about the fact that in straight cash terms, people at the top would get much bigger absolute tax cuts than those at the bottom, as long as, proportionally, everyone up and down the line got about the same percentage cuts. In other words, his tax-cut proposal was (to use today's pejorative term) classic "trickle-down" economics. Since JFK was no ideologue, he was able to understand that if one wants more savings and investment, one has to provide substantial new incentives to those most likely to save and invest, and particularly to the top 5%–10% of income-earners who account for two thirds of all individual savings and investment.

Kennedy made this original tax-cut case in words and phrases that would have delighted both Andrew Mellon and Ronald Reagan, but which were nevertheless couched in a kind of supply-side Keynesian exegesis that subsequent presidents unfortunately ignored:

> The most direct and significant kind of federal action aiding economic growth is to make possible an increase in private consumption and investment demand—to cut the fetters which hold back private spending.

> In the past, this could be done in part by the increased use of credit and monetary tools. . . . It could also be done by increasing federal expenditures more rapidly than necessary—but such a course would soon demoralize both the government and the economy.

> If the government is to retain the confidence of the people, it must not spend a penny more than can be justified on grounds of national need, and spent with maximum efficiency.

The final and best means of strengthening demand among consumers and business is to reduce the burden on private income and the deterrents to private initiative which are imposed by our present tax system . . .

He then presented to Congress a two-year tax-cut proposal that was every bit as "favorable to the rich" as the one Ronald Reagan introduced in 1981, cutting tax rates right across the board, top to bottom. Congress gave him nearly all of his cut—though tragically, posthumously accepting Kennedy's contention that this was the way to "get America moving again."

He was, it turned out, exactly right:

- Personal savings, which had been declining, suddenly jumped from an average annual growth rate of 2% to 9% over the next six years.
- Business investment zoomed from 2% annual growth to more than 8%.
- Not surprisingly, the Gross National Product (GNP) growth rate increased by 40% within two years.
- Job growth more than doubled.
- Unemployment declined by nearly 33%.
- And the per capita disposable-income growth rate tripled.

Because the tax cut was as good percentagewise to the wealthy as it was to those with lower incomes, Kennedy got just what he wanted: massive new savings and investment—just what the United States needs so badly today.

What the skeptics conveniently ignore, of course, is that by cutting all tax rates Kennedy also got *more* tax revenues as the economy boomed and money was moved out of "shelter" into productive tax-paying investment. Following the JFK cuts, with marginal rates reduced by an average of 23%, tax revenues from every class of taxpayers above $10,000 shot up enormously, and the biggest increases came in the highest tax brackets. Total revenues also rose in 1966 by their fastest rate in postwar history.

Even Walter Heller, the Keynesian economist who had privately argued against the Kennedy tax cut when it was first broached, was forced to admit in testimony to the Joint Economic Committee in 1977 that the tax cut did "pay for itself in increased revenues," because "it did seem to have a tremendously stimulative effect, a multiplied effect on the economy," an effect, incidentally, that completely overturned the Treasury's preliminary predictions.

Thus it was that almost exactly 40 years later, a brilliant young liberal president essentially stole a leaf right out of Andrew Mellon's 1926 book *Taxation: The People's Business*—and, as after Mellon's cuts, revenues rose. The most striking result of the Kennedy-Johnson tax cuts was that even though the top rates (on the rich) were cut from 91% to 70%, a reduction of 25%, the total taxes paid by the top income brackets actually rose by 72% in the three years after the tax cut (after having declined 5% in the three years before the cut). Once again the government got the rich to pay more taxes than ever before, by cutting their tax rates and making it more profitable for them to invest in productive industry. At the same time, the resulting economic progress reduced the percentage of those Americans living below the poverty line from 22% to 13% (1960–68), the best results in poverty reduction in our history—and virtually all of this was accomplished before the Great Society was implemented!

Above all, the JFK cut revealed the basic bankruptcy of the principle of soaking the rich to help the poor. For three years, prior to the Kennedy tax cuts, the amount of revenue collected from the rich (at the 91% rate) had actually declined. But, after the rates were lowered, the revenues collected from each high-income group soared, and this in turn had a highly progressive effect on the actual tax burden.

As with the Mellon cuts of the 1920s, the Kennedy cut actually shifted the tax burden very substantially from the backs of the 80% who earned less than $10,000 a year to the 20% who earned more.

These two across-the-board tax-cutting experiences demonstrate the utter bankruptcy of so-called progressive tax theories. They also debunk the demagoguery that has characterized the political and media assaults on the so-called Kemp-Roth tax cut, which in every way was a mirror-image of the Kennedy tax cut, except for the fact that the 1963–64 cut gave an even greater share of tax reduction (in static analysis) to the rich than the 1981–82 version. Not only do high marginal tax rates discourage economic growth for everyone, but they invariably produce sharply lower rates of tax-revenue growth from the upper-income brackets. This means that these high rates merely force the middle- and lower-income groups to shoulder more of the tax burden, whereas cutting those rates across the board is the sure way to get the rich to shoulder more of that burden.

This becomes clear when we compare the 1964–69 experience with what happened in the 1974–79 period, when we actively pursued a redistributional taxation approach. (See Table 3-3.) During the latter period virtually all of the tax cuts were targeted to the lowest income groups, while "tax reform" consisted mainly of assaults on higher-income taxpayers. With these "percolate-up" (as opposed to "trickle-down") theories, we managed to turn the once productive U.S. economy into an inflation-riddled basket case. Personal savings, business investment, and economic growth all fell off sharply to levels worse than existed before the Kennedy tax cut of 1963–64.

Furthermore, since 1974, despite massive bracket-creep (which has driven most Americans into 50% higher marginal tax rates than before), federal tax revenues actually rose by less than half the rate at which they grew in 1964–69.

The Capital-Gains Tax Experience

The experience with the nation's capital-gains tax since 1961 also exactly bears out Mellon, Keynes, and Laffer. When the top marginal tax rate on capital gains was 46% (1946–63), or nearly double Mellon's maximum range of 25%, the taxes paid on capital gains steadily declined from 1961 through

TABLE 3-3

JFK "TRICKLE-DOWN ECONOMICS"
(all data based on constant dollars)

	6 years before JFK tax cut 1958-63 (inclusive)	6 years after JFK tax cut 1964-69 (inclusive)	6 years of "percolate-up" economics 1974-79 (inclusive)
Average tax revenue growth	+2.4%	+6.2%	+3.5%
Average GNP growth	+3.4%	+4.5%	+2.5%
Average business investment growth	+2.0%	+8.0%	+2.1%
Average personal savings growth	-2.5%	+8.8%	-6.0%
Average job growth	1.0%	+2.4%	+2.3%
Average unemployment	6.0%	4.1%	6.8%
Average per capita disposal income growth	1.2%	3.6%	1.8%
Average CPI	1.5%	3.0%	8.6%

SOURCE: President's Economic Message, 1980.

1963. Then, as a result of the Kennedy across-the-board tax cut of 1963–64, the top marginal tax rate on capital gains was reduced from 46% to 35%–a cut of 24%. The revenues from this tax steadily rose, by 25% in 1964 and 27% in 1965. By 1968 they had nearly tripled in constant dollars, at a substantially lower marginal tax rate.

Unfortunately, this growth in capital gains and investment was hit hard, first by a surtax in 1968–69, and then by an increase on capital gains put through by Senator Edward M. Kennedy in 1969, which had the effect of raising the top marginal tax on capital gains to its highest level in U.S. history, 49% in 1970. The results were immediately destructive. Tax revenues from capital gains plummeted, and over the next eight years remained consistently at a level nearly $1.5 billion lower than they were in 1968.

Within a year of this tax increase, the entire equity capital market for small companies (which account for over 80% of all new jobs and 65% of new inventions) fell apart; and it continued to disintegrate over the next eight years. In 1969, before the tax hike, there were nearly 700 new stock offerings by small companies, with a total 1980 value of nearly $3 billion. But by 1977 this equity market had shriveled to only 13 offerings and less than $55 million—a compound annual decrease of nearly 40%, the worst collapse in equity sales in modern U.S. history.

For all intents and purposes, Senator Kennedy's innocent little tax hike had virtually killed off the small-business equity market and countless thousands, even millions, of jobs along with it. The impact of this huge

TABLE 3-4

EQUITY CAPITAL RAISED BY COMPANIES HAVING
A NET WORTH UNDER $5 MILLION
(millions of dollars)

Year	Number of offerings	Current	Constant 1980 dollars
1968	358	$ 745.3	$1,643.3
1969 Kennedy	698	1,366.9	2,869.5
1970 tax hike	198	375.0	747.3
1971	248	550.9	1,044.5
1972	409	896.0	1,631.2
1973	69	159.7	274.8
1974	9	16.1	25.3
1975	4	16.2	23.2
1976	29	144.8	197.0
1977	13	42.6	54.8
1978 Steiger	21	89.3	106.9
1979 tax cut	81	506.5	570.3
1980	237	1,401.0	1,401.0

SOURCE: American Council for Capital Formation, Vol. 6, No. 2,
February 1981.

decline in capital formation and productivity was devastingly direct. From 1948 until 1970, the ratio of U.S. capital investment to labor had remained firm at a constant 3% annual growth rate; but in 1970 this ratio began to drop sharply, and by the period 1975–79 it was actually declining about 1% per year. (See Chart 3-B.)

Since capital is directly related to productivity, and productivity to inflation, it is not surprising that both indicators deterioriated sharply in the 1970s, as workers were given fewer new tools to work with and unit labor costs began to rise. It is no accident that this dramatic fall-off in capital-to-labor formation began within one year after the increase in the capital-gains tax in 1969.

As we might have expected, considering the Mellon and JFK tax-cut data, the 1969 tax hike did not extract more tax revenues from the rich as Edward M. Kennedy had predicted. (He forecast that it would increase capital-gains tax revenues by at least $2 billion a year.) Instead, it actually reduced tax revenues by $1.7 billion per year. By 1978, some nine years later, at the height of an economic boom, the real (constant-dollar) tax revenues from this source were 21% lower than they had been in 1969, and all at a 40% higher top marginal tax rate.

It was perhaps the best illustration of the Laffer Curve in action—so good, in fact, that a young Republican congressman, the late William Steiger of Wisconsin, decided in 1977 to try to convince an overwhelmingly Democratic Congress to repeal this massive mistake by showing his colleagues that as much as half of the new equity capital for the nation's fast-growing high-technology industries was, by now, coming from overseas rather than from our own equity markets.

The dramatic fall, both in capital-gains tax revenues and in equity

CHART 3-B

RATIO OF CAPITAL STOCK TO LABOR FORCE

Ratio scale, thousands of constant (1972) dollars
per person

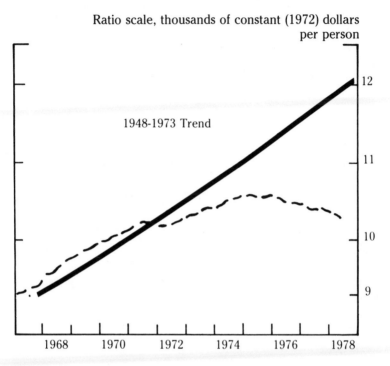

Prepared by the American Council for Capital Formation.

SOURCE: Federal Reserve Board.

investment, convinced the Congress to turn down President Carter's own surprising plan to increase the capital-gains tax rate still further (to 52.5%) and instead to adopt Congressman Steiger's amendment, which cut the rate from the 49% level down to 28%—a 43% tax reduction.

The Carter administration, in an unsuccessful attempt to block this bold move, had warned that the Steiger Amendment could reduce Treasury revenues by more than $2 billion during the first year. Instead, the Steiger cut actually *raised* capital-gains tax revenues modestly in 1979, the first year following the 43% reduction, as the number of new equity offerings suddenly jumped from 20 per year to 81 in 1979. Then, during 1980, a recession year, 237 companies offered stock to the public for the first time (the greatest number since 1972) and sold $1.4 billion in shares—a huge increase from the 81 new companies that had sold $506 million in 1979.

In just two years, one individual tax cut had done more to stimulate the formation of new companies than any corporate investment tax credit had ever done before.

Why are individual tax cuts so much more important to stimulating savings, investment, and productivity than corporate tax cuts? Simply stated, we can't have capitalism without capitalists. To a degree, it doesn't really matter what the tax rate on business income is. Most of that tax is ultimately paid by workers and consumers, not by those who provide its equity capital. What is important is the tax rate on capitalists, not on corporations. Let us ask ourselves how much capital would ever be raised by corporations if the tax rate on individuals was 100% while the tax rate on business was 0%.

Now we can understand why Great Britain, which has some of the lowest corporate-tax rates in the West and the greatest number of corporate-tax breaks—but the highest individual tax rates—has the worst capital formation.

Ultimately, all capital raised by business must come from individual savings or from what some politicians so scornfully treat as "unearned" income. If the tax rates on individual income and capital gains are too high, then individuals will find it more attractive to spend their savings on leisure or on inflation hedges than to invest them in risk enterprises. More important, since small companies create 80% of the real growth in new jobs in this country, the individual income-tax burden is far more important to the small entrepreneur than corporate taxes.

During the middle 1960s, when economic growth and productivity were at their peak, corporate income taxes accounted for an average of 23% of all federal taxes, while individual income taxes accounted for 43%. But in the 1970s, corporate income taxes provided only 16% of total federal tax revenues, while individual income taxes rose to 46% of a much higher and more rapidly rising tax burden. Thus economic growth and capital formation tapered off in exact proportion as the tax burden on individuals rose, while the relative tax burden on business actually declined. The great mistake of the Reagan tax plan of 1981 was in giving too much to business and not enough to individuals.

The Tax Wedge

One of the problems facing the United States today is the continuing failure of our basic personal-savings rate. The principal reason for that is the declining amount of discretionary income left to Americans after the impact of inflation on rising marginal tax rates.

When Henry Ford first decided to raise his auto workers' pay to $5 a day (a big boost for those days), he could be sure that 95% of this daily pay would be available to spend—and some of it on his cars. In other words, his labor costs were almost the same as the workers' take-home pay. By contrast, in 1981, the Ford Motor Company paid over $22 per hour for labor costs, but the individual worker was lucky to take home $9 per hour out of his own gross pay of $12. The take-home pay for auto workers was now less than 45% of the actual labor cost.

This vast difference between the $22 in gross labor cost and $9 in take-home pay is known in economic circles as "the wedge." It consists primarily of federal income and payroll taxes, plus the costs of special incentives, fringe benefits, pensions, health care, and so forth, some paid by the worker and most by the employer, but all paid by the consumer.

Over the years since 1930, this wedge has grown steadily from less than 5% to its present average level of nearly 33% of total labor costs—for some industries, like autos, it is now over 80%—with most of this growth having taken place since 1950. More important, as the wedge between labor costs and what workers can take home to spend has expanded, workers have had to ask for higher and higher wage settlements, just to keep pace with rising prices—themselves fueled by rising labor costs in a vicious spiral. Even so, average weekly wages, which used to rise 3% a year in real purchasing power, by the late 1970s were losing ground, in constant dollars, to price inflation and taxflation, and forcing still higher wage demands and labor costs.

It is this rising wedge which supply-side economists Arthur Laffer and Robert Mundell contend is the chief reason for our nation's chronic bouts with inflation and recession, or stagflation. They also argue that the combination of inflation and the bracket-creep of the progressive income tax automatically inflates this wedge still faster, forcing the economy to work harder and harder just to "climb up the Laffer Curve" (as Jude Wanniski puts it), until real disposable income starts to sputter and the economy slides into recession again. Then, because the recession temporarily lowers the tax burden, there is temporary productivity and inflation relief, and recovery. But unless something is done to slow down the rising tax wedge, either through tax-rate cuts or tax indexing, the whole deadly cycle begins again, but at higher and higher levels each time. Thus, the long-term effect of this accelerating wedge is to reduce incentives, lower basic productivity, reduce real income growth, and engender permanently higher inflation rates.

In the 1950s, for example, the wedge averaged 17%, inflation averaged 1.5%, and productivity growth over 3.3%. But by the end of the 1970s, the wedge had increased to 33%, inflation was up to 13%, and productivity growth down to 1%. This means that unless basic tax rates and the wedge are cut substantially and permanently, inflation will go higher and productivity will continue to be hamstrung.

Monetarists, such as Milton Friedman, view all of this with some skepticism. They argue that the only thing that really causes inflation is rapid growth in the money supply. Reduce the money growth, they argue, and inflation will go away.

Supply-side economists say: Yes, that may be true, but what is it that is driving up the money supply growth? Their answer lies in the wedge. They argue that the Federal Reserve has had to increase the money supply faster and faster simply to accommodate the rapid rise of labor costs, themselves primarily caused by the tax and fringe-benefit wedge. If the Federal Reserve

TABLE 3-5

HOW THE WEDGE PRODUCES RECESSION
(in percentages)

Period 1950-54	Employee Wedge	Employer Wedge	Total Wedge	Rise in Real Per Capita Disposable Income	Real GNP
1950	9.1	5.0	14.1	5.9	8.7
1951	11.3	5.4	16.7	0.9	8.3
1952	12.5	5.3	17.8	1.1	3.7
1953	12.3	5.3	17.6	2.3	3.8
Recession					
1954	11.2	5.6	16.8	−0.6	−1.2
1955-58					
1955	11.4	5.9	17.3	4.1	6.7
1956	11.9	6.2	19.1	2.6	2.1
1957	12.1	6.7	18.8	0.3	1.8
Recession					
1958	11.7	6.9	18.6	−0.5	−0.4
1965-70					
1965	12.0	8.7	20.7	4.8	6.0
1966	12.7	9.3	23.0	3.8	6.0
1967	13.0	9.4	22.4	3.0	2.7
1968	14.5	9.7	24.2	3.1	4.6
1969	15.3	10.0	25.3	2.0	2.8
Recession					
1970	14.3	10.3	24.3	2.8	−0.2
1971-75					
1971	13.4	10.8	24.2	2.4	3.4
1972	14.8	11.5	26.3	2.9	5.7
1973	14.1	12.3	26.4	5.8	5.8
Recession					
1974	14.6	12.8	27.4	1.7	−0.6
1975	13.4	13.4	26.8	1.0	−1.1
1976-80					
1976	14.3	14.3	28.6	2.6	5.4
1977	14.7	14.6	29.3	2.5	5.5
1978	15.1	15.0	30.1	3.3	4.8
1979	15.6	15.4	31.0	1.9	3.2
Recession					
1980	15.8	15.8	31.6	−0.5	−0.2
1981	16.2	16.3	32.5	1.1	1.9

SOURCE: President's Economic Message, 1982.

had not accommodated this wedge growth, the nation would have been condemned to much higher rates of unemployment and slower growth, since higher wages would have butted heads with tight money. (As they do today.)

Some of the faster money-supply growth was the direct result of faster wage-increase rises, which went from 3%–4% a year in the 1950s to 8%–10% a year in the 1970s. The supply-siders argue that much of this increase in basic wage-rate inflation represented a perfectly legitimate effort on the part of workers to catch up with the growing gap between what their labor cost their employers and what they actually could take home and spend on their employers' products.

Table 3-6 shows how this worked in the four-year "boom-bust" cycle,

TABLE 3-6

HOW RISING TAX WEDGE PROMOTES INFLATION
(in percentages)

Year	Federal tax % of personal income	Rise in wage rates	Rise in productivity	Rise in labor costs	Rise in CPI
1976	23.8%	8.6%	3.5%	5.0%	5.8%
1977	24.4%	7.7%	1.9%	6.0%	6.5%
1978	25.1%	8.4%	0.5%	8.0%	7.7%
1979	25.4%	10.1%	-0.9%	10.4%	11.3%
1980	25.1%	10.2%	-2.2%	11.7%	12.3%
1981	26.0%	10.0%	1.0%	8.9%	10.4%

SOURCE: President's Economic Message, 1982.

1976–80. The basic federal tax burden on personal income rose from 23.8% in 1976 to 26% in 1981. To pay for this rising wedge of taxes (coupled with rising fringe costs), the basic wage-rate increases rose from 8.6% to 10.2%. This, combined with declining productivity, meant an increase in unit-labor costs from a 5% rise in 1976 to a 10.4% increase in 1980—and inflation rose to match.

Table 3-5 and Chart 3-C also show the way in which the escalating wedge on both employees and employers has resulted in periodic slowdowns, or recessions, coming every three to five years, in disposable or spendable income and, therefore, in the GNP. The clearest case was 1971–75, when the total wedge rose from 24.5% to nearly 28% in just three years—a colossal growth—causing an ultimate failure in real per capita spendable income and in the GNP.

It is also interesting that the one and only time we missed a recession (in its usual place) was 1963–65—the period affected by President Kennedy's cut of income-tax rates by 23% across the board. The effect of that cut was to increase buying power by stopping the upward growth in the employee tax wedge (which had reached nearly 13.5% in 1963) and to reduce it to 12.0% in 1965. This undoubtedly forestalled another recession like that of 1958, and it generated a long period of sustained economic growth from 1963 to 1970. Then, once again, the wedge shot up from 20% of total labor costs to nearly 26%, causing a very deep recession in 1970.

This process of "climbing up the Laffer Curve" seems to precede every recession, unless government finds a way to slow down the tax wedge. It also has a counterproductive effect on government revenues and deficits (as Ronald Reagan discovered from the delay in actually implementing his tax cut).

In the four budget years of Carter's term (1978–81 inclusive) the U.S. Treasury was forced to borrow $260 billion more from the public. That mounting sea of red ink came in spite of the largest tax increases of any four-year peacetime period in U.S. history—from 18.3% of GNP in 1976 to nearly 22% in 1981. (See Table 3-7.) It was, in its own way, a strange proof of Professor Laffer's much-maligned curve. The higher we pushed the tax rates,

CHART 3-C

RECESSION AND MISERY INDEX

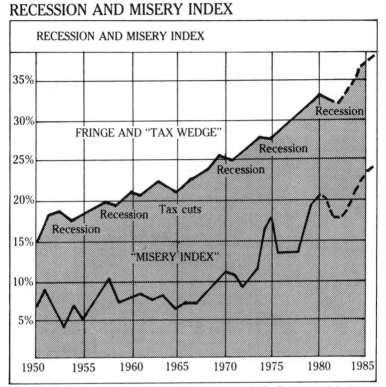

RECESSION AND MISERY INDEX

SOURCES: U.S. Department of Commerce; U.S. Bureau of Labor Statistics; President's Economic Message, 1980.

the more red ink ensued, because the economy itself rebelled against those tax rates with declining productivity and output. In other words, even though President Carter tried to balance the budget by increasing taxes, the economy forcefully imposed its own unique form of tax-cutting in the form of a slowdown and recession in economic activity, with much higher deficits, slower revenue growth, and even higher tax rates.

That was nothing new. The modern history of every industrial nation demonstrates that periods of rising tax burden invariably produce corrective recessions, in which the tax burden is eased arbitrarily by the recession itself if not by cutting the rates. Conversely, every major tax-rate reduction has increased economic growth and tax revenues.

Chart 3-C shows how the ever-rising fringe and tax wedge has led to progressively higher levels of stagflation, or what we now call the "misery index"—the combination of inflation and unemployment rates. From 1950 to 1968 the misery index hovered at about 6% to 7%. But as domestically

TABLE 3-7

HOW RISING TAXES PRODUCE RISING DEFICITS

Fiscal year	Federal tax burden (% of GNP)	Federal deficits* (billions)	GNP growth†
1976	18.2	$73.7	5.4%
1977	19.1	53.6	5.5%
1978	19.2	49.2	4.8%
1979	19.7	40.2	3.2%
1980	20.1	73.8	−0.2%
1981	21.0	78.9	1.9%

SOURCE: President's Budget Message, 1982.
* Includes off budget.
† Calendar years.

stimulated inflation began to push people into higher and higher tax brackets, and the cost of both the Vietnam war and the Great Society programs drove up government taxes and spending, the good effects of the 1963–64 Kennedy tax cuts were soon overwhelmed, as the tax wedge pushed to new heights and steeper growth rates in the 1970s. As a direct result, the misery index has in recent years climbed to the 12%–20% range.

The Mounting Case for Fundamental Tax Reform

In a way, the whole history of the so-called progressive income tax has been one of progressive misery, both for the economy and for the average middle-class family, who have found themselves on a taxflation treadmill. While periodic tax cuts have helped modestly to slow the inevitable upward bracket-creep, they have done nothing to change the essentially discouraging character of this tax system which punishes hard work and rewards nonwork and leisure. No wonder Milton Friedman has had such widespread popular response to his case for dropping the graduated tax code altogether and substituting a flat-rate tax system. As Friedman contends, "the law is riddled with so many loopholes, so many special privileges that the high [marginal] rates are almost pure window dressing. A low flat rate—less than 20%—on all income above personal exemptions . . . would yield more revenue than the present unwieldy structure." He points out that everyone would be better off, taxpayers (who could avoid the costs and problems of sheltering income), the economy (from better resource allocation), and the government (from higher revenues at less collection costs). "The only losers," Friedman says, "would be lawyers, accountants, civil servants and legislators," who "would have to turn to more productive activities . . ."

Friedman's idea is so sensible, so obviously advantageous, in terms both of revenues and of economic growth, that, by contrast, it makes the present graduated system seem foolish. As we shall see, by providing adequate levels of basic personal exemptions, it can easily be made just as "progressive" in its effective distribution of the tax burden as our present system. That being so, why do we cling to the anachronism that is punishing us so? Why not try such a fundamental tax reform?

The answer, simply, is the argument that a flat-rate tax would not redistribute income enough from rich to poor. The underpinning of the graduated income-tax system in the last analysis is the politics of *envy*—the notion that the good of one group can be improved only by taking away some of the good of another, that success should be punished to compensate for lack of success.

Unfortunately, no nation or individual ever became rich through envy. Nothing useful or constructive was ever created through envy. No business ever succeeded through envy. No jobs were ever created through envy. Envy in reality is the single most impoverishing attitude of thought. It is the linchpin of Marxism, and the antithesis of individual incentives and initiative that made this nation and its people the social and economic model for the rest of the world.

Unfortunately, the politics of envy, so long practiced by the intellectually impoverished and economically backward nations of the Third World, have been enthusiastically embraced by populist politicians and the media in the United States who see the federal government primarily as a massive agent for transfering more and more money from the most productive segments of society to the less productive. To the individual struggling on a modest wage, or the poor living on welfare, this can seem to be a very appealing idea. The only trouble is that it doesn't really work, and it never has.

Despite our relatively steep levels of tax graduation, despite a colossal growth in social transfer spending, and despite double taxation of corporate profits, the distribution of wealth in our nation changed very little over a period of 30 years. Not only was the redistribution slight but the trend in recent years has actually modestly reversed itself, even as the tax burden grew moderately more progressive. Thus, during the 1970s, when the total level of U.S. social transfer spending reached its highest levels (rising from 13% of the GNP to nearly 19% in 1979), the relative cash-income lot of the lowest percentile of U.S. income groups actually declined, while the top 40% actually strengthened its position modestly—this in spite of a concerted effort to shift the tax burden upward.

Why is this? The answers, I feel, are essentially twofold. One is practical and the other philosophical and fundamental. From a practical standpoint, the graduated income tax is not a tax on the rich. It is primarily a barrier to upward mobility—to everyone who wants to be rich. According to Peter Gutmann, of the Economics Department of Baruch College of the City University of New York, "It is too easy to stay rich and too difficult to get rich. That, to put it bluntly, is what's the matter with our present tax system."

If the rich in this country had been trying to design a method to keep the lower and middle classes down, they could not have invented a better system than the graduated income tax. As Professor Gutmann puts it, "The tax system is creating a class system. It establishes a solid barrier to social and

TABLE 3-8

DISTRIBUTION OF INCOME AMONG FAMILIES,
1947-77

PERCENTAGE SHARE

Year	Lowest Fifth	Second Fifth	Middle Fifth	Fourth Fifth	Highest Fifth	Top 5%
1947	5.0	11.9	17.0	23.1	43.0	17.5
1952	4.9	12.3	17.4	23.4	41.9	17.4
1957	5.1	12.7	18.1	23.8	40.4	15.6
1962	5.0	12.1	17.6	24.0	41.3	15.7
1967	5.5	12.4	17.9	23.9	40.4	15.2
1972	5.4	11.9	17.5	23.9	41.4	15.9
1977	5.2	11.6	17.5	24.2	41.5	15.7
Highest	5.6	12.7	18.1	24.2	43.0	17.5
Mean	5.1	12.2	17.6	23.8	41.3	16.0
Lowest	4.5	11.6	17.0	23.1	40.4	15.2

SOURCE: *Current Population Reports*, Series P-60, No. 118,
Table 13.

economic mobility, upward and downward. Those who aspire to rise in society through work, savings, and capital accumulation have most of it taxed away. They have a tough time rising. The tax system keeps those who are down, down, and keeps those who are up, up."

Largely because of taxflation, it is taking nearly 50% more actual effort (workers per family) on the part of middle-income families today just to maintain the income level they earned 20 years ago. As Professor Carolyn Shaw Bell of Wellesley College points out, "If income is regarded as the return to productive effort, it takes more effort today to be in the top half of the income distribution. Conversely, low incomes are received with less effort than formerly, because of the rapid growth of income-transfer programs." So while we are punishing hard work, we are subsidizing nonproductivity. All we have succeeded in doing is not transferring real wealth and income but slowing down the growth of the total economic pie.

Real Wealth Cannot Be Redistributed

More important, the whole notion of using the tax system as a method of redistributing wealth rests on a fallacy—namely, that wealth is money, and that all one has to do to transfer wealth is to transfer money.

The trouble with that hypothesis is that money is nothing more than a medium of exchange. Real wealth is the total productive output of the economy in the form of services and goods, which are in turn the product of the energy, resources, and talents of the people who produce them. Thus merely passing money around does little to change a nation's real productive output or wealth, nor does it change the inherent "wealth capacity" of individual citizens. All it does is to reduce the real value of the money itself, through inflation.

Yet we hear a leading liberal senator, on a television panel, repeat the oft-told myth: "The poor are poor simply because they have no money. The problem in alleviating poverty is really very simple: Just get money into the hands of the poor." If that were really true, we could easily wipe out poverty just by running the federal printing press.

To understand the fallacy of the senator's notion, consider an example of two different 21-year-olds, both broke, that is, "having no money." By that simplistic definition, both are equally poor. Yet one of them has just finished college and is trained to go out and earn a good living as an engineer. He is motivated, eager, intelligent, and ready to strive. The other man is a high school dropout with no skills, no motivation, and no training. Which one is really poor?

Although both have no money, only one is poor, while the other has unlimited wealth potential. Merely by giving each of these two "poor" men $10,000, the chances are that at the end of the year one of them would have run through his money and would still be poor, while the other would have increased his wealth potential still more. But, nothing really would have changed.

The attempt to redistribute wealth by redistributing money through the progressive tax tables only winds up keeping the poor poor, the rich rich, and the middle class struggling even harder to keep up with taxflation. Although Kennedy-Reagan-style tax-rate cuts are useful, they don't change the fundamentally punitive nature of the graduated tax code or defuse its inflationary potential (in the form of bracket-creep). Even indexing the tax tables merely confirms inflation instead of fighting it. Above all, none of the tax-cut plans does anything to eliminate the necessity for the whole distortionary process of tax loopholes. As long as top marginal tax rates remain in the punitive 40%–50% range, and as long as most workers have to pay taxes at the 20%–40% marginal rates, there will be political pressure for tax relief for such things as home mortgage interest and taxes, capital gains, energy conservation, and other purposes.

Yet there is now a nearly universal feeling among the public that the tax system should not be pulled and hauled in this political way; that it should be a more straightforward, fair-minded method of raising revenues, and not an instrument of social or economic policy. That is why the most universally attractive plank in the 1976 Democratic platform was its call for "fundamental tax reform". It always elicited public applause.

Ironically, it was the only issue on which Jimmy Carter stumbled when he campaigned in Massachusetts in 1976, when he almost casually and correctly suggested that deductions for real-estate taxes and mortgage interest would disappear under "broad-based tax reform." While the liberal upper- and middle-class property-holding audience gasped, Carter tried to explain that this would be more than offset by "other reforms in the tax system." He was conceptually right, but of course he wasn't heard. Too many "oxen were gored," and that year Carter went down to a dismal defeat in the Massachusetts primary.

TABLE 3-9

FEDERAL TAX EXPENDITURES
(in billions of dollars)

Fiscal 1981 category	Amount
Income security (Social Security, unemployment compensation, pensions, disability, etc.)	$46.84
Mortgage interest & property tax	22.34
Capital gains (including home sales and investment credits)	25.43
Health and medical care	19.27
State and local taxes (other than property)	17.31
Municipal tax exempt bond interest	3.87
Charitable institutions (churches, etc.)	8.86
Education, job training & child care	4.43
Consumer credit interest exclusion	4.24
Energy & housing construction loans	4.17
Total	$156.75

SOURCE: Special Analysis of 1981 Federal Budget.

The horrified reaction to Carter's proposition reveals the basic difficulty in bringing about really comprehensive tax reform by "closing loopholes." Of the $157 billion in 1981 loopholes in the personal income-tax system listed by the Senate Finance Committee, less than $18 billion was specifically designed for upper-income groups. All the rest was available to, and used by, the vast majority of American taxpayers. (See Table 3-9.) This does not mean that the present tax system is not fraught with privilege, inequities, and distortions. It is. It does mean, however, that many of these distortions are very widespread—affecting the interests of most taxpayers. As the marginal tax rates on average incomes have soared, the entire tax system has become nothing but "loopholes," pushing the interests of one group or another, promoting or stimulating the economy in one direction or another, and, in the process, raising all sorts of ethical, moral, and political problems:

- Should the family which has to rent because it can't afford a down payment on a house get no tax credit for its $500-a-month rent payments, while another family gets full tax credit for $500 a month in mortgage and tax payments?
- Should a union member get fully prepaid health insurance as a tax-free fringe benefit, while the middle-income white-collar worker can deduct only 50% of his own health insurance costs?
- Should a family receiving more than $12,000 in welfare, unemployment benefits, and food stamps pay no income and Social Security taxes, while an unskilled factory worker pays full taxes on the same income?
- Should people who don't believe in organized religion, or those who don't support the ideas of the myriad tax-free political and social foundations, have to carry the burden of the tax benefits enjoyed by those institutions and their beneficiaries?

We have turned our tax system into a giant political, social, and economic "buffet," one which caters to nearly all the special interests of the entire nation.

Given the broad base of these tax favors, and the political clout of the thousands of interest groups now favored in the tax system, how can we ever accomplish the serious tax reform that has been promised so often in vain?

The difficulty of this challenge was vividly illustrated by the adverse congressional reaction to former Secretary of the Treasury William E. Simon's radical proposal of January 1976 calling for complete elimination of all but the basic personal and "need" exemptions such as health care and disability. Simon showed that, by the elimination of all loopholes, the basic tax range could be reduced from the present 14%–70% to a range of 4%–30%, or even less.

While the public response to this idea was immediate and affirmative, the congressional reaction was a mixture of horror, disdain, and contempt. Senator Russell B. Long (Democrat of Louisiana), then head of the Senate Finance Committee, called it "political naiveté" and proceeded to write his own 1977 "tax-reform" bill which came out 1,600 pages long and added more loopholes than it closed.

What Congress has created is not a tax system at all but a 40,000-page compendium of political favors, subsidies, and handouts, a veritable pork barrel of goodies for every political constituency, from rich to poor. In the process it has also profoundly confused the public about who really bears the tax burden.

Back in 1977, at a town meeting, in Clinton, Massachusetts, President Carter repeated his popular charge: "Our federal income-tax system is a national disgrace." And it drew predictable applause. Unfortunately, one got the distinct impression that much of this applause stemmed not so much from impatience with the sheer intractability of our income-tax laws as from the feeling that "Rich people don't pay their fair share." This partly arises from the annual announcement of the number of very wealthy individuals who paid no federal income tax at all. For example, in 1977 the Treasury Department announced that, in 1975, some 230 of the nation's wealthiest individuals with incomes of more than $200,000 a year paid no taxes at all. Unfortunately, what the public did not hear was that the 230 who paid no taxes were only .07% of the 34,131 individuals with incomes of more than $200,000 that year who actually paid huge taxes at an average "effective tax rate" of over 63%. This notion that rich people don't pay their "fair" share of taxes is simply a fraudulent political myth, which is totally dispelled by the accompanying table compiled from the 1981 summary of income-tax distribution, which shows that the top 4.4% of the taxpayers now pay 33% of the taxes, a very progressive distribution.

While the system can and must be simplified and loopholes closed, unless the entire rate structure is reduced dramatically there will be no bonanza awaiting the average taxpayer just from closing loopholes.

The best proof is that during the period 1967–81, when all "tax cuts" and "reforms" were aimed at cutting taxes on the very lowest income groups and

TABLE 3-10

1981 TAX BURDEN BY INCOME CLASS

(in percentages)

Income class	% of returns	% of taxes paid	Effective rate*
Under $10,000	37.0	2.2	2.1
$10,000-$20,000	26.0	13.9	9.3
$20,000-$30,000	18.2	20.7	13.3
$30,000-$50,000	14.4	30.3	18.8
$50,000-$100,000	3.7	18.2	28.0
$100,000 and over	0.7	14.8	48.8

SOURCE: U.S. Treasury, Office of Tax Analysis.
*Prior to 1981-82 tax cuts.

closing loopholes for the very richest, the family at the median income (currently about $20,000) saw its top marginal tax rates rise from 17% to 28%, while the family with double the median income went from 23% to 43%—as an average 7% inflation pushed whole legions of average income-earners up through the tax tables at an astonishing rate.

Since every 1% in inflation (and personal income growth) means a 1.6% growth in federal income taxes, the faster the rate of inflation, the faster the growth in tax revenues. From the standpoint of the economy, this is like pedaling faster and faster on a racing bicycle while gripping the hand brakes harder. Economists call this effect "fiscal drag." Jerry Hausman of MIT terms it "deadweight loss."

Hausman's work for the National Bureau of Economic Research shows that the present graduated tax system, with its high marginal rates, has a tremendous negative impact on the willingness of men and especially of women (as second-earners) to work additional hours. With half of all Americans paying top marginal rates in the 30%–50% range, Hausman finds that this cuts the total hours worked by husbands (or first wage-earners) by about 8% (from what they would be willing to work at lower marginal rates) and by wives (or second-earners) by about 30%. Because of these losses, caused by high marginal tax rates, Hausman finds that the economic cost of raising a dollar of revenue by the income tax is about 25 cents on average in terms of lost welfare to the economy and that the marginal cost of raising each additional dollar of revenue by this means is approximately 40 cents. The tax system is costing the economy a loss in productivity and this, in turn, reduces tax revenues.

The deleterious effects of rising marginal rates thus make the graduated income tax a very costly way of raising revenues with a very high deadweight loss ("the amount that an individual needs to be given [in added income] to be as well off after the tax as he was before it, minus the actual revenues raised").

Hausman estimates that the average deadweight loss to the economy from our present high marginal tax rate system, as a proportion of the tax revenues actually raised, is almost 29%. This is such a high cost, he contends, that it outweighs the redistributional values and goals of the system. "The large amount of redistributive expenditure by the federal government is being done at relatively high economic cost," and because this deadweight loss is (in his mathematical model) in direct proportion to the *square* of the marginal tax rate, it "will grow quickly (geometrically) as marginal tax rates rise." For the layman this means that the graduated income tax is a ladder of progressive destruction, not merely for the taxpayers but for the economy as a whole.

Hausman's research has led him to conclude that the economic cost of "progressive" income-tax schedules far outweighs their "redistributional advantages" (if any), and he now argues for flat-rate income tax without any loopholes but with generous personal exemptions for all taxpayers, amounting in 1982 dollars to about $8,000 for an average family.

At that level he finds that a 20% flat rate (or what he calls equal-yield-linear-income-tax) would not only raise just as much money as the present system, but would cut the deadweight loss to the economy from 28.7% down to 14.5%, and that "all taxpayers are made better off by this type of linear income tax system."

Since his analysis is based on much lower average 1975 tax rates (before the last six-year mammoth increase in rates), it becomes even more cogent when he finds that the substitution of such a system would add, on average, more than 160 working hours a year to each husband's effective output, or a net gain of nearly 9%, and some 300 hours to each married female worker, an increase in their labor supply of nearly 30%. At today's high tax levels, the increases would be even greater.

Hausman's research supports Milton Friedman's long-held position that a 16%–20% flat-rate tax system (without loopholes) would actually produce a much more progressive distribution of the tax burden, as well as more revenues, without concomitant loss of incentives and distortions of the present monstrous system.

We experimented with Hausman's thesis by applying a 15% flat-rate tax using a basic deduction of $8,800 for a family of four and then comparing the "effective tax burden" with the actual effective rates as worked out by Professors Edgar Browning and William Johnson of the University of Virginia in 1979. As the Table 3-11 shows, the flat rate provides a far more progressive tax distribution than our present system actually does, despite the enormous range of our present marginal tax rates. This degree of "progressivity" could be further increased simply by raising the flat rate and by increasing the basic exemptions.

The advantages are too obvious to enumerate. More than $600 billion in personal income, now sheltered or hidden from taxation, would come back into the tax and economic system, and the terrible economic distortions that the present 40,000-page tax code now promotes would be eliminated. The "underground economy" would quickly surface, as much lower tax rates made tax evasion far less attractive. In 1982 IRS Commissioner Roscoe Eggar told Congress that more than $90 billion in tax revenues was being lost through such evasion, principally by middle-income Americans now facing punitive 30%–40% marginal tax rates, once reserved only for the rich. A flat-rate tax

TABLE 3-11

PROGRESSIVE TAX VS. FLAT-RATE TAX EFFECTS

Income decile	Total household income*	Top federal marginal tax rate	Average effective tax rate	Flat rate of 15%	Effective tax rate† flat rate†
1 & 2	$6,195	16%	1.1%	15%	0.0%
3	8,827	19%	2.6%	15%	0.2%
4	11,250	22%	4.0%	15%	3.3%
5	13,893	22%	5.5%	15%	5.5%
6	17,893	25%	6.9%	15%	7.4%
7	20,681	28%	8.1%	15%	8.6%
8	25,183	32%	9.1%	15%	9.8%
9	31,997	36%	10.2%	15%	10.9%
10	63,644	52%	11.6%	15%	12.9%

SOURCE: Edgar Browning and William Johnson, *The Distribution of the Tax Burden* (American Enterprise Institute, 1979).

* Includes all transfer income which is nontaxable.
† Uses a basic family deduction of $8,800 (family of four) and flat-rate tax of 15% on all income above the basic deduction.

would immediately reduce deficits, even as it cut tax rates more than Kemp-Roth (the 1981 Recovery Act) did.

The irony is that a flat-rate tax of 16% (with an average $8,000-per-family basic exemption) would actually have raised more revenues in fiscal 1980 ($256 billion) than the old system raised ($240 billion), even though the old system had top marginal rates of up to 70%. In other words, with a 16% flat rate, we could cut the marginal tax rates of all taxpayers (except the very lowest) and yet increase the revenues raised, simply by tapping into the more than $600 billion that now goes untouched either through shelters or in the underground economy. At 16%, there would be no advantage in tax evasion.

The Challenge of Ideological Myths

Even though there is now growing public enthusiasm for it, the great challenge would be to get such a plan enacted, in a country that is still so steeped in the populist ideology of the progressive income tax despite the clear evidence that such a tax does very little to hurt the rich and very much to punish the rest of us.

King Frederick the Great of Prussia once said, "If I wished to punish a province, I would have it governed by philosophers." For the past half century or so the U.S. economy has been punished again and again by too much social philosophy and too little common sense.

It is ironic that during an address to the Urban League in the 1980 presidential campaign, immediately after the third heckler from the Communist Workers Party had been hauled from the room, Jimmy Carter launched a frankly Marxist attack on Ronald Reagan's tax-cut plan. Calling it "rebates for the rich," Carter vowed to "turn the table on this trickle-down economics."

Whenever populists use the pejorative term "trickle-down," they are referring to classic supply-side economics. But the plain truth is that in any free society, through invention, creativity, and enterprise, a comparatively small part of the population still contributes the major share of economic growth. In this largest and richest of all industrial democracies, it is still safe to say that 80%–90% of the new jobs and economic growth is contributed by the efforts, imagination, energy, and initiative of less than 5%–10% of all individuals, through whose creativity the great wealth of this country still "trickles down" to the economy.

In the process, of course, this top 5%–10% has become very rich, and not always very nice; but genius seldom seems to equate with meekness and charity. Yet without those well-rewarded individuals who often have risked everything to create the one new enterprise in ten that succeeds, our economy would become stagnant, and trickle-down would quickly be replaced by dole-out, as it has in Poland, Russia, China, Cuba, or even England.

This may sound very unegalitarian, and it is. Egalitarianism is an interesting ideal, but it is also a denial of human reality. Liberals like to scorn supply-side economics as trickle-down, because it encourages the few who are entrepreneurs to generate growth and wealth more rapidly so that the majority of us can have better jobs and a higher standard of living. Yet trickle-down is really the natural order of things, not merely in economics and business, but in nearly every other facet of life as well. We are all blessed by the genius of relatively few.

Many thousands of books are published each year, but only a few hundred survive the test of time. The world's greatest music is still the work of a comparative handful of great composers, and most of the world's great art is the product of a few hundred brilliant talents. The Bible is the compilation of the ideas and inspiration of a few dozen prophets, yet it enriches the lives of billions.

It is easy to forget this in a populist society where "listening to the people" often has become a maudlin way of suggesting that great wisdom, great ideas, and great progress can, in some way, percolate up from the masses or out of government bureaucracies and committees. Yet a few man-in-the-street interviews, a few radio talk shows, public opinion polls, and "Real People" shows can quickly rid one of that notion. Real progress, real breakthroughs, real economic and social well-being do not emanate from populist movements, turgid technocratic bureaucracies, or community action. They come through individuals, sometimes working with other individuals, as often as not, working alone.

So, of course, countries that have provided the most individual freedom and the greatest incentives tend to generate the greatest wealth—economic, technological, cultural, and sociological. And the quickest way to dry up this flow of wealth is to take away both freedom and incentives. Anything that does that will surely turn the spout into a trickle.

That is precisely what we have been doing in the United States, the historic center of economic creativity in the Western world—and we have been doing it primarily through our tax system, which, contrary to the rhetoric emanating from the left, has been getting steadily more punitive to the "tricklers" and steadily more restrictive to the initiatives of today's budding enterpreneurs.

True tax reform in the form of a genuine flat-rate tax system with a top rate of 16%–25% would not only reindustrialize the U.S. economy quickly; it would turn trickle-down into a floodtide of individual economic growth and opportunity and make the United States the magnet for world-wide investment. Anyone who still doubts that simply hasn't studied history closely.

4

Inflation and the Crisis in Confidence

By a process of inflation governments can confiscate, secretly and unobserved, an important part of the wealth of their citizens. There is no subtler, no surer means of overturning the existing basis of society, than to debauch the currency. The process [of inflation] engages all the hidden forces of economic law on the side of destruction, and does it in a manner that not one man in a million is able to diagnose.

—*John Maynard Keynes*

Once trust in money has been lost through whatever circumstances, the freedom of the men and women in society will be correspondingly diminished or ultimately destroyed.

—*S. Herbert Frankel*

Regardless of a nation's economic system, its total wealth is a direct function of its faith in the future—the "substance of things hoped for." Without faith, without confidence, wealth is not generated, risky investments are not made, crops are not planted, businesses are not founded, and poverty ensues. Anything which corrodes that confidence can lead to economic decline, regardless of "objective economic circumstances or natural resources."

That is the supreme danger of Keynesian or "macro" economics—the process of stimulating consumer demand by deliberately expanding the nation's money supply and by deficit spending to "create jobs." The impact of such policies on public trust is infinitely more serious than the actual objective effects that technical economists might expect of such policies. A $50-billion budget deficit may, in fact, have a very salutary short-term impact on consumer demand and economic performance, but a whole series of such deficits, even if not statistically significant, can so erode public trust in the nation's money that the long-term effect can be seriously debilitating.

Money is, after all, an expression of trust, and depends for its usefulness on the public's willingness to exchange work and goods for paper which they perceive will be worth something in terms of future goods and services. As soon as the public perceives that the government is actively manipulating that paper money for its own purposes, people who lend money want higher interest, people who work want higher wages, people who manufacture want higher prices.

Through this auto-mechanism of fearful expectations, inflation—which is itself an underlying cause of diminished faith and confidence—becomes its own spiraling effect, as the threat of rising prices drives both prices and wages up still faster.

If this cycle of fear feeding fear is not stopped, the nation's real substance will be depressed, as faith in the future is diminished and freedom is threatened.

History demonstrates that the surest long-term result of continuous unchecked inflation is government tyranny from either the left or the right. Not only does inflation ultimately force the imposition of draconian measures of government control; it undermines economic liberty itself.

According to Herbert Frankel, the Oxford economist, "A trustworthy, disciplined monetary system is indispensable for the free unfolding of the division of labor on which the growth of world economies depends. Free economic endeavor can be fostered only when there is sufficient security to sustain it." So long as workers and businessmen have a currency they can trust, they are free to earn their economic livelihood without danger of loss and destruction by forces beyond their control. But let inflation loose upon the land, and the economic freedom of every individual is at risk from the policies of politicians and governments.

That is the main reason why governments generally have been so unsuccessful at fighting inflation. It is the chief source of growing power and revenues for politicians and bureaucrats. The more rapid the inflation, the more dramatically taxes rise and the more obsequiously people must turn to government for help—which is a little like asking the Mafia to control crime.

Banks are the only other institutions in society that genuinely profit from inflation. For bankers, like politicians, create only one product—money itself. And the more they create of it, the better they do and the more powerful they get. Bankers and politicians have always been eager promoters of unbacked paper money, reluctant inflation-fighters, and, in recent years, closet Keynesians.

Prime Minister Margaret Thatcher found, to her dismay, that she could not trust the bureaucrats of the Bank of England to calm Britain's raging inflation by slowing the rate of money growth. They had too much stake in inflation. She also discovered (as we have) that while the monetarists (economists who believe that the money supply is the key to inflation) have been wonderfully correct in defining inflation's underlying cause, they have been somewhat less than efficient in their efforts to curb it without excessive and unacceptable pain.

For example, under the strong influence and impetus of strict monetarism, Federal Reserve Board Chairman Paul Volcker adopted specific and much lower monetary growth targets in August 1979, and abandoned the Fed's decades-long practice of trying to use (targeted) interest rates as the control-ling mechanism. Since that time, the United States has been on an interest-rate roller coaster, and even the money-supply growth rates have gyrated wildly between 12% and 20% for months on end, followed by no growth at all for similar periods.

While inflation and money growth have been cut sharply, the primary effects of this strict monetarism, thus far, have been massive instability in the financial markets (adding nearly 3 to 5 points to the interest rates them-selves) and two painful recessions in less than 18 months, something of a record in itself. As this book was being written, Wall Street and the economy were in a nearly constant state of schizophrenia about the weekly monetary growth rates for fear they might be "above the target," even as they worried about whether the economy would get enough money to recover! Both the private and the public sectors were being held hostage to an as-yet-unproven monetary policy under which the greatest danger had suddenly shifted from hyperinflation to depression-level deflation.

Economists on the supply side of the argument contend that the mone-tarists' fixation on strict monetary targets is bound to produce such instabil-ity, since, if the supply of any commodity is held constant, the only thing that can fluctuate is the price. Since the natural effect of a lower inflation rate is to make people want to hold more dollars (rather than fewer), the Fed's strict money-supply limits automatically produce the anomaly of very high interest rates in the midst of very low inflation. This, in turn, makes the dollar even stronger and more attractive to hold, even as the economy is driven into depression, in a kind of monetaristic Catch-22.

Although the sources of this dilemma are technical and complex, not to mention controversial, I suggest that the primary cause lies in our continued tendency to look at money as something in and of itself, a force to be manipulated for national economic benefit or pain. The monetarists (with whom I have genuine sympathy) seem to be as absorbed in this abstract notion as are the Keynesians. It is necessary to remind ourselves, as we wrestle with the inflation/monetary problems, that if we were to destroy every piece of paper currency in the world, and every bank account entry, we would not have destroyed one shred of real economic wealth. Indeed our "real" economy might quickly recover if it were released from what econo-mists now call the whole "money illusion."

As Herbert Frankel writes, "Abstraction is the Achilles' heel of advanced monetary systems. It causes money to be regarded as exercising powers of its own—powers that individuals possessing it can allegedly wield, irrespective of political, social, and economic circumstances." "But," he continues, "actually money has no such independent powers. It merely reflects cost and value relationships in the present and expectations concerning them in the future. Governments and individuals are always tempted to resist reality by overlooking or ignoring the inescapable fact that money in itself is nothing . . ."

Inflation, then, is the process by which banks and governments attempt to make something out of nothing; and, in the process, they use their power to create artificial money as a means by which to transfer both wealth and power away from the people and to themselves. So subtle and so effective is this process that most of the public and even many politicians and so-called economists do not understand how it is done. But this subtlety ultimately undermines the trust upon which a free society must rest.

Even more venomously, inflation feeds envy, as a wind fans a brush fire. In an inflationary economy, all wages, prices, and profits appear to be exaggerated. People soon begin to cast green, accusatory eyes around to see who is ripping them off.

The politicians, sensing political capital with every rise in the price index, seek out appropriate scapegoats to castigate: big business, lawyers, doctors, middlemen, multinational corporations, and supermarkets among them.

- Big business points to big labor, whose own wage and fringe demands have outraced prices for years without the productivity gains to match.
- Farmers complain of extortionate middlemen, and they demand subsidies, price supports, and parity.
- Supermarket owners, with operating margins squeezed by rising taxes, complain of lowered net profits and demand higher prices from consumers.
- Investors complain of the diminished value of the dollar and demand higher dividends to compensate them for inflation.

In a chain reaction, each group attempts to use its political and economic muscle to assure itself its own fair share of the devaluing pie—in a self-defeating spiral of envious demand and counterdemand. Inflation thus is nothing more than blown-up envy, a green monster threatening to debase us all.

This is no accidental metaphor, since inflation itself has its fundamental roots in the politics of envy—specifically, in the federal government's well-meaning but clumsy efforts to redistribute income from the rich to the poor.

The problem is that today there are not enough rich people around to pay for the more than $500 billion in social spending. Everyone must pay; and since politicians don't like to tax everyone, inflation has become the acceptable but hidden method of transfer.

Each rise in this transfer spending load has increased the tax burden on the entire middle class—and when politicians are afraid to load this tax burden fully on the voters, they resort to increasing use of deficit financing and to printing paper money to accommodate it. Is it really any wonder that the money they print is *green*?

Unfortunately, in this highly sophisticated economy, with our complex banking systems, credit cards, and computers, we easily take our eyes off our real wealth (productivity and ideas) and concentrate on its illusionary symbol. In the process we are lured into a set of false economic theories that seem delightfully sophisticated and attractive, until we get snakebitten by the inflation they cause and the havoc they wreak.

The Failure of Keynesianism

It was John Maynard Keynes who lifted money out of its natural role as a medium of exchange or barter and gave it a new economic and political significance by calling it "aggregate demand" and by theorizing that the major reason for boom-and-bust business cycles was the unevenness of aggregate demand, and the failure of this demand to keep the economy moving, particularly during recessions. He proposed that the government could smooth out the business cycle simply by more clever management of the aggregate demand (alias money supply), pumping it up during periods of recession and tightening down during periods of boom, using the combination of government spending and money-supply control as the basic tools in the process.

Unfortunately, the politicians heard only the first part of Keynes's proposition—the part that called for stimulating the economy by monetary and fiscal expansion, and it wasn't long before this one-sided and simplistic pursuit of Keynesianism produced rapidly rising inflation and rapidly deteriorating investment. In the process, the entire complexion of the U.S. economy has been altered. Prior to 1965, our average real annual growth rate was 3.5% and our average inflation rate was 1.9%—while our money supply grew less than 3.5% per year. Since 1966, however, our average real growth rate has fallen to 2.5%, and our average inflation rate is now more than 8%. GNP growth has dropped by 30% and inflation has more than quadrupled, while money growth has surged to 8% or more.

Fifteen years of stimulating consumer demand in this fashion painted our economy into a very tight corner, with the result that in 1980 and again in 1981 we had to witness the tragic process of throwing over 3 million men and women out of work solely to attempt to restore both the Federal Reserve's and the dollar's credibility. After churning money out like a gusher (right through Carter's failed reelection bid in November 1980), the Federal Reserve finally slammed the gates for good in the spring of 1981 and drove the U.S. economy into its most dangerous recession in 40 years.

In this way, 3 million Americans who had been put back to work by the highly stimulative monetary policies of 1977–79 suddenly found themselves being sacrificed to fight the double-digit inflation which these deliberately inflationary policies had produced, as the economy was once again dragged through the wringer for the sake of saving the value of an otherwise worthless paper dollar.

The Death of the Phillips Curve

If William Jennings Bryan had been alive when Jimmy Carter ran for office, I think he'd have been tempted to invent a new slogan: "You shall not crucify the working man and woman on the Phillips Curve."

The Phillips Curve is an economic model designed by British economist A. W. Phillips. In a paper published in 1957, he showed that there was an entirely predictable relationship between rising unemployment and declining wage demands, and vice versa—a relationship that actually worked rather well over the last hundred years in Britain and America, right up through the middle 1960s, but fell apart in the 1974–75 recession.

Although the curve originally illustrated the traditional capitalist method of dealing with excessive wage demands and inflation by inducing economic slowdowns, this original purpose was quickly perverted by the Keynesians, who used it as a reverse premise for using "a little inflation" to fight unemployment.

As Congressman Jack Kemp points out in *An American Renaissance*, "Insofar as it ever worked, the Phillips Curve was based on the unwholesome idea of deceiving workers into taking a hidden cut in real income [as money was being printed and devalued]. Prices [through inflation] would supposedly rise faster than wages—cutting real wages, boosting profit margins, and making it profitable to hire still more workers."

The idea was beguiling: Instead of waiting for investment to produce jobs, one uses deliberate inflation to reduce real wages, so that companies will then hire more people, instead of building more plants. Rather than letting workers adjust their wage demands voluntarily to suit the market, one simply devalues their wages by creating money. MIT Professors Robert Samuelson and Robert Solow, in 1960, actually encouraged fiscal policy-makers in this direction by suggesting that "in order to achieve the non-perfectionists' goal of no more than 3% unemployment, the price index might have to rise by as much as 4% to 5% per year." A "little inflation" would be used to cut unemployment. (It would also be used to destroy the gold standard under Bretton Woods.)

The theory was that the workers would either not see, or not mind, this deception, but would readily accept the trade-off of lowering real wages to put more people to work. As Keynes himself put it with devious logic but dramatic lack of foresight: "Reductions of real wages arising in this way are not, as a rule, resisted, and no trade union would dream of striking on every occasion of a rise in the cost of living."

Keynes badly underestimated the trade unions.

By the early 1970s, virtually every major U.S. union had fought back by writing into its contract cost-of-living adjustment (COLA) escalators. As a result, nominal wages, which had been rising in the early 1960s at an annual rate of 4%, suddenly started rising at an annual rate of more than 7% in the early 1970s, and more than 9% from 1977 on, thus institutionalizing the inflation started by the Keynesian planners. The same COLA's were written into major government entitlement programs as well, especially Social Security.

It was at this point that the Phillips Curve became moot. Wage rates, instead of being linked to productivity, or to labor supply and demand, became tied to the Consumer Price Index. Suddenly we found ourselves with the debilitating malaise of stagflation—high inflation and high unemployment at the same time. Throughout the deep 1974–75 recession, even as unemployment shot up to 9%, wage rates were still rising at 8%, and the Phillips Curve flattened out and formally died.

Simply stated, the deep recession of 1974–75 failed to relieve the underlying pressure on inflation from wage rates. Throwing nearly 4 million people out of work cut only 2 points off the nation's underlying inflation rate—and absolutely nothing from future wage rate demands, which continued to rise gradually.

Unfortunately, President Carter came into office in 1977 naively believing that stimulating the economy would be a simple, safe tool to "put the nation back to work," and thinking that because there was so much unemployed slack capacity, there was no danger of rising prices.

In September 1976, during Carter's first presidential campaign, I was shocked to discover that both Charles Schultz (who later became Carter's chief economic adviser) and Professor Lawrence Klein of the University of Pennsylvania (who headed Carter's campaign economics committee) still apparently believed in the Phillips Curve, in reverse.

In the light of subsequent history, it is useful to go back and consider the opposing arguments of Professor Klein (now a Nobel laureate) and William E. Simon (President Ford's Treasury secretary) in October 1976 about the "trade-off" between inflation and unemployment, in separate interviews which we then spliced together for publication:

QUESTION: Which do you regard as the more serious problem for the country, inflation or unemployment?

KLEIN: Both problems are serious, but unemployment is much the greater problem and needs the most immediate attention.

SIMON: I am convinced that our whole productive society will collapse if we continue to permit inflation to dominate our economy. If we are to increase the output of goods and services, and reduce unemployment, we must first make further progress in reducing inflation.

KLEIN: I just don't think the world really functions that way. The cause of unemployment is mainly too little fiscal stimulus and monetary support for the economy. We need faster monetary growth.

SIMON: I disagree. I think it's a hoax to suggest that more jobs can be created by "printing money." The record of the past decade shows very clearly that excessive fiscal and monetary stimulus only leads to rising rates of inflation and a "boom-bust" cycle.

KLEIN: I disagree. Unemployment is much too high for another inflationary cycle. Government programs to stimulate the economy do not need to contribute to inflation—particularly if these programs take people off the dole and make them taxpayers. That kind of stimulus pays for itself.

QUESTION: Professor Klein, what measures do you think should be taken by the government to reach your unemployment target of 4% to 4½%?

KLEIN: Well, in the first place, there should be general monetary expansion, and that means "easier money." There should also be some kind of direct government fiscal stimulation, which could be a mixture of either tax reductions or additional government expenditures, or both.

QUESTION: Professor Klein, don't you feel that there's a serious risk of restimulating inflation by pursuing easier money?

KLEIN: Not in our slack economy. Once the economy does near full employment and stays there year after year, then that risk would build up. But right now, we're not in that situation.

SIMON: No matter what you call them, these monetary proposals are nothing more than a call for "printing money." The moment the politicians get their hands on the money supply is the moment when you begin to destroy the economy and the society. And the people who get hurt the most are the poor, the elderly, and those on fixed incomes.

QUESTION: But what about the high interest rates?

SIMON: Some critics claim that more rapid rates of monetary expansion would reduce interest rates, but this is not true. Businessmen and consumers always react negatively to excessive money expansion because they know the ultimate result will be inflation, so they raise interest rates to match.

It was a classic confrontation between two very different economic views of the world. As it turned out (unfortunately for the country), Simon was prophetically right, but his boss (Ford) lost the election, while Klein turned out to be wrong, and his boss, Jimmy Carter, won, with dismal results for all.

The Easy-Money Myth

One of the economic fallacies that has long beguiled populist politicians (and a surprising number of Keynesian economists) is the notion that easy money (rapid money creation) produces low interest rates.

The reason this myth persists is that neither the politicians nor the public really understand the difference between short-term interest rates, which the Federal Reserve can control to a degree, and long-term interest rates, which it really can't. Nearly all major personal and business borrowing (mortgages, etc.) is done at long-term rates (one-year or more).

The long-term interest rate depends almost entirely on the basic inflation rate and is only modestly affected by short-run changes in the money supply. For this reason, the long-term rate is more the result of the policies of big-spending politicians than of those of hard-hearted bankers.

When politicians tell us that they want to lower our interest rates by "easy money" (monetary expansion), they are kidding us—no, they are actually lying to us—because exactly the opposite is the case. Easy money pursued as policy always raises interest rates in the long run.

While the present loan-shark interest levels Americans are now confronting (15%–20%) have indeed been exaggerated by the instability of the Federal Reserve's heavy handed crackdowns on money growth, they are the direct result of easy-money politics pursued more or less steadily by the Federal Reserve since 1968, under pressure from government.

Consider a simple set of facts: From 1955 to 1965, the nation's basic money supply (M-1: currency, plus demand deposits and NOW accounts) grew at an average annual rate of less than 2.5% (compared with nearly 8% since 1970).

TABLE 4-1

THE CARTER RECORD

(annualized rates)

	Fall 1976	Fall 1980
Inflation (CPI)	4.8%	12.6%
Prime rate	6.8%	21.5%
Mortgage rate	8.9%	14.5%
Money growth rate (last quarter)	5.1%	16.8%
Wholesale Price Index (PPI) last quarter	5.7%	11.6%
Unemployment rate	7.7%	7.6%
Unemployed	7,448,000	8,165,000
Housing starts	1,768,000	726,000
Productivity growth	+3.5%	−1.9%
Average weekly earnings (1967 dollars)	$102.95	$96.25
Average federal tax burden on middle income family	16.6%	20.8%
Spot oil price-OPEC	$11.10/bbl	$31.60/bbl
Price of gold	$125.30/oz	$684.00/oz
Value of dollar on world markets (index)	105.7	84.6
U.S. rate of personal savings	6.1%	3.6%

SOURCE: President's Economic Message, 1981.

During that time, interest rates seldom exceeded 4.5% and inflation averaged 1.6%.

In the 1970s the money supply grew over 7% per year, on the average, and interest rates averaged 8% and more. The faster the money growth, the higher the interest rates.

When President Carter took office in January 1977 the prime interest rate (the rate charged by banks to their best customers) was 6.8%, and basic money growth in 1976 had been down to 5.5%. By 1979 money growth was up to the 8%–9% range, inflation rose to double-digit figures, and interest rates soared to a range of 15%–20%.

In other words, the "easier" the money supply gets, the higher the long-term interest rates go. Conversely, countries with the lowest long-term interest rates also have been those with the tightest rein over money growth. West Germany, for example, has had the tightest money in Europe and the lowest interest rates (and inflation rates) to match. Great Britain has had the easiest money in Europe and the highest interest rates.

Why is that? Why does an increase in supply of money raise the long-term price of money? Why doesn't a bigger supply of money reduce its price? Because money is not a commodity but a medium of exchange. When its value goes down (as a result of too much printing), bankers have to start charging more just to protect their assets, regardless of supply and demand. So the basic interest rate (long-term) is composed of two things: the long-term inflation rate, plus the risk rate for particular loans. Thus as inflation (devaluation or printing of money) rises, interest rates have to rise to match.

Chart 4-A shows that, to a very large extent (and up until 1981–82), the

CHART 4-A

INTEREST RATES FOLLOW INFLATION

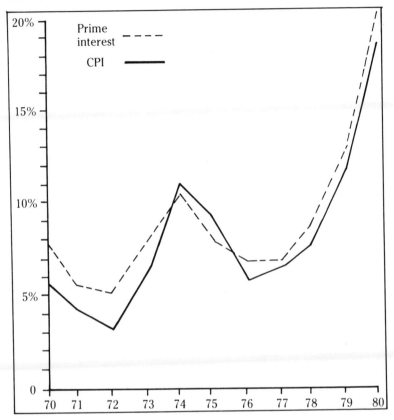

SOURCES: U.S. Bureau of Labor Statistics (inflation); Federal
Reserve Board (interest rates).

prime rate has tended to follow the inflation rate and has remained close to it,
irrespective of temporary tight money situations. The easier the money, the
higher the rates went.

Inflation and the Falling Dollar

After his firing, in September 1979, Treasury Secretary W. Michael Blumenthal said that the reason the Carter administration had done such a poor job
fighting inflation was that "the liberals in the administration believe that
high interest rates are bad, and that fighting inflation hurts poor people."

In Plains [in December 1976], all the talk was about the necessity to stimulate the American economy [with easy money and larger deficits]. We underestimated the basic strength of the American private economy. The real problem was not a major slowdown, but it was really an endemic, in-built, growing, inflationary pressure. But we occupied ourselves with developing stimulus packages.

So, in 1977, the Carter administration, with the full advice and approval of the Democratic leadership in Congress (including Senator Edward M. Kennedy), set about to inflate the U.S. economy deliberately, and as a matter of policy. Furthermore, convinced of the rightness of their easy-money policies, the Carter economic team journeyed in 1977 to Europe and Japan to try to convince those nations to inflate their economies right along with us.

Fortunately (for them but not for the dollar), neither Germany nor Japan bought this idea. Both had just been through the wringer of cutting their own inflation rates and strengthening their own currencies, by very careful tight-money policies in the middle 1970s. Germany, especially, was not about to travel down the "hyperinflation" route ever again—having experienced the horror in the 1920s sufficiently to have an indelible memory of it. So even as America plunged ahead with expansionary monetary policies, our two largest trading partners were carefully keeping a rein over their own monetary affairs.

Predictably, the dollar began in late 1977 and early 1978 to plunge in value in the world money markets, but most Americans, including President Carter and his advisers, seemed not to understand what the falling dollar could do to domestic inflation.

One morning on ABC–TV for example, John Kenneth Galbraith told Americans that the only people who would feel any impact from a falling dollar were "the rich who might find the price of imported wine or Rolls-Royces would rise."

That, of course, is utter nonsense, as the people of Great Britain know—having lived through several major devaluations of the pound sterling since 1965 and having experienced the enormous inflation that these devaluations have always brought them.

As the British discovered, we no longer live in a world of insulated national economies. We live in a world market economy, governed entirely by world pricing mechanisms. As the dollar rises or falls, relative to other currencies in the world, we have either deflation or inflation, compared with those other countries.

It is in this way that the devaluation of any national currency becomes an automatic conduit for inflation into every sector of that economy. That is why Great Britain found that a 10% devaluation of the pound sterling led to a 10-point increase in its total inflation rate—not immediately, but within the next 15–20 months.

This process was documented in a doctoral thesis written in 1975 by Dr. Moon H. Lee, a young Korean economist, who concluded: "Devaluation of one currency, vis à vis others, produces inflation vis à vis those other currencies' inflation rates."

Thus, if our dollar more or less annually declines 10% against the German mark, our own domestic inflation will tend to rise to 10 percentage points higher than Germany's. Dr. Lee supports his thesis with 72 years of currency history which shows that there is an absolute "one-for-one relationship between the average change in currency values with the dollar, and the inflation rates."

As Arthur Laffer writes, "The efficiency of world markets dictates that the single predictable consequence of devaluation is a rise in the level of prices in the devaluing country, compared to those it devalues against." This is why, Professor Laffer warns, "the single most important lesson of the past decade is that an unhinged monetary system (floating exchange rates) results in global inflation."

To get a feeling for how this works, suppose you are living in Germany but are being paid in U.S. dollars (say, as a serviceman). The inflation rate for you would be the German inflation rate, *plus* whatever the dollar is losing in value against the Deutschmark (DM), or *minus* whatever it's gaining. If the German inflation rate were 5%, and the dollars in your salary were losing 5% each year against the DM, your personal inflation rate would be 10%. On the other hand, if the dollar were gaining 5% a year against the DM, your inflation rate would be zero. For you, there would be an exact one-for-one relationship between the rise and fall of the dollar and the ups and downs of the inflation rate in Germany.

If you understand this, you are now prepared to make the next step, which is to realize that, even though you do not live in Germany, you do live in a world market—where the price of all of our commodities is more or less governed by world conditions. In this world market, where currencies are allowed to "float," our own U.S. inflation rate will automatically be the world's inflation rate, plus or minus the relative value of the dollar. If the world inflation rate is 10%, and the dollar is losing 4% a year (against the composite of all world currencies), our own inflation rate will be 14%, on average, allowing for a lag of about one year in overall price adjustments.

But, you may object, "Only 15% of our goods are imported. How does that small 15% influence the other 85% of our domestic consumption?" The answer is that not only are all basic commodities (metals, food, oil, etc.) priced in the world market, but the prices charged by overseas companies which sell their manufactured products (automobiles, computers, etc.) here have a direct competitive bearing on our own domestic prices. Any attempt by domestic manufacturers, or by the government, to support or control prices either above or below this world market will immediately cause big distortions in supply and rapid increases or decreases in demands for exports and/or imports that would thwart such controls. Oil has been a classic case. We have, in fact, been paying the world price since 1973, despite lower domestic price controls. (Since oil decontrol in January 1981 there has been no net change in domestic consumer prices.)

The effect of a floating exchange-rate system (of paper currencies) is to transmit inflation quickly from country to country. More important, the system quickly punishes those countries that print too much of their own currency and rewards those that pursue hard-money policies. That is why monetarists prefer the floating exchange-rate system. They say it forces market discipline on domestic monetary and fiscal policy without the rigidities of a fixed-exchange system. There is real merit in that free-market argument.

The trouble comes when we get a president, such as Richard Nixon or Jimmy Carter, who doesn't fully understand this, and tries to run counter to it. As Table 4-2 shows, under Nixon, from 1970 through 1974, the United States was on a money-printing binge, as a result of which the dollar's value decreased in the world markets by 21%. That, in turn, drove U.S. inflation to record heights (12% in 1974) and forced the Federal Reserve to tighten up drastically in 1974–75. The effect of that tightening was the restoration of over half of the dollar's lost value by 1976, and thus the lowering of U.S. inflation rates. But in 1977, when Carter came into office and proceeded to reinflate or stimulate the U.S. economy with big new deficits and rapid money creation, the effect was immediate and dramatic: The dollar plunged 36% against the yen, 27% against the DM, and almost 20% against the French franc, producing a worldwide monetary crisis on 31 October 1978 and forcing the Federal Reserve to start its long slow turnaround, which finally culminated in the "credit crunch" of spring 1980.

Unfortunately, as Table 4-3 demonstrates, American consumers paid a devastating price for this Carter monetary policy. As the dollar declined relative to other currencies, our inflation one year later began to show an immediate upward surge. In fact, our own money expansion and falling dollar actually helped other countries (which didn't follow this approach) to keep their inflation rates even lower, since so many world commodities (such as oil) are priced in dollars.

Conversely, the rapid rise in the dollar following the November 1980 elections (reaching over 25% by March 1982) had the opposite effect, lowering our inflation rate dramatically from 11.5% down to less than 4%, while at the same time fueling renewed inflation in countries such as France, Canada, and Italy whose currencies were so devalued by the dollar's strength.

As Chart 4-B shows, the actual trend of the U.S. dollar has, with only a six-month lag, been a marvelous forecaster and mirror image of our CPI inflation rate. Since the fall of 1980 the dollar has gained an average of more than 6% per year against the major Western currencies, and our inflation rate has now fallen to a level more than 6 points below the trade-weighted inflation rate of about 12%, a nearly precise one-for-one relationship.

The relationship becomes clear in Table 4-4, which shows that (allowing for a one-year lag) the average differential in the U.S. inflation rate against other countries was nearly one-for-one with the average loss in the dollar's value against the currencies of those countries. In the period 1976–79, for example, the dollar lost an average of 7.6% per year against the German

TABLE 4-2

THE SINKING DOLLAR

Value against selected currencies

Date	Yen/$	DM/$	Franc/$	Composite index
May 1970	360	3.66	5.55	100
March 1973	262	2.81	4.51	83
March 1975	288	2.32	4.20	79
December 1976	295	2.38	5.00	91
September 1978	190	1.97	4.37	77
March 1979	206	1.86	4.29	76
December 1979	240	1.73	4.06	74
May 7, 1980	232	1.79	4.20	75
% changes high to low	−47%	−53%	−27%	−26%
December 1976 to low (Carter dollars)	−36%	−27%	−19%	−18%

SOURCE: Federal Reserve Board.

TABLE 4-3

HOW THE SINKING DOLLAR AFFECTS U.S. INFLATION

AGAINST JAPANESE YEN

	Dollar index	Japanese inflation	U.S. inflation
1975	100	8.4%	9.1%
1976	99	9.2%	5.8%
1977	89	6.2%	6.5%
1978	70	3.8%	7.7%
1979	74	3.6%	11.3%
1980 1st qtr.	81	9.1%	18.3%

AGAINST GERMAN D/M

	Dollar index	Japanese inflation	U.S. inflation
1975	100	6.2%	9.1%
1976	101	4.0%	5.8%
1977	93	3.8%	6.5%
1978	80	2.7%	7.7%
1979	74	4.1%	11.3%
1980 1st qtr.	75	5.2%	18.3%

SOURCES: Federal Reserve Board; U.S. Bureau of Labor Statistics; Merrill Lynch-Economics.

DM—and the U.S. inflation rate averaged, in 1977–80, about 7.1% above the German rate.

Even as oil prices (in dollars) were rising in the United States, oil prices in Deutschmarks were actually declining in Germany until 1979. This hurt our inflation rate and helped theirs. The relationship was direct and measurable.

So direct is that relationship that it is safe to say that one of the leading causes of our high inflation rates in 1979–80 was the sharp decline in the U.S. dollar in 1977–79—a decline directly caused by the policies of President Carter and Secretary Blumenthal. Blumenthal admitted as much in the fall of 1979, when he told the Washington Forum, "We did not appreciate early and fully enough, the potential for trouble in the currency markets."

CHART 4-B

INFLATION AND THE DOLLAR, 1975-82

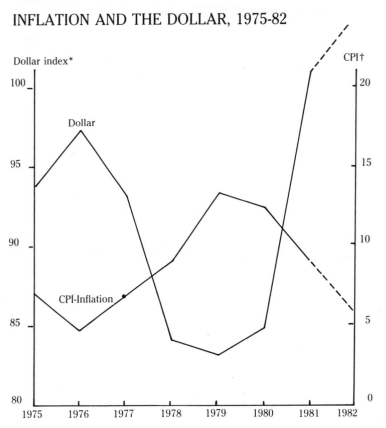

SOURCES: Federal Reserve Board; U.S. Bureau of Labor Statistics.

* Multilateral trade-weighted value of U.S. dollar (March 1973=100).

† CPI measured from December to December, to provide "lagged" effect.

Behind the Gold Panic

Indeed they didn't. In March 1978, in a column entitled, somewhat melodramatically, "Are We Headed For a Crash?" I warned: "A lot of investors think the widely forecast recession for 1979 could turn out to be a serious crash." In late October 1978, just eight months after that column was written, the collapse of the dollar in the world markets was so serious that "we came within hours," according to one French market economist, "of an international monetary crisis of serious proportions."

That's when the Federal Reserve was forced to step in with heavy measures to stop the dollar's slide—measures which eventually triggered the 1980 recession. But by that time the most serious damage had already been done. The dollar had lost 18% of its value against world currencies. The world was fleeing from the dollar to other currencies (marks, yen, and even the pound sterling), and by the fall of 1979 investors were getting out of all paper currencies and into gold. When that happens, the entire communications and monetary credit structure that undergirds the world economy is threatened. The economy, as I've pointed out, is built on mutual confidence and trust, and the purchase of gold is an act of fear and distrust.

The trouble was that few in Washington seemed to realize just how serious the situation was. Even a leading economist like Paul Samuelson (who pooh-poohed the 1977–78 dollar slide) downplayed the gold panic of 1979. Samuelson—one of the nation's leading Keynesians, and the man partly responsible for the "pump-primed" inflation we were experiencing—called the gold panic "tulip-mania," referring to the craze that struck Dutch investors three centuries ago, when they speculated on tulip bulbs.

Most liberal economists blamed the dollar slide and the gold panic on OPEC, forgetting that the two largest drops in the value of the U.S. dollar took place in 1971–73 (before OPEC raised its prices) and in 1977–78 (when OPEC's prices were frozen). They were also forgetting that the strongest world currencies were the yen and the mark, from countries that import virtually all their oil from OPEC.

Their argument suffers from two basic flaws: First, the rising *real* cost of energy is not inflation but impoverishment, since inflation is, in the final analysis, a monetary devaluation, not a price phenomenon. Second, energy costs, as much as they have risen, have played a remarkably small role in the nation's long-term price index, as Table 4-5 demonstrates.

How, for example, is one to explain why the United States (which imports only 35% of its oil) has had double the inflation rates of Germany and Japan (which import over 90% of their oil)? Even so, gasoline at $1.30 per gallon in June 1981 was only 6.8 times its price of 19 cents in 1940, while all other prices had risen 6.4 times and wage rates had risen 9.6 times. Oil and gasoline, have not escalated any faster, over the long term, than other price and wage indices.

As Table 4-5 shows, without any impact from energy cost increases, the basic inflation rate doubled from under 5% in 1976 to more than 10% in 1980. OPEC price rises contributed less than 10% of the total inflation doubling in this period.

We all tend to ignore the fact that inflation is not the product of someone raising prices, but at the root is the process by which nations debauch their currencies by printing too much of them—and that debauchery inevitably takes place unless these currencies are tied in some way (through gold or silver) to real goods or commodities, and thus are removed from political manipulation.

That was the underlying purpose of the Bretton Woods agreement of 1944, which tied the world to the dollar and, in turn, tied the dollar to gold—at a

TABLE 4-4

DOLLAR LOSS EQUALS INFLATION GAIN

	Average annual dollar loss 1976-79	Average differential inflation rate 1977-80
Against all industrial countries	2.75%	2.8%
Against Japanese yen	6.7%	5.2%
Against Deutschmark	7.6%	7.1%

SOURCE: Federal Reserve Board; U.S. Bureau of Labor Statistics; Merrill Lynch-Economics.

TABLE 4-5

OPEC INFLATION

Inflation rates with and without energy (in percentages)

	YEAR TO YEAR		DEC. TO DEC.	
	with energy	without energy	with energy	without energy
1974	11.0	9.8	11.9	11.0
1975	9.1	9.1	7.0	6.4
1976	5.8	5.8	4.8	5.0
1977	6.5	6.3	6.8	6.6
1978	7.7	7.8	9.0	9.2
1979	11.3	10.0	13.3	11.3

SOURCES: President's Economic Message, 1980; U.S. Bureau of Labor Statistics.

fixed rate of $35 per ounce in the international market. That agreement served the United States (and the world) fairly well (with minimal 1%–2% inflation) until the late 1960s, when, under the influence of the Keynesians and the fiscal pressure of the war in Vietnam and the Great Society, the United States began actively to inflate its own currency.

The natural result of this rapid expansion in the U.S. money supply was to encourage a world-wide run on our own gold reserves, dropping them from $24 billion in 1947 down to less than $10 billion in 1971.

As Jude Wanniski writes, "In the spring of 1971, as the Federal Reserve tried desperately to expand the U.S. economy by flooding it with dollars, the rest of the world came, demanding our gold. On August 15, 1971, Richard Nixon ordered the Gold Window (at the Federal Reserve) closed, ending the international currency's link to gold for the first time in 1,500 years. There began the worst inflation of the century."

Six months later, in Geneva, in January 1972, the original "supply sider," Professor Robert Mundell, one of the nation's leading experts on international monetary policy, correctly warned that, as a result of leaving the gold standard, "the price of gold, and oil and other commodities will soon soar." From 1971 to 1973, before OPEC raised its oil prices, the price of gold nearly tripled to $98—and the value of the dollar declined nearly 20% against world currencies. The soaring gold price then acted as a magnet pulling oil and other commodities up. Hence, the price of oil followed (not caused) the upward price of gold, by about two years—with the result that an ounce of gold (at $160) in July 1974 bought about the same number of barrels of oil that an ounce of gold (at $35) had bought back in 1970.

The Golden-Oil Standard

Indeed economists such as Professor Roy W. Jastram of the University of California at Berkeley and Robert Mundell have hinted that the 1979 initial rise in oil prices to the $18–$20 range resulted largely from the plunging dollar in 1977–78, and not just from the crisis in Iran.

CHART 4-C

THE GOLDEN MAGNET

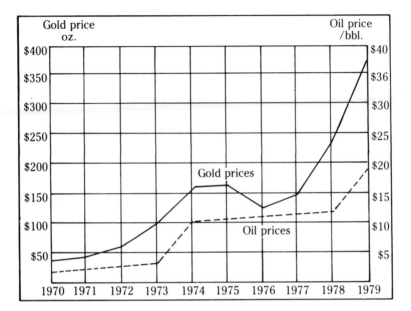

SOURCES: Dow-Jones; Wall Street Journal; U.S. Statistical Abstract.

While the price of OPEC oil to the United States had risen 43% from 1975 to 1979, the price of OPEC oil to the West Germans had risen only 1%, and to the Japanese only 7%. The reason for this huge disparity was that the United States had been systematically devaluing its currency through domestic inflation, and the members of OPEC (who price their oil in dollars) had not caught up. As Table 4-6 shows:

- From 1975 to 1978 U.S. inflation was 21%. During that time the OPEC price rose only 10%, or half as fast. So the "real" price of OPEC oil went down 10% in that period.
- In fact, during the time of the 18-month OPEC price freeze on oil (June 1977 to December 1978) the U.S. inflation rate rose from 6% to 9.8%—with no rise in oil prices.
- As a result of this inflation, the U.S. dollar was dropping on the international monetary market, falling 25%–30% against the major Western currencies.

Because OPEC prices its oil in dollars, this meant that by 1978 its member countries had lost 20% of their 1975 purchasing power in the world market—and 10% of their purchasing power in the U.S. market. In June 1979, for example, it took 3,870 yen to buy a barrel of OPEC oil on the world market,

TABLE 4-6

THE "REAL" PRICES OF OPEC OIL

	1975	1978	June 1979	% change
Dollars/barrel	$12.60	$13.80	$18.00	+43
Japan				
Yen/dollar	287	196	215	−26
Yen/barrel	3,616	2,705	3,870	+7
Germany				
Marks/dollar	2.61	1.97	1.85	−29
Marks/barrel	32.90	27.20	33.30	+1
Switzerland				
Francs/dollar	2.56	1.85	1.67	−35
Francs/barrel	32.25	25.50	30.05	−7
United States				
Consumer Price Index	161	195	216	+34
OPEC price in 1975 dollars	$12.60	$11.40	$13.43	+7
OPEC price in real world purchasing power (1975)	$12.60	$10.10	$12.60	———

SOURCES: Dow-Jones; U.S. Bureau of Labor Statistics; U.S. Department of Energy.

TABLE 4-7

GROWTH-RATE MULTIPLIERS

	Output	Money supply	prices
1957-67	1.46	1.75	1.19
1967-77	1.33	2.31	1.82

SOURCE: President's Economic Message, 1979.

compared with 3,616 yen in 1975—only 7% more in four years, or about one third the Japanese rate of inflation. For the West Germans, the pinch was even milder. In June 1979 they paid an average of 33.3 Deutschmarks per barrel for OPEC oil, only 1% more than they paid in 1975.

One primary reason for low and declining inflation rates in Germany and Japan had been the weak U.S. dollar, which resulted in a steady lowering of their fuel costs up until spring 1979. That is why OPEC, like many other international traders, gave up the dollar standard and returned to a kind of "golden-oil" standard. From 1970 to 1981 the price of gold rose 1,219%—the price of oil 1,291%. That's no coincidence.

So when we see the price of gold going up or down on the nightly news, we could be looking at the future trend in the price of oil, and while it is impossible to determine which commodity is affecting which price at any given moment, it is factually true that gold and oil have been "chasing each other" ever since the Bretton Woods Agreement formally ended in 1971 and the world deserted the international gold standard.

In 1970 an ounce of gold ($35) would buy 15 barrels of OPEC oil ($2.30/bbl). In May 1981 an ounce of gold ($480) still bought 15 barrels of Saudi oil ($32/bbl). In fact, in February 1981 President Reagan scooped the experts

CHART 4-D

THE CASE FOR THE INTERNATIONAL GOLD STANDARD

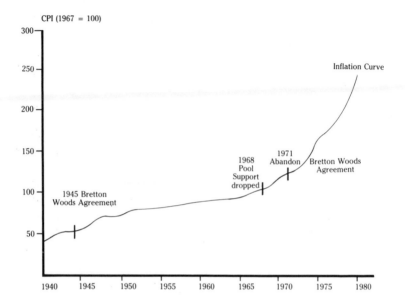

CPI (1967 = 100)

when he predicted that oil prices would soon fall because the price of gold had dropped over 20% since his election. By December 1981 the domestic spot price of oil was nearly $8, or 20% lower than one year before.

Ever since 1971, when President Nixon abandoned the international gold standard, the price of oil (and other commodities) has followed the rising (or falling) price of gold.

To this day, few Americans realize that one of the original motivating forces behind the OPEC price escalation in 1973–74 was the Arabs' correct perception that they were being taken to the cleaners by Western nations, who were actually devaluing their own currencies and thereby cutting the real price of oil. When they woke up, recounts economist Robert Mundell, "Confidence in currencies in general declined, and a shift out of paper money into land-based minerals began. A worldwide scarcity of land and land-intensive products, including raw materials, emerged. Within two years the price of metals, foods, and minerals more than doubled."

The startling effects of cutting our final tenuous links to gold can be seen in Charts 4-D and 4-E, which show how suddenly U.S. inflation (CPI) and the prices of export-import commodities began to soar when we first abandoned the pool-price supports (on gold) of the Bretton Woods Agreement in 1968, and then when President Nixon formally ended that entire compact in

CHART 4-E

PRICES OF U.S. EXPORTS AND IMPORTS

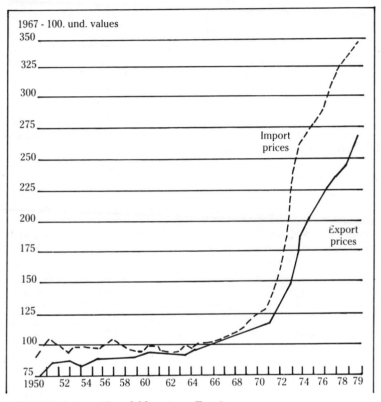

1967 - 100. und. values

SOURCE: International Monetary Fund.

August 1971, when he closed the Federal Reserve's "gold window." This huge upsurge in commodities prices and the consumer price index did not start with OPEC's price hikes of 1973–74, but nearly three to five years *before*.

As Roy W. Jastram pointed out in *The Wall Street Journal*, 12 December 1979: "The [research] does suggest that the present turbulence in world monetary relationships started well before OPEC's embargo. Looking at this [research], those who assert that the rise in energy prices is a *cause* of our inflation must ask themselves if the rise in energy prices, at least initially, has been a *result* of inflation."

Inflation and the Money Credit-Explosion

Yet, in spite of this painfully obvious scenario, most Americans, (including

Jimmy Carter) still thought that OPEC was causing U.S. inflation and the weak dollar, instead of the other way around. We easily forget that first, last, and always, inflation is a monetary phenomenon—caused by the deliberate expansion in the money supply faster than real output of goods and services.

As Table 4-7 shows, from 1957 to 1967 this nation expanded its money supply about 19% faster than its real output of goods and services (1.75 ÷ 1.46 = 1.19) in a total inflation rate for the ten-year period of about 19%. From 1967 to 1977, however, our money-supply growth jumped enormously, while the growth rate in our output of goods and services fell 10%. As a result, we created money about 75% faster than we produced goods. Not surprisingly, our inflation for this total period was 82%. In other words, our inflation rate almost exactly equaled the percentage difference between the speed with which we have expanded the money supply and the growth rate of our production of goods and services.

The Credit Explosion

One driving force behind this rapid money-supply growth has been an exploding level of demand-side credit, fueled in large measure by deliberate government policies and by an accommodating attitude at the Federal Reserve. The idea behind these policies was that one could get much more "bank for the buck" by expanding consumer demand through government deficits and federally assisted borrowing than by the slower process of waiting for (or encouraging) private capital investment in productivity (supply). Their effect can be seen in Table 4-8 which shows just how drastically the nation's basic credit markets shifted from supporting supply (corporate and farm investment) to promoting consumer demand (consumer and government credit).

Throughout the 1960s (the decade of our best, and least-inflationary, growth), the supply side of our economy got 55%–60% of all the credit, while the demand side got only 40%–45%, and government took only 9%-12%. But in the 1970s the demand side took over, with 60%–65% of all credit going, not to productivity (plant and equipment), but to stimulating consumer demand, with government taking 25% of all credit dollars.

As Table 4-8 shows, during the period 1970–78, the total credit market in the United States expanded by 263%—more than twice the total GNP growth of 114% and seven times as fast as the real growth in goods and services of only 35%. More important, the demand-side credit grew nearly three times as fast as the supply-side credit, with consumer credit growing 486% in just eight years, when even inflated consumer purchases grew only 117%. In other words, consumer credit grew four times as fast as total consumer purchases and 11 times as fast as real goods output, as the nation moved to a credit-card economy, tremendously expanding demand beyond real supply.

What the public does not realize is the degree to which the explosion in

TABLE 4-8

INFLATION AND THE CREDIT EXPLOSION

(billions of inflated dollars)

	DEMAND SIDE CREDIT				SUPPLY SIDE CREDIT		TOTAL
	Government	Consumer	Total	Share	Business/Farm	Share	Credit
1970	$23.2	$24.9	$48.1	49%	$49.8	51%	$97.9
1971	42.6	45.2	97.8	66%	60.6	34%	148.3
1972	29.6	64.3	93.9	55%	78.1	45%	172.0
1973	21.5	80.9	102.4	52%	95.2	48%	197.6
1974	27.3	49.2	76.5	44%	97.0	56%	173.5
1975	98.6	48.6	147.2	76%	47.7	24%	194.9
1976	87.5	89.9	177.4	71%	74.4	29%	251.8
1977	82.7	139.6	222.3	68%	106.0	32%	328.3
1978	85.4	145.9	231.3	66%	124.0	34%	355.3
% change 1970-78	268%	486%	381%	+35%	149%	-33%	263%

Growth in total inflated GNP, 1970-78 114%

Growth in total consumption, 1970-78 117%

Growth in real output of goods, 1970-78 35%

SOURCES: President's Economic Message, 1979; Federal Reserve Board.

consumer borrowing was directly assisted by federal programs (housing, education loans, etc.). In addition to the more than $400 billion in direct new federal debt issued to the public in 1969–81 to cover deficits, the federal government also added more than $290 billion in federally assisted or guaranteed credit to the consumer markets, mostly in housing. In 1978 alone, for example, $51 billion of the $145.9 billion in new consumer credit was directly sponsored by the federal government, in addition to the more than $59 billion borrowed directly by the U.S. Treasury to cover budget deficits.

It is this explosion in demand-side credit (accommodated by the Federal Reserve in money growth) that has fueled the U.S. economy's unprecedented combination of declining productivity (weakening supply) and double-digit inflation (accelerating demand).

At the very time when rapidly rising marginal tax rates were choking private investment, savings, and real economic growth, the U.S. credit markets were also under heavy siege by the federal Treasury. At the very time when interest rates should have been coming down to allow for investment in recovery, the U.S. economy faced a credit crunch. While part of that credit crunch resulted from the Federal Reserve's somewhat "yo-yo" efforts to get the raging money supply under control, a significant share of it stemmed from the mounting federal demands on U.S. credit markets.

As OMB Director-to-be David Stockman warned with prescience in December 1980, "President Reagan will inherit thoroughly disordered credit and capital markets, punishingly high interest rates, and a hair-trigger market psychology poised to respond strongly to early economic policy signals in either favorable or unfavorable ways." What worried Stockman was the degree to which much of the federal borrowing had nothing to do with the federal budget but consisted of off-budget items in the form of loan guarantees and federally-sponsored credit, mostly through the Federal Financing Bank

TABLE 4-9

THE EXPLOSION OF FEDERAL CREDIT, 1967-80

(in billions of current dollars)

Funds raised	1967	1970	1975	1979	1980	% Change
Total raised under federal auspices	$1.1	17.9	64.8	81.2	104.5	9,400%
Direct federal borrowing	$2.8	5.4	50.9	33.6	51.0	1,721%
Federal loan guarantees	$2.1	8.0	8.7	26.1	35.8	1,605%
Federally sponsored agencies	$ − 3.8	4.5	5.3	21.4	17.7	(infinite)
% share of total credit raised	1.8%	19.1%	35.7%	19.8%	26.1%	

SOURCE: Special Analyses of Federal Budget, 1977-81.

(FFB). The FFB had been created by Congress in 1974 for the express purpose of taking out of the discipline of the Budget a whole range of federal credit activities, ranging from commodities to housing. The direct annual cost of this "off-budget" activity passed $18 billion in 1981, and Congress had no effective control over it.

As Table 4-9 shows, of the $104.5 billion raised in 1980, only $51 billion was raised to cover the federal budget deficit. The rest went to cover the mushrooming explosion in loan guarantees (like those to New York City and Chrysler, and housing subsidies) and to other federally sponsored credit agencies. These off-budget areas of federally sponsored credit and borrowing took off under the Carter administration, leaping from $12.5 billion in 1970 and $14 billion in 1975 to $53 billion in 1980. As a result, the total federal credit outstanding nearly doubled between 1975 and 1981, and the major share of that growth came off-budget. (As of 1981, it stood at more than $1.1 trillion.)

"It's a classic budget scam," Stockman told The Wall Street Journal, "a money-laundering device." The importance of getting this "money laundry" under control becomes evident when we consider that throughout the 1960s (the period of our best economic growth) the federal government took on average less than 10% of the nation's available credit. But during the 1970s this escalated to nearly 50%, while the corporate and farm share (the supply side) steadily dwindled.

From 1977 to 1981, the annual assault on the credit markets for federal loan guarantees quadrupled, and for sponsored agency loans more than tripled. Virtually all of this growth was away from congressional and public scrutiny.

The pressure that this undisciplined credit expansion creates on the money supply is clear: Just as politicians have discovered they can pass out goodies merely by monetizing their debt, they now provide cheap credit without paying for it in unpopular taxation.

Can We Ever Restore Sound Money?

This is why bankers and politicians responded with such enthusiasm to the presentations of Keynes, who transformed government-sponsored counterfeiting (printing money) into "compassionate" macroeconomic policy. Keynes was surprisingly untroubled by the fundamental immorality of government deliberately destroying the value of personal wealth and savings through this process—even though he well understood what he was proposing. Yet through his demand-stimulation process of deliberate government inflation, pursued by the United States since 1970, and especially since 1976, Americans have seen much of their real wealth stolen from them by government. In 1977–81 alone, nearly half a trillion dollars worth of private pension wealth in bonds and savings were wiped out by this deceptive process. That's why every working man and woman has a big stake in the struggle for the radical reestablishment of sound money.

As Lewis Lehrman warned in *Harper's*, "without real money, savings evaporate, investment languishes and the future is impoverished." The working men and women who carefully save have a right to expect that the future value of these savings match the present value of the labor it took to achieve them. But without an objective regulator of discipline (such as gold), paper money will always deteriorate in value, since it costs nothing to produce in the first place and since neither politicians nor bankers can resist giving "something for nothing."

The Professional Employees Federation, a union in New York State, in 1982 proposed the following language in its contract with the state:

Recognizing the possibility of uncontrollable inflation and the serious loss of credibility and purchasing power of the dollar, the employer, upon union's demand, will remunerate employees in mediums of exchange other than the presently used U.S. Federal Reserve dollar. Such alternative mediums of exchange include, but are not limited to, gold, silver, platinum, bullion and coin, and/or one or more foreign currencies.

As one of the union leaders told *The Washington Post*, "We're not suggesting the governor pan gold in Colorado and pay us in gold dust. We want to be paid in the value of gold or silver, or another (similarly definite) index of value."

If we are genuinely to put the inflation genie back into the bottle, we must combine a supply-side fiscal and tax policy (lower taxes and spending) with an equally forceful plan to take the control of our money away from the bankers and the politicians and impose the true discipline of a commodity-based monetary standard. Otherwise, we may be doomed to lose our liberty and our economic system to the totalitarians among us.

"In fact," warned Lehrman in 1980, "without serious monetary reform, tax reduction, as necessary as it is, cannot do the job of restoring a healthy and stable economy." Lehrman argues that while the income tax is, indeed, an "engine of inflation" (because it progressively punishes productivity, savings, and investment and rewards government for inflation), the fuel for this engine is being too generously provided by the Federal Reserve, despite "all its talk about tight money." It is Lehrman's thesis that the important thing to remember about the Federal Reserve is that "it is, first and last, a bank, and a bank's basic business is to create credit."

Unfortunately, when the Federal Reserve Bank creates credit, through loans to its members and customers, it creates money for the entire economy. It does this even during periods when it is supposed to be trying to cut the nation's money supply. This is why Lehrman has never paid as much attention to the so-called monetary aggregates as he has to the outstanding Federal Reserve bank credit, which has been expanding at about 8.5% a year (compounded) for the past 20 years, with no appreciable let up, even in periods of supposedly tight money. Lehrman argues: "If, instead of a specific quantity of money (which it can't control anyway) the goal of the central bank were primarily price stability, the Fed would promptly reduce the amount of credit it made available to the commercial banks. As the Fed credit growth contracted, so would the money stock . . . and prices would generally stabilize."

Undoubtedly the best proof of Lehrman's thesis came in 1981–82, when the growth in Federal Reserve bank credit dropped sharply from the 8% range to about 4%, the lowest rate in more than a decade, and the pace of inflation dropped from double-digit to less than 6%.

But since the Federal Reserve ultimately derives its power from the politicians in Washington, it cannot long be trusted to impose a true monetary standard on the country. It will always be tempted or forced to manipulate the money supply, however clumsily, for political, economic, and social purposes, and just because it is a bank.

Lehrman's step-by-step plan to deal with this weakness was outlined in January 1980 in a private monograph which has been widely circulated in economic and financial circles, the most important thrust of which involved the restoration of a fixed monetary standard:

- "Announce the restoration of dollar convertibility to gold within the next 12 to 18 months at a fixed rate to be determined in the market-place, but at a level which in no circumstances would reduce nominal wages."
- "Convene an international monetary conference under the leadership of the U.S. with the goal of establishing a true gold standard, one which would rule out the special privilege of official reserve currencies, and thus remedy the most profound defect of the Bretton Woods exchange-rate regime."

Whether or not it is possible to return to the gold standard or whether some other commodity-based standard would work better than gold is too complex for discussion here and is really irrelevant to the central issue, which is sound money. The only possible way this can ever be achieved in the long run is to return our monetary system to some independent discipline or standard (such as gold or silver) and let that standard act within the impartial forces of the marketplace to control the supply of money. In that way it does not arbitrarily outrace the supply of goods and services which it is supposed to represent. One way of doing this short of a full gold standard is to have the Federal Reserve gear its monetary policies to the support of a fixed price of gold, a kind of "proxy gold standard" which would have the same effect.

Herbert Frankel points to the extraordinary expansion of world trade in the 19th century (when the world was on the pound sterling and it, in turn, was based broadly on gold) as evidence of "a self-denying act by democracy to curb the power of government so as to ensure monetary trust across national frontiers." Frankel argues that this discipline of gold did more to promote the world economy "than any other monetary system," but, in the last analysis, it depended on the willingness of the public in all countries to accept the definite constraints which such a system imposes. This, he says, is the real difficulty of restoring such a system in today's more permissive atmosphere: "The monetary predicament of the free world can be dealt with by none other than its citizens. If they attempt to do so, can they afford to overlook the classical idea of virtue: the need to control the passions, to moderate envy, greed, lust for power, and the love of ease at the expense of others, and of freedom itself?"

Inflation as a Moral Issue

In 1981 the federal debt crashed through the $1-trillion ceiling, nearly quadrupling since 1972.

Thinking about this monument to fiscal incontinence, I am reminded of the apocryphal story of the Georgia dirt farmer with 12 hungry children—and another on the way. When asked why he didn't exercise more restraint, he said, "Whenever I get to lovin' I feel like I can feed every child in Georgia."

In a way, this story describes the underlying cause of our continuing inflation syndrome. Like the Georgia dirt farmer, our politicians get to lusting after political power, and suddenly feeling that they can "feed all the children in Georgia," they make their promises accordingly. But in the process of trying to make good on their promises by irresponsible fiscal policies, they are merely spawning more helpless, hungry, and dependent children—and an economy riddled with inflation, caused by massive federal deficits and devalued currency. In this sense, inflation is the outward symbol of swollen pride and ego and a false sense of compassion, the effect of heady promises made during the heat of political lust, the logical outcome of unrestrained passion.

It is easy to blame this on the politicians. They are, after all, extensions of our will and reflect our desires. It is our own lust for a government that can provide us with economic security without effort or responsibility that has fed the age-old political lust for more power, achieved not through genuine productivity, but by means of a printing press.

It is we who have shunned those few politicians with the guts to tell us that there is no free lunch, and who have fallen instead for those who will promise us anything but give us phony greenbacks.

It is we who have chucked aside the traditional moral restraints of self-discipline and opted for a permissive society in which there is no right or wrong, no value judgments, only the pursuit of self-gratification. There is, after all, very little difference between the debasement of our currency through the adulteration of the money supply and the larger debasement of our moral currency through unbridled greed, irresponsible living, and the adulteration of human relationships and ethical standards.

It seems no coincidence that the motto "In God We Trust" was struck on our national coins. It is a fitting reminder that our currency is worth no more than our fundamental sense of trust and faith, a faith based on the higher set of moral laws that underlies our Constitution and its Bill of Rights. It was Moses who argued that such moral laws are the only sure guide to the promised land of milk and honey (economic well-being) and that ethical principles, strictly adhered to, are the only substantial "currency" any nation would ever need.

Is it not inevitable that a nation whose human and moral values are declining will soon find its currency losing value, too? Does it not seem logical that financial devaluation is merely the outgrowth of ethical and moral devaluation? Ultimately, it takes the same kind of self-discipline to preserve the value of a nation's currency as it does to preserve the ethical value of human life itself.

5

Ideas vs. the
Babel of Bureaucracy

If we do not halt this steady process of building commissions and regulatory bodies and special legislation like huge inverted pyramids over every one of the simple constitutional provisions, we shall soon be spending billions of dollars more.

—*Franklin D. Roosevelt*

In 1981 a national public television news show took an in-depth look at the new field of biogenetics and the promise it holds for a new level of productivity in agriculture without chemicals and petroleum. Scientists and entrepreneurs showed how the technology of recombinant DNA was now being used to develop new feed grains that fertilize themselves by conserving their own nitrogen, using fewer petroleum-based fertilizers, and eliminating the need for pesticides.

Then, all too predictably, the interviewer turned to a dour-looking young lawyer who was identified as representing one of those myriad public-interest lobbying groups (which so many of our tax dollars now support) and who immediately began pouring cold water all over our enthusiasm with alarming predictions and imperious demands that Congress and the federal government "get in and control this whole process, before it gets too much further along." When he was asked what he meant, he was unambiguous. "Well, let's just say we ought to be sure first that these procedures aren't simply going to be used to make a profit." The program then degenerated into the usual populist discussion about the dangers of "allowing new technology to fall into the hands" of those dreadful profiteering people—who developed it in the first place—and the predictable call for a new government agency to control its development.

It was, in its own way, a perfect metaphor for all that is now trying to stifle U.S. economic growth and productivity, the mounting triumph of regulation over ideation, of bureaucracy over creativity. In an economy whose wealth is increasingly metaphysical (ideas, inventions, high technology) and whose greatest capital resource is the *individual*, the greatest single threat to economic growth and dynamic development is the growing bureaucratization of our society in both the corporate and the governmental spheres. This was why the best economic news in an otherwise dismal 1981 was that, for the first time in nearly 30 years, government employment had gone down, not up.

It is no coincidence that the productivity of the U.S. economy has declined in almost precise proportion to the rapid buildup in government employment which, between 1950 and 1980, soared by 168%—from 6 million to 16 million. While private employment grew by only 90% during the same period and employment in manufacturing by only 34%, government bureaucratic jobs multiplied six times as fast as blue-collar jobs.

Because each rise in government bureaucracies has generated a corresponding rise in corporate bureaucracies, it is also no coincidence that the period of greatest corporate merger and concentration of power exactly paralleled this gigantic government expansion. In turn, it is no happenstance that this trend toward centralization of both governmental and corporate power and bureaucracy has exactly coincided with the rise of . macroeconomic policies.

Perhaps the most important distinction between demand-side and supply-side economics is that the perspective of the first is collective (or macro) and the perspective of the latter is individual (or micro). Keynesians tend to view the economy as a single "macro-machine" in which government-manipulated "demand" (alias deficit spending and money-printing) is used to bring about the necessary supply responses from individuals and businesses. In other words, government manages the economy, using the federal budget and the Federal Reserve.

The supply-siders argue that the real economy is the sum of *individual* entrepreneurial efforts and enterprise which generate supply and that that, in turn, creates its own demand. The principal impediments to the process, from this point of view, are government interference and too much bureaucratic structure in corporate affairs.

Irving Kristol best described the Keynesian "macro-mentality" when he pointed out that in it, "the economy and business are two different things. In this brave new world, businesses are run by businessmen, and the economy is run by economists (alias bureaucrats)—as if businessmen are like mice, doing what they are told by the economists." "This is, of course, nonsense," Kristol concludes, with the ultimate supply-side premise, "The economy is business"—and especially small business, which is the real engine of economic growth.

An MIT study found that between 1969 and 1976 nearly two thirds of the new jobs in the economy were generated by businesses with 20 employees or less, yet these companies accounted for less than 10% of total sales. The MIT study also showed that the Fortune 1000 companies contributed less than 2% of the total growth in jobs in that period. The other 98% was contributed by the unknowns outside of the big-business elite.

A Commerce Department survey showed that between 1969 and 1974 the large mature corporations averaged an annual job growth rate of less than 1%. The innovative corporations like IBM had a job growth of 4.3% during that same period. But the biggest job growth rates were found in the innovative young high-technology companies, where annual job-growth rates ran as high as 25% to 40%.

Most important, studies by both the Commerce Department and the Office of Management and Budget have concluded that over half of all scientific and technological developments come from small businesses with 100 employees or less.

The National Science Foundation studied the period from 1953 to 1973 and found that small firms produced about four times as many inventions and innovations per research and development dollar as the medium-sized firms and about 24 times as many as the largest firms.

This clear-cut innovation and technology advantage for small business was absolutely crucial to the nation's productivity problems in the immediate past, and will be even more crucial for the decades ahead.

One of the nation's leading merger consultants, Arthur Burck, told the House Sub-Committee on Small Business in 1978:

America needs a continual flow of creative entrepreneurs, ready to challenge new horizons, but in recent years the obstacles have often been unsurmountable. Starved of capital, deprived of incentives, submerged in bureaucratic red tape, and surrounded by the burgeoning bigness of the corporate giants, the small business sector has become a victim of the upheavals and recessions of the 1970s.

The rapid growth of big government has also meant the parallel rapid growth of big business and, by inversion, the decline of the fortunes of small businesses, which have watched their share of the U.S. economic pie steadily dwindle, while the billion-dollar corporations increased their share of total assets from less than 30% in 1960 to more than 50% in 1976.

What most Americans may not realize is that this growing concentration of power in the big corporations is not merely hard on democracy; it is even worse for productivity and economic growth. It is noteworthy that the decade of the greatest merger growth, the 1960s, was followed by the decade of the worst slowdown in productivity in U.S. history. Obviously, big business is as dangerous to economic dynamism as are the turgid bureaucracies of central government. They feed each other, even as they drain away the metaphysical capital of enterprise. It is this kind of symbiotic development of "corporate socialism" that came up in an interview with F. A. Hayek in 1980, when he warned:

. . . technological progress in these last 80 years has occurred almost exclusively in the non-socialist countries, and the former industrially advanced countries that have become socialistic have lost their technological leadership, and are now largely living on what technology they can import from the still market-organized countries.

I am personally pessimistic of what would happen to our capacity to increase production, if ideas continue to move in the same direction in which they have been moving. . . .

Not only do regulatory bureaucracies in government, and their counterpart compliance bureaucracies in industry (and the legal profession), act as a tax on economic growth, but through their socializing impact they act as a brake on the most important component of the productivity equation—innovation.

Few of us remember that the Data Generals, Digital Equipments, Xeroxes, Polaroids, and Prime Computers of this world were, not very long ago, small companies and that their own most vigorous competition is today coming from new firms whose names mean nothing to most of us. Yet it is precisely these small companies that now find the regulatory burden from Washington so competitively onerous. It is easier for the large conglomerates simply to add to their own already substantial legal staffs and compliance bureaucracies, and to absorb regulatory costs into an already vast overhead.

But companies with only ten to 500 employees soon discover they are spending more time coping with the *Federal Register* than perfecting and marketing new product designs—more money on lawyers than on research engineers.

Conversely, the large corporations have discovered that the hidden advantage of the regulatory explosion is that it limits their own vulnerability to competition from below and allows them to leave more innovation to government, to tax-subsidized universities, and to struggling small companies, rather than risk heavy outlays for basic research themselves. It is safer and more profitable "to play defense" than offense, to merge when new products are needed.

Not surprisingly, the dramatic drop in the nation's commitment to basic research and development during the 1970s coincided exactly with the regulatory and litigatory explosion of the late 1960s and 1970s. As Tables 5-1 and 5-2 show, the 1960s and the 1970s were decades in which corporate America at all levels moved out of the lab and into the courtrooms, and went on the defensive. The tables also show the degree to which, in the 1970s, scientists and engineers took a back seat to regulators and lawyers. Executive suites were emptied of innovators and venturists and filled up with defensive accountants, comptrollers, lawyers, and technocrats. As Catholic University Professor Norman Ornstein told us, "The '70s produced an incredible expansion of regulations and of the bureaucracies on both the corporate and government sides to manage them."

Indeed, if we want to know why the United States is not growing and producing as it should (and used to), we might just find the answer in the single fact that American universities are now graduating twice as many lawyers as engineers and scientists. In Germany and Japan, our two strongest

TABLE 5-1

RESEARCH AND DEVELOPMENT TRENDS

(in constant dollars)

	1960-70	1970-79
Total research and development	44.0%	12.1%
Total research (basic and applied)	64.5%	12.4%
Basic research	120.6%	7.2%
Federal share of all research	31.1%	38.6%
Federal share of basic research	13.4%	16.1%

SOURCE: National Science Foundation.

TABLE 5-2

REGULATORY-LITIGATORY EXPLOSION, 1950-79

	1950	1960	1970	1978	% change 1960-70
Pages in the Federal Register	10,286	11,687	20,032	61,283	424%
U.S. District Court civil cases	47,600	59,300	87,300	138,800	134%
U.S. Appeals Court civil cases	1,922	2,322	7,001	11,162	381%
U.S.	708	788	2,167	3,928	398%
Private	1,114	1,534	4,834	7,234	372%
Lawyers	228,000	286,000	356,000	436,000	52%

SOURCES: U.S. Statistical Abstract; Federal Register.

competitors, the ratio is exactly reversed. Not surprisingly, the two greatest challenges now facing the U.S. high-technology industry in the 1980s are (1) a shortage of engineers and scientists and (2) a glut of litigation and obfuscation from the bureaucracies and courts of government.

A great irony of our times is that even as our industrial plant is operating well below its capacity, there is a huge backlog of court cases, particularly in the federal courts. More than twice as much corporate money now goes to litigation as to research and development.

This theme was touched on by President Carter when he addressed the American Bar Association in Los Angeles in April 1978—where he meta-phorically stole a leaf from Shakespeare's *Henry VI, Part II*, Act 4 and implied that to get the nation back on its feet, "the first thing we do, let's kill all the lawyers." But, blaming excessive litigation on lawyers is like blaming inflation on high prices and wages. The clogged courts of the nation are only the superficial symptom of the underlying cause: proliferating government. We are over-litigated and over-lawyered because we are over-regulated and over-lawed.

It is after all, the passage of laws and the issuance of regulations that creates the demand for lawyers, not the other way around. The chief cause of too many lawyers is too many laws and the resulting legislation. Every time Congress or a state legislature passes a new law it generates a geometric progression of new regulations, which in turn spawn a whole new demand for

TABLE 5-3

BALLOONING BUREAUCRACIES OF CONGRESS

	1970	1979	% change
House and Senate personal staffs	6,833	10,679	55%
Committee staffs	1,337	3,547	165%
Congressional research	332	847	155%
Library of Congress	3,848	5,390	40%
General Accounting Office (GAO)	4,704	5,303	13%
Total direct staff supporting Congress*	10,273	17,229	68%

SOURCES: American Enterprise Institute; U.S. Bureau of the Budget; GAO; Library of Congress.

*Includes congressional research and 30% of GAO. Does not include officers of Congress and housekeeping.

litigation, both from the regulators and the regulated. This is the primary cause for "lawyer inflation."

In 1977, for example, Congress enacted some 223 new laws, but the federal bureaucracy issued more than 7,568 new regulations—a ratio of about 34 to 1. Is it any wonder that U.S. lawyers will earn a net income of more than $30 billion this year? Nearly 40% of this income is derived just from the problems of compliance with the federal government's 40,000-page Tax Code.

Mr. Carter should have given his speech not to the lawyers in the American Bar Association but to all those lawyers on Capitol Hill (more than 70% of our representatives and senators) who have built the fastest-growing bureaucracy of all. The American Enterprise Institute (AEI), under the innocuous title *Vital Statistics on Congress, 1980* (an exhaustive tabulation of the activities, workload, costs, and politics of Congress), tells us why we are in the mess we are now in:

- From 1946 to 1980, the cost of Congress has swollen from $54 million to $1.3 billion. Since 1970 alone, the cost of Congress has risen 260%, nearly triple the rate of inflation.
- The primary reason for this has been the explosion in staff personnel. As Table 5-3 shows, between 1970 and 1979 the total congressional bureaucracy rose by 68% and the committee staffs soared by 165%. There are now 32 nonelected bureaucrats for every member of Congress, six times as many as in 1948.
- Naturally, the workload has increased, as well, from 11,000 bills introduced in 1947–48 to 19,000 in 1977–78.
- At the same time, fewer bills actually get passed—from 3,400 per session down to 1,100. "More and more activity is combined with fewer and fewer products," the authors conclude.

But the most ominous statistic of all is the scope and detail of the bills that do get passed, rising from an average of 2.5 pages per statute to 8.5 over the last 20 years.

The growth in the complexity and detail of laws has meant that the output in pages of law passed by Congress increased by 85% in the 1970s alone.

Naturally, this legislative gusher forced an even greater profusion of regulations, written by executive office bureaucrats, interpreting and translating congressional laws into new mountains of inflationary red tape.

In 1936 the New Deal at its peak got along famously with only 2,355 new pages in the *Federal Register*. By 1970 the number of pages had increased to 20,032. In 1980 almost 90,000 pages were pumped out. (In 1981 Reagan administration officials were pleased when they cut the output back to some 68,000 pages—still *triple* the 1970 rate!)

In the 91st Congress (1969–70) each law written averaged 4.2 pages, and each page produced another 13.8 pages of regulations. By the 95th Congress (1977–78) this had blossomed to an average of 8.5 pages per law and more than 23 pages of federal regulations per page of law.

Interestingly, there is a remarkable correlation between the explosion in federal regulations and laws in the 1970s (85%) and the dramatic upsweep in the Consumer Price Index (78%). Throughout the 1950s and early 1960s the *Federal Register* averaged about 10,000 new pages per year and inflation averaged about 1.6%. But from 1965 to 1972, this average jumped to 20,000 pages a year, and the inflation rate rose to 3%. Since 1972 this average has tripled to more than 60,000 pages per year and the inflation rate has spiraled to 10% and higher.

Yet all these regulations are merely the outward symbol of the way in which the substance of our government has been so drastically altered from a representative democracy to an unelected and imperial bureaucracy, which has the power (and is using it) to deaden our entire economy and the creation of new ideas, new products, and technological breakthroughs.

As Meg Greenfield, editorial page editor of *The Washington Post* put it, "there is a profound and pervasive commitment in this country to not letting anything happen, a kind of national institutional inertia in which competing bureaucracies and think tanks endlessly study and analyze each other's ideas until they lose both their vitality and their constituencies and finally exhaust themselves in that great 'memory hole' of Potomac politics, the presidential commission (or worse, a cabinet department)." Then, Greenfield concludes, "everyone can settle back and make the situation [which the ideas were supposed to solve] whatever it was, a little worse and get paid for it." What Greenfield is describing is the perfectly predictable result of 40 years of centralizing (and expanding) all governmental functions in Washington, a process which the writers of the Constitution never envisaged and greatly feared.

It was Alexis de Tocqueville who sensed the validity of that concern when he warned of "a new kind of servitude" when government, "having successively taken each member of the community into its powerful grasp, and fashioned him at will . . . then extends its arm over the whole community. It covers the surface of society with a network of small complicated rules, through which the most original mind and most energetic characters cannot penetrate to rise above the crowd."

Indeed, Tocqueville could have been describing 1981 America and Washington when he added, "The will of man is not shattered, but softened, bent and guided; men are seldom forced by it [the bureaucracy] to act, but they are constantly restrained from acting."

The mounting flood of legislated inhibitions to new ideas and creativity and its mushrooming regulatory and compliance bureacracies now trying to stifle our economic rebirth bring to mind the 12th chapter of Revelation, in which John depicts an allegorical "woman clothed with the sun . . . being with child [symbol of new ideas] . . . and pained to be delivered." In John's imagery we find standing before the woman a symbolic "great red dragon" waiting to "devour her child as soon as it was born," and casting out of his mouth "water as a flood after the woman that he might cause her to be carried away of the flood." Like this great red dragon, the Washington establishment (both public and private) seems eager to devour any newborn ideas, policies, or even products before they can get into their swaddling clothes, let alone out of them.

It is no coincidence that our national economic decline began in the same decade that Washington replaced New York as the richest per capita metropolis in the United States. As Washington has grown more powerful and rich, the country has grown weaker and less prosperous. As power has become more centralized, the nation has become more fragmented and less dynamic. The process is as old as Methuselah.

In the 11th chapter of Genesis, we are told of a people who were "of one language and of one speech." Instead of trusting this marvelous idea of unity to hold them together, they said: "let us build us a city and a tower, whose top may reach unto heaven; and let us make us a name, lest we be scattered abroad upon the face of the whole earth." In other words, "Let us institutionalize this idea—put it into structural form. Through this structure or organization we can preserve our unity." They didn't trust the idea by itself. They had to have a bureaucracy to protect it. Yet, as a result of their false trust and pride of institutionalism, they lost that unity, their language was confounded, and they were scattered abroad "upon the face of all the earth."

The lesson of the Tower of Babel seems clear. The greatest threat to unity and to the power of ideas is nearly always from the institutional structures which such ideas engender. From the moment of conception, from babies to inventions, from companies to compositions, ideas inevitably fall prey to the debilitating process of structural accretion, the smothering tide of material organization, the entropy of bureaucracy.

It was probably inevitable (given the Second Law of Thermodynamics) that America, whose inspired ideas were captured in the Constitution and the Declaration of Independence, would someday face the danger of losing those ideas in the proliferation and aggrandizement of their entropic institutional outgrowths.

A few years ago, Murray Lincoln, the founder of CARE and a leader of the American cooperative movement, wrote, "It seems to be inevitable that people start out working with all their hearts for a great cause. Then the cause becomes an institution and they work for that. Next, they wind up working for their own place in that institution." Lincoln was describing with vivid accuracy the most compelling and frustrating challenge to human progress—the constant tendency for structure (institutionalism, bureaucracy, organization) to swallow up and destroy ideas; for institutions to replace causes, for bureaucratic self-promotion to replace purpose and commitment, for rote and ritual to replace inspiration and vision, for human empiricism and hierarchical logic to obscure intuition and revelation.

Or as John Gardner of Common Cause once put it, "One of the deep tidal currents—perhaps the most fateful—is the movement toward the creation of ever larger, more complex, more organized social groups. It threatens the freedom and the integrity of the individual; and the capacity of the society for continuous renewal depends ultimately on the individual." But Gardner warned, "It is futile to hope this movement will reverse itself. A modern society is and must be characterized by complex organization. This is what makes the problem difficult and interesting. Organization serves man and rules him, increases his scope and hems him in."

Unfortunately government bureaucracy today seems to be doing more ruling than serving, more "hemming in" than increasing scope. It should not seem surprising that in this age of mindless bureaucratic growth, the disease most prevalent in public concern is cancer—which, simply described, is growth without purpose or function, structure feeding on structure, anything bad or harmful that spreads and destroys.

In the private marketplace such bureaucratic cancer is usually (though not always) neutralized by the antibodies of competitive pricing, innovation, and the discipline of profitable survival. But in government no such antitoxins exist. All of the incentives are for growth without purpose, for structure without function.

With government bureaucracies what count are not measurable results but rosters of employees. Power derives not from performance but from personnel—and as personnel counts soared, "performance" fell apart. From 1950 to 1979 government bureaucracies grew by 159% and service bureaucracies by 218%, while the productive sector of the economy (manufacturing, mining, construction, transportation, and utilities) grew by only 41% and manufacturing by only 38%. And the number of jobs in agriculture actually dropped by 50%. As a result, comparatively fewer and fewer workers in the productive sector are carrying an ever-increasing load of bureaucratic structure in the service sector.

It is not hard to see why such a development, combined with soaring taxes, has steadily diminished the nation's productivity, increased its effective unit-labor costs, and dramatically expanded inflationary pressures on money policy. What we have been witnessing is the slow destruction of the U.S. body economic and politic, by the cancer of meaningless institutional growth, not because bureaucracy in and of itself is malignant, but because so much of our nation's institutional growth has been totally unrelated to the genuine life support of the American ideal of individual self-government. Too much has been growth for its own destructive sake.

As Tocqueville described it, "Such a power does not destroy, but it

116 THE ECONOMY IN MIND

TABLE 5-4

JOB TRENDS VS. PRODUCTIVITY TRENDS

(in percentages)

	TOTAL	PRODUCTION			SERVICE SIDE			PRODUCTIVITY TRENDS		
		Manufacturing	All production	Government	Services	Finance	Wholesale – retail trade	Total Private	Non-Farm	Manufacturing
1950-60	19.9	10.2	8.6	38.6	37.7	39.2	21.4	2.6	1.9	2.8
1960-70	30.8	15.3	14.8	50.3	56.5	38.6	32.0	2.9	2.4	3.5
1970-79	26.3	8.3	13.0	24.4	47.6	36.2	33.9	1.4	1.3	2.9
Total change 1950-79	98.1	37.6	40.9	159.1	218.1	163.0	114.6			

SOURCE: U.S. Bureau of Labor Statistics.

prevents existence; it does not tyrannize, but it compresses, enervates, extinguishes, and stupefies a people, until each nation is reduced to be nothing better than a flock of timid and industrial animals of which government is the shepherd."

The Seduction of Serfdom

There is a story about a herd of wild pigs which a group of farmers were trying in vain to domesticate. After they had made numerous abortive attempts to round up and trap the pigs, a soft-spoken stranger asked for a chance to try something different. Within a few days the entire herd was not only in the pen, but perfectly domesticated, eating out of the stranger's bucket. When the astonished farmers asked him how he did it, the stranger merely explained, "I just made them dependent on me."

The story is a useful reminder that, in most cases, people give up their freedom not to external force or aggression, but by gradual, and eventually willing, consent. Throughout history, far more slavery has been accepted than imposed. In this respect the drug addict and the alcoholic provide useful similes. Not only do they obtain their state of dependence voluntarily, but they do not even know when they have passed the point of no return when the sirenic lure of the drug or alcoholic "high" is stronger than the sweet aroma of sober and independent action.

The subtle promise that lures them is not overt slavery but false freedom. The drug addict and the alcoholic feel that their habit releases them from worry, anxiety, tension, responsibility, and care. It gives them a kind of security; and this false lure of release overcomes the basic but more subtle desire for independence and freedom.

As with individuals, so it is with nations and governments. Politicians and governments, like dope pushers and good-time Charlies, are forever promising "happy days" of security and release from individual responsibility through promising social programs. What they promise, of course, is not freedom at all, but bondage and dependence. They offer the false hope of freedom from responsibility, but what they deliver is slavery to the state. The promise is beguiling, and we the people are easily tempted to take "just a little dose" at first—a program here and a program there.

We do not realize that the government is feeding us a kind of fiscal methadone. The high of inflation and handouts is very hard to give up, even harder to come down from. Gradually, as our dependence on government grows, we lose our confidence to go it on our own. Our insecurity, ironically, has been fed by the promise of government security—and the more insecure we feel, the more we demand the enslaving medicine of government security.

By this time, of course, we may begin to understand our plight. We may even realize that we have been had by the false promise of material security—but it is too late. We have passed the point of no return and there is no turning back. This is the actual experience of nations such as Britain and Sweden—countries which have found that once major social programs get started there is no turning back. There is, as with drugs, only escalation of the addiction. Even when these nations reach the point of near bankruptcy, they seldom repeal or seriously reduce their social programs—they just tax more, inflate more, control more, and enslave both the worker and industry ever more to the false god of government.

In such situations, real two-party democracy disappears, as the political debate is reduced to squabbles over which coalition is better able to deal with the economic crisis and run the bureaucracy. Indeed, the bureaucracy has grown so large, it, not the politicians, runs the country and takes a dominant chunk of private income.

What is worrisome is that, even with the 1980 elections, we may already have passed that point of no return. No one now seems to have the will to hold down the growth of government spending in present programs, at least not more than for a single budget, before the screams of protest weaken political resolve.

We are, it would seem, no longer proud and free wild boars, but domesticated little piggies, feeding at the public trough, hoping that our benevolent keepers (the bureaucrats and politicians) will hurry up and give us some more goodies. But, of course, we want them to do it more responsively, and with less waste and fraud.

I have purposely exaggerated the situation. The United States is quite clearly not as far along the road to serfdom as is Great Britain or Sweden, but to be able to defend freedom for the world we cannot afford to go any further.

It is really only in the last 30 years or so that Americans have rather swiftly traded in the original concept of self-government by law, for government by burgeoning bureaucracy. It was not until the 1930s that government began to play a more prominent role in individual lives. Even so, in 1939, after six years of the New Deal, the federal share of the GNP was still only 7% (it was 23% in 1981), and all forms of government took only 15% of personal income (compared with over 40% today).

In 1940, only 8.7% of U.S. employment was in government, about 4 million people out of a total employment of some 47 million. By 1981 nearly 16 million (out of a total employment of 98 million) worked for government—more than 16%, one in every six jobs. And when one adds in government contracts, the figure jumps quickly past 20%.

In 1950, less than 25% of us were dependent, directly or indirectly, on government for jobs or income. By 1960 the number had escalated to more than 42%, and by 1977 it had become a national majority of nearly 54%. It is now estimated that by 1990, 60% of our population will be drawing all, or a significant portion, of their livelihood from the public sector.

To put it another way, 40% of us will soon be supporting to some degree, 60%. That 60% will have the political power to expropriate the productive wealth of a diminishing private sector work force.

The Great GNP Con Game

The surprise is that this very heavy government presence sneaked up on us so quickly and so largely unnoticed. That is due, at least in part, to what I call the "great GNP con game," the process by which we are routinely told that "government's share of the GNP is really not growing that much"—even as we are *not* told that the GNP *includes* the cost of government although that cost contributes nothing much to real economic growth. This means that every time government grows, the total economy grows, even though the productive private sector might be stagnant.

The effect, of course, is to understate government's presence in the economy by burying it in the GNP and then measuring it against itself. As hard-pressed taxpayers we may be astonished to know that between 1965 and 1980 government's total share of the GNP rose only 6 points from 27% to 33%, even as taxes for Social Security rose over 500%, marginal tax rates doubled, and federal spending rose 50% faster than the national economy.

When we take government out of the GNP, and measure it as a "ratio" (rather than an embedded share) to the residual private sector, we get an altogether different picture in which government's real presence in the economy becomes more apparent. This picture shows that government is now actually 50% as large as the private sector that supports it (instead of the 33% the "con game" would have us believe) and its actual rate of growth is 50% faster than we are told.

If we want to know why the U.S. economy is looking a lot less prosperous than the raw GNP figures suggest it should, we must remember that without that huge "leviathan" of government resting in it (swamping it), it really hasn't grown all that much in the last seven or eight years, and for the individual wage-earner it has actually gotten smaller by about 8% in the last decade. Despite a fall-off in productive growth, the individual American worker has been producing more goods, but, after taxes and inflation, he has actually been taking home less pay. This violates the fundamental rule of economics that (until 1970) successfully governed this country. Real wages should grow as fast as real output or productivity.

TABLE 5-5

THE FLIGHT FROM INDEPENDENCE

Government vs. nongovernment beneficiaries
(in percentages)

	1960	1977
Total government beneficiaries as % of population	42.3	53.5
Government employees & dependents including military	12.9	13.0
Private employment due to government spending	10.2	8.3
Government transfer & pension beneficiaries	18.4	30.4
Government pensions	.8	2.2
Veterans pensions	1.7	2.1
Social Security	9.7	16.5
Welfare	1.9	5.3
Unemployment compensation	1.0	1.1
Dependents of transfer beneficiaries	3.3	3.2
Other recipients of government benefits	.7	1.9
Total percentage *not* dependent on government	57.7	46.5
Employees and proprietors	26.4	26.5
Dependents	31.3	20.0

SOURCE: A. Gary Schilling & Company, Economic Consultants.

TABLE 5-6

GOVERNMENT SHARE

(in percentages)

	In the GNP
1965	27.3
1977	33.0
% change	20.5

SOURCE: President's Economic Message, 1978.

Between 1960 and 1970, for example, there was a 34% growth in worker productivity, and real (uninflated) wages grew 36%, or just a fraction more than real output. From 1970 to 1980, however, the average worker in America increased his productivity by about 12%, but his average real take-home pay actually declined by about 8%, a complete reversal of normal economic history.

Anyone who seriously doubts the impact of these figures on economic growth and individual freedom is taking an ostrichlike view of the world as it really is.

In his compendium of essays by leading economists, *The American Economy in Transition,* Martin Feldstein observes: "The first two decades of the postwar period (1947–67) were a time of stability and optimism. The contrast between the strength and achievement of the economy during those years and its poor record since then signals a major change in the performance of the economy in the postwar period."

What caused this major change? Feldstein puts it succinctly: "The expanded role of government has undoubtedly been the most important change in the structure of the economy in the postwar period." But in order to throw off a tyranny, we must understand that it is tyranny.

The Dilution of Democracy

One of the most disturbing trends in American politics is the steady decline in public interest in the whole political process, evidenced by a steady downward trend in the percentage of people voting. Only 52% of those eligible voted in the 1980 presidential election.

The polls show that the basic reason for this disinterest in the political process is a "gut feeling" by many Americans that they no longer have much real voice in the control of their government.

They are right. More than 40 years of centralization and bureaucratic buildup at both the state and federal levels have created a situation in which unelected government employees vastly outnumber and outpower the people's elected representatives.

Today, well over 90% of all the rules, regulations, policies, and "guidelines" that intrude upon our lives emanate, not from elected representatives, but from unelected government employees, who are responsive to none of us and whose sheer numbers are too great for either Congress or the state legislatures to control.

Table 5-7 shows that as we move from local government to state, and from state to federal, there is a sharp decline in the effective control of the individual voter and his elected officials over government. At the local level, there are only 18 bureaucrats for every elected official; at the state level, 256; and at the federal level, 5,400.

Every time a program or an activity is moved toward the central government (either state or federal), the citizen loses political control, while the relative power of the nonelected bureaucrats automatically increases. That is why—not always, but most of the time—programs run by state and federal government are far more costly and more wasteful than programs run at the local level. The reason is not ideological but logistical.

There are two prime examples of this, welfare (see Chapter 7) and education, both of which have gradually been shifted in both spending and control from local to state and then to federal levels. Each move has proven enormously costly both in dollars and performance. Public education is perhaps the perfect illustration.

As Table 5-8 shows, since 1950 the funding of public education has changed dramatically from predominantly local to predominantly federal and state. Today the majority of the funding of public education comes from taxes raised, controlled, and spent by federal and state education bureaucracies. For all intents and purposes, most school districts have lost control over the

TABLE 5-7

RATIO OF NONELECTED BUREAUCRATS TO ELECTED OFFICIALS AND REPRESENTATIVES

	Nonelected bureaucrats	Elected officials	Ratio
Federal government	2,950,000	537	5,400:1
State government	3,350,000	13,038	256:1
Local government	9,300,000	508,720	18:1

SOURCE: U.S. Statistical Abstract, 1978.

TABLE 5-8

FUNDING OF PUBLIC SECONDARY EDUCATION (in percentages)

	Local	State and Federal
1950	66	34
1960	61	39
1964	58	42
1970	55	45
1976	48	52
1979	45	55

SOURCE: U.S. Office of Education.

content, curriculum, and techniques employed in the education of their children.

Has this major change in the control and funding of our public education improved performance or productivity?

The answer is obvious.

Since 1950 the cost of public secondary education has risen from $6 billion to 1981's total of more than $100 billion, an increase of more than 1500%. Even discounting inflation, we are spending over three times as much per child for public education today as we were in 1954 and more than twice as much as in 1960.

The primary reason for this cost explosion has been a tremendous growth in the education bureaucracy in public schools, both teaching and nonteaching. In 1950 there was one full-time educational employee for every 20 students. Today the national rate is 1 to 10. In 1950 there were 28 pupils for every full-time teacher in the public school systems. Today in most urban systems there are 18 per teacher.

Thus, the price of moving the funding of public education gradually to state and federal control has been a doubling in the size of the total bureaucratic input into public education and a tripling of the real per-pupil cost.

Has all this increase in cost and input been worth it? Has it produced better educational results?

The answers are dreary—and well known.

What is not so well known is that the national decline in educational performance has almost exactly coincided with the rise in the role of the state and, in particular, the federal education bureaucracies.

It may be hard to believe now that this nation was on a long upward course in educational performance that ran from the 1930s (when measurements first were made systematically) to the early 1960s. But, with the birth of federal aid to education in 1962–63—and the steady growth of both state and federal control over education—the test scores in almost every school system across the country began to decline. (See Table 5-9.)

If we were to plot on a graph the rise in the share of state and federal education funds, we would find that it almost exactly coincides with the leveling off and decline in national educational performance. And this is true of most state education test-program results other than the SATs. In Iowa, for

TABLE 5-9

SCHOLASTIC APTITUDE TEST (SAT) RESULTS

	Math	Verbal
1950	479	455
1956	497	473
1963	502	481
1970	489	460
1976	474	436

SOURCE: Educational Testing Services, Inc., Princeton, N.J.

example, from 1956 to 1964 the average IBTS scores rose 1.6% per year for all grades and percentiles, but from 1964 to 1971 the average IBTS scores declined almost 0.2% per year for all grades and percentiles. In New York State from 1956 to 1966 there was a 13.6% total gain in reading scores and a 16% gain in math scores, but from 1966 to 1976 there was a 13% drop in reading and an 18% percent drop in math. And if space permitted, we could document this decline for dozens of other states. Suffice it to say, the arrival in 1964 of the U.S. Office of Education and the rise of the state education bureaucracies almost exactly coincided with the decline in education performance and led to the recent trends of parents shifting children to private schools.

Now, if there *is* a causal relationship here (as we suggest), it should follow that states that have kept more control over education spending at the local level should have better performance and lower costs—and vice versa. Table 5-10 provides a vivid illustration of this theory. It shows three states in which the use of state funds in education varies widely, as do the cost per pupil, the amount spent on education as a percentage of personal income (PI), and the SAT performance scores.

The table shows:

• New Hampshire, which spent the least per student and had the lowest state education contribution, had the highest SAT scores of the three states—well above the U.S. average.

• Massachusetts, which spent the most per student, had the lowest test scores.

• Vermont, which spent more of its personal income on public education by nearly 28% than New Hampshire, had lower SAT scores.

• Massachusetts, which spent the biggest share of its personal income on secondary education of all three states (and much more than the U.S. figure) had the poorest SAT performance of the three.

• New Hampshire had as good a teacher-to-pupil ratio as the other states, but had far lower administrative costs.

One lesson from this table is clear: Local funding and control are not detrimental to the quality of public education. Indeed, they are probably an asset, because they keep the control of the public schools out of the hands of both state and federal education bureaucracies and they hold down the bureaucratic cost. They also provide the one thing that is so essential in keeping any bureaucracy honest—accountability through efficient competition.

TABLE 5-10

ELEMENTARY AND SECONDARY PUBLIC EDUCATION PERFORMANCE
AND FINANCING, 1974-75

	Cost/ pupil	% of personal income on education	Pupil/ teacher ratio	Ratio of state aid*	SAT scores Verbal	Math
New Hampshire	$1,175	4.3%	17.0	16%	449	484
Vermont	1,398	5.5%	16.1	27%	439	477
Massachusetts	1,690	5.9%	18.2	24%	434	469
United States	1,251	5.5%	21.0	39%	436	474

SOURCE: U.S. Office of Education.

*Percentage of school budget provided by state aid.

Competition in Government

Without the hot breath of competition, government, like monopolistic business, grows complacent with waste, inefficiency, and excessive bureaucratic infrastructure, and it becomes less and less responsive to the people it is supposed to serve. That tendency to unresponsiveness was supposed to have been solved by the only system in the world today that provides for real competition in government—federalism, which says that the essential and primary responsibility for the government of domestic, internal affairs lies with the individual sovereign states and, within those states, the individual cities and towns.

Theoretically, the only power the federal government really has is the power that is delegated to it by the states. The Constitution specifically limits this power to national defense, foreign affairs, and those domestic issues that affect interstate commerce. Through this ingenious idea, the writers of the Constitution built into government the principle of competitive interplay, which should prevent monopolistic central governmental power. A state or a city that manages its affairs effectively will attract population, industry, and wealth. A city or a state that runs its affairs badly will lose population, industry, and wealth because they will move to the cities and states that are well run. When this happens, overtaxing governments are forced to reform, to run their affairs better, or to lose their economics and constituencies and be replaced.

In the 1970s, for instance, Massachusetts, which had for decades managed its affairs badly, began losing industry, jobs, and people to (among other places) New Hampshire, which has been more prudent. As a result, Massachusetts was forced to reform itself, if it was to continue to have a tax base to work with. As a result of this competition, it has lowered its tax burden by nearly 20% since 1978 and is now experiencing a strong economic rebirth. (See Chapter 8.)

Another instance is the classic experience of New York City, once financially sound and well run. In 1975, after 15 years of bad management, it was losing industry and employment and it was driving away population. Forced to reform—by the pressure of the balance sheet and by healthy competition from the better-run states and cities around it—New York did so. With a new mayor and a drastically reduced bureaucracy, it cut its tax burden and produced a $250-million fiscal surplus in 1981. Now its economy is beginning to flourish again, as is that of New York State, which has cut its spending curve substantially, and its top marginal income tax rates by 40%.

The danger to this federalist system of competition in government is that over the past 30 years a growing number of Americans, confronted by bad government at the local level and the problems that result from it, have turned not to local reform but to the federal government to bail them out.

Naturally, like any good monopoly, Washington was only too happy to oblige. There's nothing that senators, congressmen, and federal bureaucrats enjoy more than increasing the scope of their own power and authority. As a result, the country is now faced with monopolistic government power, as this big, wasteful, and oppressive central government seems to dominate every aspect of our lives.

Can We Deregulate Washington?

How can we restore honest competition to government? The answer seems clear: by reviving federalism, by a gradual but definite return of power and responsibility to where it belongs—state and local government. Then let the states and communities compete in the free market for industry, for commerce, and for the people's support. Unfortunately, that is a lot easier said than done, as President Reagan has been finding out. Predictably, those more highly taxed states—especially in the Northeast and North Central regions (the so-called Frostbelt) which have been losing the competitive economic struggle to their Sunbelt neighbors—are in the forefront arguing for more central federal takeover and funding of social programs (and more revenue-sharing as well), while those states with lower tax burdens and tighter spending controls have been more receptive to Ronald Reagan's "new federalism."

One of the new stars on the Democratic left, Congressman Barney Frank of Massachusetts, framed this whole debate in an article in *The New Republic*, in which he specifically condemns "competitive federalism." While he gives some credence to the negative competitive economic effects which high-tax liberalism in the Northeast has had on those individual state economies that have embraced it, his solution is to impose this liberalism and its heavy social-spending levels on *all* states by federal mandate.

Congressman Frank wants the federal government to wipe out what he regards as "excessive governmental competition" so that states which are more frugal, or pursue a less liberal social agenda, would no longer enjoy a "competitive edge" in the economic arena. He would eliminate that edge by having all environmental standards, tax rates, welfare benefits, labor-union rules, and general business regulatory practices promulgated by the federal government rather than by the individual states. (So much for the 10th Amendment!) He warns that "state autonomy in the economic sphere . . . has become one of the most reactionary influences on contemporary public policy. Today's state experiments in reaction [i.e., conservatism] are explicitly intended to penalize the rest of the country."

Congressman Frank's solutions would be to take away, as much as possible, the power of individual states to compete for industry and commerce by lowering tax burdens, social services, and rigid environmental regulations, and by giving tax breaks to business. He proposes a *national* health insurance plan, a *national* welfare scheme, and a *national* uniform level for unemployment compensation, and would force all states to accept the same enforced protection and compulsion of big labor unions (which he himself found so problematical as a representative to the Massachusetts State House)—despite the fact that over 60% of union members themselves reject compulsory unionism and 80% of the rest of the public rejects it.

Ironically, it was Congressman Frank who argued the opposite case—for more competition—in 1979, when he appeared on the public TV program "The Advocates" on behalf of *deregulating* the trucking industry! In that performance he made the point that competition is "always good for both the economy and the consumer, while its absence ultimately penalizes everyone." He was supported by Senator Edward M. Kennedy's testimony in that debate. Yet when it comes to the worst monopoly of all, government, both Congressman Frank and Senator Kennedy seem determined to eliminate what little competition still exists and to create an even greater federal monopoly.

Either way they are afraid that in the competition of the real marketplace of ideas their own programs can't stand the test, or else they believe that statists have a natural monopoly on the truth. Indeed, Frank's *New Republic* article makes that assumption implicit, when it refers to the "reactionary policies" pursued by some Sunbelt states. Yet surely this flies in the face of the fact that the lot of all social classes in the Sunbelt states has enormously improved in the last 20 years, due at least in part to their more conservative fiscal and social policies, which have promoted rapidly rising employment and wages, while the economic well-being of those in the high-tax states has shriveled under the shadow of high-tax, heavy-handed regulatory government.

Apparently the central statists have not yet grasped the significance of what happened to Great Britain, which found that it could not shield its own stagnant socialized economy from the ravages of more productive competition from countries like Japan, where the tax burden is about half that of Britain's. The same effect can be seen intramurally in the United States.

What the Sunbelt states are now proving competitively is that low-bureaucracy low-tax environments promote internally generated high job and income growth within their own industries, while high-tax, high-bureaucracy environments dampen such growth, and most of these effects have less to do with industry state-line crossing than with freedom, incentives, and economic climate. This competition is now pushing states such as Massachusetts, New York, New Jersey, and Pennsylvania to respond by putting their own bloated government houses in order. What we need most in government today is more of what Congressman Frank argued so eloquently for the trucking industry in 1979: deregulation.

Unless we deregulate government (as well as business) by reducing the size and power of its bureaucracies, its very presence will continue to "socialize" and deaden the vitality of the whole private system as well, and force more concentration of power in business and labor to match that of government itself. This mounting organizational concentration in both the governmental and corporate sectors is the ultimate threat to individual creativity, and to ideas themselves, because it so inhibits real freedom.

Those who set out to build the Tower of Babel were inspired by a marvelous idea, the power of universal communication. It wasn't the idea but the Tower that did them in. As the French historian Élie Halévy wrote, "The socialist believes in two things which are absolutely different, and perhaps even contradictory: freedom and organization."

6

The Ecology of the Free Market

There have been more serious studies made of government regulation of industry in the last 15 years or so, particularly in the United States, than in the whole preceding period. . . The main lesson to be drawn from these studies is clear: they all tend to suggest that the regulation is either ineffective or that when it has a noticeable impact, on balance the effect is bad, so that consumers obtain a worse product or a higher-priced product or both as a result of that regulation.

—Ronald H. Coase

In reading a recent issue of a leading liberal newspaper, I was struck by the juxtaposition of two editorials that completely conflicted in their premise and conclusions. The first was a defense of more government regulation of the economy and of business. In summary it said: Our economy has now become so complex and so sophisticated, it is simply impossible to allow it to run by itself without a substantial degree of government regulation. Just six inches below was a fervent plea for environmental integrity, whose gist was: Our magnificent natural environment is simply far too complex and too delicate in its balance for mere mortals to go on interfering in "its naturally accommodative process." Such human interference, no matter how well meaning, invariably produces chaos and distortion. So, on the one hand, our economy is so complex that it must be regulated, and on the other, our ecology is so complex that we shouldn't attempt to interfere with it!

Now the true ecologist certainly does understand something fundamental about our world that is as applicable to economics as it is to our environment. The natural ecosystem is so infinitely complex and varied, and so remarkably interrelated, that even the best-intentioned efforts to regulate this environment in one way or another invariably bring about reactions and distortion throughout the system. The ecologist understands that the system itself is constantly bringing about accommodation and balance. While these accommodations are frequently painful and difficult, they are usually better in their long-term result, because nature tends to preserve, protect, and strengthen its own creation. So the ecologist opts for a hands-off policy because he has learned that "it is not nice to fool with Mother Nature."

Our economic system is, in no small measure, precisely the same kind of enormously complex interrelated system as our ecosystem. Just as there is a Mother Nature that you can't fool, there is a "Father Economy," whose infinitely accommodative laws of supply and demand you can't fool, either— laws that mere mortals cannot manipulate for their own selfish purposes; and these laws grow daily more relevant as the world economy grows more complex. In fact, the single greatest argument and case for a freer market today is precisely its growing complexity—the fact that this system becomes increasingly interrelated, more delicate in its balance, and more subject to wholly unpredictable reactions and effects by even the mildest human attempts to manipulate this system for specific political or economic objec- tives. As Leo Rosten said in a TV interview with Eric Sevareid, "We have learned that our economy is like a big, soft balloon. You put in your finger in one place and it pops out in another wholly unexpected spot."

Several years ago, I saw a study that showed that the average American family makes over 140 separate economic decisions each day. These decisions range from the minute ones of deciding whether to have cereal or eggs for breakfast, take the car or bus to work, all the way up to whether to strike, to buy a car, or to sell the house and move to Florida. That means that the 77 million American families this year will make more than 11 billion decisions a day, 77 billion decisions a week, and more than 4 trillion decisions each year. Since all of these decisions are arrived at more or less separately, by relatively free individuals, and yet, all of them are influenced by literally trillions of interrelationships and stimuli, we can begin to gauge the incredi- ble complexity and delicate balance of our economy.

Yet many people in Washington still think that somehow a central group of politicians, economists, and bureaucrats can regulate, plan and control all of this economic activity for a better result. That was precisely what the original Humphrey-Hawkins Bill called for: the establishment of a Central Planning Council and a national economic planning process, to involve all levels of government, business, labor, and consumer groups.

In 1973, the University of Miami published a *Catalogue of Research Issues for Understanding National Economic Planning.* It took a small army of scholars to come up with this list of issues, a 1,750-page, 2 ½-inch-thick volume weighing 3.5 pounds. Mind you, these were not the issues themselves, but merely a *list* of issues that would have to be considered, just to understand the complexity of central economic planning.

Their conclusion: "Not even high-speed computers—even the type we could foresee in the future—could handle the billions upon billions of computations required for the federal government to plan intelligently for the economy."

Even liberal economist Paul Samuelson of MIT warns that in the central planning process "the number of unknowns of the mathematical problem will be in the millions, and the number of steps to its solution in the billions of billions."

Perhaps it is time for the ecologist and the economist to get together, because they are both beginning to understand not only the enormous complexity and delicate balance of our economy and our environment, but that when both are left more or less alone, they usually do better than when they are interfered with.

Is Uncle Sam Becoming Aunt Liz?

I have a confession to make. About five or six years ago, during a period of enforced bedrest, I became temporarily addicted to daytime TV soap opera. One of the principal characters was a well-meaning meddler named Aunt Liz, an archetypal do-gooder who spent her life running around trying to be helpful to her friends and relatives. Four things characterized Aunt Liz's efforts: First, she was always well-meaning, self-righteously so, wanting only what was best for her loved ones and friends. Second, she was often dead right in her diagnosis of the problems she perceived in the lives of others, or of the impending disaster of some of their actions. Third, she invariably made things still worse by her helpfulness than they would have been if she had never meddled in the first place. She turned problems into disasters with charming regularity. Fourth and finally, she never learned from the disasters she created but went right on, chin high and resolve undaunted, wreaking more and more havoc on the people she loved. Aunt Liz so typified the actions of our present regulatory government, I found myself asking, "Is Uncle Sam turning into Aunt Liz?"

The symptoms are ominous. Hardly a day goes by that we don't learn of some new "impending disaster" or "serious crisis" in our economy or environment that only government (Aunt Liz) can solve for us. Usually these warnings seem highly plausible and are backed up by detailed studies and masses of statistics. No sooner does Aunt Liz (government) identify the problem for us, but she then tells us exactly how she's going to help us solve it. A program is developed; regulations are issued; sometimes an agency is created; money and politicians gush; and chaos invariably results. Further studies then show that all of this well-intentioned meddling has created an even bigger mess than existed before and has ironically caused an even bigger demand by Aunt Liz to meddle still further in order to "solve" the problems she has already created.

A prime example was the case of TRIS, the fire-retardant chemical banned for use on children's sleepwear in 1977. A few years before, in 1974, the government, and some well-intentioned consumer safety advocates, announced that certain kinds of polyester sleepwear were hazardous to children because of their highly flammable character. Instead of merely publicizing this fact and warning consumers that polyesters, like other synthetics, would burn faster than cotton or wool, they prescribed an Aunt Liz solution: Require the treatment of all cotton and polyester garments with a flame-retardant chemical. Several government studies actually recommended a particular chemical compound for this retardant, which turned out to be TRIS. It wasn't long before all the nation's garment manufacturers were complying with Aunt Liz and slapping lots of TRIS on their children's sleepwear. Then Aunt Liz became aware that TRIS was very bad for our health—that while it retarded fires, it promoted something much worse. So she immediately issued an edict that all garments treated with TRIS must be removed from the market. Everyone was in a tizzy. Hundreds of millions of dollars were at stake. Jobs were on the line. Department store inventories were suspect. Parents were confused. Politicians were irate. Small companies went bankrupt. Aunt Liz had struck again!

TRIS was only a small example of what Aunt Liz does every day. Her well-intentioned meddling in our lives and economy is now costing us literally tens of billions of dollars, and who knows how many jobs? Not because Aunt Liz is evil, but because she is so self-righteously good.

Unfortunately, she isn't content with just telling us about the problems and then letting us deal with them in our own way. You see, she doesn't really trust us. She doesn't think we can be counted on to do the right thing. She feels that someone else wiser and more caring has to take action to do something to protect us from our own foolishness or ignorance.

Even as this book was being written, Congress was investigating the actions and connections of Mary K. Bruch, an Aunt Liz who worked at the Food and Drug Administration and who one day became convinced that contact-lens wearers couldn't be trusted to prepare their own salt solution for cleaning and storing their lenses. So she ordered salt pills (used for this purpose) taken off the market altogether. This, in turn, created a new market for the manufacturers of preserved saline solutions (such as the Burton-Parsons Company, whom *The Washington Post* reported having entertained Ms. Bruch for fancy dinners in Georgetown). Eventually, when hundreds of contact-lens wearers began to complain about paying six times as much for saline solutions as for the salt pills, Congress looked into the situation and found no basis whatever for taking the salt tablets off drugstore shelves. Doctors told the House subcommittee looking into this that it was almost impossible to use the salt tablets improperly, whereas many contact-lens wearers had complained of physical reactions to the preserved solution. Once more the "protection" was much worse than the "problem."

Without taking anything from the useful accomplishments of consumer advocates, usually in highly specific and technical areas, I have found that most corporations have more respect for the intelligence of the average consumer than do most consumer advocates. If they didn't they would soon go out of business.

No major business can survive on first sales alone. Success depends on the repeat customer. The evidence is overwhelming that very few customers will buy a product the second time that didn't satisfy them the first time or whose safety has received unfavorable publicity. Although advertising and promotion do help in selling a product to a new customer, only the product's overall quality, performance, and price relationship will hold this consumer's continued loyalty. This is one reason why the proportionate share of sales devoted to consumer advertising budgets has actually been declining modestly over the past 20 years and is now less than 1.5% of total sales.

Companies know that, over the long haul, American consumers buy the products that perform the best at the fairest prices. Companies with good products survive and grow, while those with poor products fail. Although advertising and marketing are important, product is still the crucial element. The best hard evidence of this is a study I made a few years ago for one of my advertising clients which showed that there is a nearly 80% correlation between the market position of leading consumer products and their price-performance ratings by *Consumer Reports*, the leading consumer magazine and product-rating service. Again and again the top-rated product was also the top-selling product, even when the product enjoyed only modest advertising and marketing support. This, in spite of the fact that *Consumer Reports* reaches only a tiny fraction of the consuming public and that frequently its ratings are made long after a major share of the consumer buying decisions have already been registered in the marketplace.

Today's supposedly helpless consumers are actually making the same intelligent buying decisions in the marketplace that the experts are making with the help of extensive testing and evaluation in consumer laboratories. The best examples have been in consumer durable goods such as appliances, where over a span of ten years, 1960–70, the brands rated as "best value" by *Consumer Reports* were consistently the top sellers in the market, even though they enjoyed the lowest level of national brand advertising of the top five brands. With a circulation of less than half a million there was no way *Consumer Reports* could have influenced that result. The consumers simply proved their own innate judgment, based on experience with the products and the companies involved, not to mention hearsay advertising (the chief ingredient in Volkswagen's remarkable early success).

This comes as no surprise to consumer-goods manufacturers, most of whom long ago discovered that they can often better predict consumer sales performance from extensive consumer testing than they can from the size or scope of their promotional programs. One canned food manufacturer I once consulted for was able to forecast with considerable precision future Nielsen sales reports for a well-established product, simply by watching the consumer quality-control figures in his own plant. And a leading candy bar manufacturer I consulted for lost half of a brand's market share after making what seemed to be only a minor adjustment in a product, using a new synthetic-coating ingredient without adequate market testing. No government bureaucrat needed to warn the consumers. They simply stopped buying the product, because it no longer satisfied.

The very high failure rate on new products (nine out of ten don't make it) and the turnover of established products, combined with the huge investments required both to introduce and market consumer goods nationally, have become the best possible safeguards against frivolous or malicious abuse of the consumer marketplace. Even Procter and Gamble can't afford many experiences such as the one with Rely, the tampon product which ultimately had to be removed from the market when its safety was challenged.

Unfortunately, the chief effect of growing regulation by the various state and federal agencies and of tax-subsidized litigation in the courts has been to reduce markedly both the variety and the pace of innovation of virtually all new products now being offered to consumers. Small companies (which have always been the source of most real innovation) can no longer afford the costs and the process of securing product compliance or adequately insured protection from new liability laws and class-action suits.

Meanwhile, the largest conglomerates (whom Naderites profess to hate) are enjoying all of this respite from entrepreneurial competition and are increasingly avoiding the regulatory hassle and playing it safe with proven product winners, instead of taking risks or responding to the marketplace creatively. Instead of genuine breakthroughs, we are seeing more and more in consumer products what we have seen in television shows: safe spinoffs, frequent ripoffs, and modest variations on past success models.

Government regulation also reduces competition in other ways. By setting elaborate and detailed standards and guidelines for products and processes, it automatically decreases either the necessity to produce better products or the incentive for real innovation. Government standards tend to become industry norms, and corporations tend to devote more attention to preserving the status quo than beating the standards. The standards also tend to be set by those companies which are large enough to lobby the bureaucracy or (as in the famous case of the General Motors catalytic converter) are so dominant that large capital investments and employment are at stake, and everyone else is forced to fall in line, even with a less-than-satisfactory solution.

The effect of such regulation is always to reduce the consumer's ability to force better products and lower prices through the free market, which is the democratic and natural process of supply meeting demand. Fortunately, a growing share of the American people and its political representatives are waking up to the wholly negative impact of constant consumerism. In a lopsided 321–63 vote, the House of Representatives on 27 November 1979 clamped a tight muzzle over one of Ralph Nader's favorite (and most active) regulatory busybodies, the Federal Trade Commission (FTC), informing that agency that every new rule it promulgates will now be subject to review and veto by Congress. (Most economists now regard the FTC as almost irrelevant, and it may well be in the process of quiet self-immolation.)

Nader was understandably stunned by this reversal. He called it "a classic case of the robbers [corporate America] chasing the cops." Happily, he was quite wrong. Congress simply recognized that his 15-year-long chorus of consumer complaint had produced highly mixed blessings. When Nader began his crusade in 1964, the country's economy was extraordinarily healthy:

- Productivity was rising 3.3% per year.
- Inflation was 1.3% per year.
- Disposable personal income was rising 3.8% per year.
- Total federal employment was under 2.3 million.
- Total regulatory costs to business (and the consumer) were less than $5 billion a year.
- New federal regulations were less than 10,000 pages a year.

By 1980, after more than 15 years of massive Nader-inspired consumer legislative and regulatory growth:

- Productivity was now rising 0.8% per year, the lowest in the Western world.
- Inflation was averaging 10%, even without including OPEC oil price rises.
- Real disposable personal income was growing less than 1% per year.
- Federal employment had ballooned to 2.8 million, with more than 100,000 now in economic regulation alone.
- The annual costs of federal regulation to consumers and business exceeded $130 billion, and had been rising 15% per year.
- The federal government was publishing over 80,000 pages a year of new regulations—over 500,000 new pages since Nader entered the picture.
- Consumers were (according to Roper and Gallup polls) far less satisfied with the quality of products than they were 15 years before.
- Esteem for private corporate enterprise was at an all-time low.

Most ironic of all, largely because of the mounting costs of regulation (and compliance with it), corporate America was more concentrated in fewer hands in 1980 than when Nader started.

Not that Nader was responsible for this debacle—but as the most vocal and successful advocate of rising federal regulation he must share some responsibility for its bad effects as well as its good ones. And the bad effects are legion, as industry after industry has been bruised by excessive regulatory and economic interference.

Auto Industry Woes Started in Washington

Probably the most visible example of the wreckage of Naderist regulation is America's ailing auto industry, with its 16%–20% unemployment rate in Detroit and other Midwest industrial centers. When Jimmy Carter took office in 1977 (and appointed Nader-assistant Joan Claybrook to regulate it) the U.S. auto industry was earning record profits, producing 9.5 million cars a year, and fewer than 2,500 auto workers were unemployed. By 1980–81 Detroit was awash in red ink, and 200,000 United Auto Workers members were on long-term layoffs, most without much hope of ever being rehired.

In the rush to judgment of this demoralizing situation, the liberal pundits (including Nader) heaped all of the blame on bad management and greedy unionism in the auto industry and heavy competition from "smarter" overseas companies which were more farsighted in anticipating the boom in small cars due to the rising cost of gasoline. Surely, there is some truth to these accusations, but only *some*. How could an industry that made record profits in 1977 and 1978 suddenly fall apart in 1979 and 1980? How could management that was so correct in judging consumer demand in 1977 suddenly become so stupid so fast? How could labor that was market-effective in 1978 be so badly overpriced in 1981?

The answer, of course, can be found almost as much in Washington as in

TABLE 6-1

U.S. GASOLINE PRICES AND CAR SALES

	1960	1965	1970	1973	1974	1976	1977	1978	1979
Gasoline price (current)	30c	31c	36c	40c	55c	59c	63c	63c	86c
Gasoline price constant 1972	44c	42c	39c	38c	47c	44c	44c	41c	52c
V-8's share of U.S. sales	57%	73%	84%	82%	68%	69%	76%	67%	58%
Automatic transmission share of U.S. sales	72%	81%	91%	93%	90%	92%	95%	93%	88%
Air conditioning share of U.S. sales	7%	23%	61%	73%	67%	76%	82%	81%	68%
Miles/gallon (average for entire U.S. fleet)	14.3	14.1	13.6	13.3	13.7	13.9	14.2	14.3	14.8
% Import share of car market	5.8%	6.0%	24%	21%	23%	22%	24%	23%	26%

SOURCE: Chilton Company.

Detroit, as much in the halls of Congress as in the design shops of Chrysler and General Motors. The same politicians and pundits who successfully fought every effort to decontrol gasoline prices in 1974–78 were the ones who began pointing fingers at Detroit in 1980. Yet it was their failure in 1974–75 to decontrol domestic energy and gasoline prices, more than anything else, that led Detroit down the path to its deep troubles in 1980.

Table 6-1 tells the story graphically. From 1960 to 1973 the price of gasoline in America, in constant 1972 dollars, fell steadily. Not surprisingly, the American demand for big V-8 cars with automatic transmissions and air conditioning steadily increased while average mileage per gallon continued to slide. And why not? Cheap gasoline enabled both consumers and Detroit to indulge their desires (and profit motives) for luxury, so much so that most of Detroit's efforts in the 1960s and early 1970s to promote small cars proved costly and ineffective. While the small imports were capturing a growing share of the second-car market, big cars were still the overwhelming choice of the first-car buyers in this country.

Then came the 1973 OPEC embargo, and the real cost of gasoline jumped by about 10 cents a gallon. Suddenly the market for V-8's dropped from 82% to 68% in 1974, and the U.S. auto industry had to move quickly into small cars in 1975. But a funny thing happened on the way to this necessary revision in Detroit's auto-marketing policy: Congress refused, in 1974, to decontrol domestic gasoline and oil prices. (At that time, decontrol would not have been nearly so costly as it was in 1980–81.) As a result, from 1974 through 1978 gasoline prices (in constant 1972 dollars) steadily declined and by 1978 were a full 6 cents below what Americans had paid in 1950 (47 cents) and a full 24 cents below the 1940 price.

To no one's surprise, Detroit suddenly found the demand for its big cars soaring again and its small-car sales dropping like a stone. By 1977 V-8's were back up to 76% of total sales, and automatic transmissions and air conditioning reached new sales highs.

Today we forget that all over America in 1977 car dealers (especially

Chrysler dealers) were stuck with huge inventories of small low-priced domestic cars, which they couldn't sell except at disastrous discounts. As a result, many U.S. small-car plants were expensively retooled to turn out big cars again for 1978. Small wonder that the industry was stunned, when the big OPEC price surge came in 1979 and 1980, a surge brought on and abetted by foolish shortage-causing price regulations of the Department of Energy.

The sad truth is that the principal blame for the Detroit debacle must still be placed, not as much with the companies as with the "yo-yo" energy policies pursued by Congress for nearly a decade.

The mess in Detroit was really just another proof of the disastrous results of government-pricing intervention in the marketplace. The unemployed auto workers have only their own politicians to blame.

Those who doubt this need only examine why both Japan and Germany went to fuel-efficient cars long before we did. They will find their answer in the fact that the price of gasoline in those countries has always been at least double the price in America—and at times, triple. That kind of price signal can do wonders toward concentrating the manufacturing mind.

The Rental-Housing Crisis

Even before the 1980–81 credit crunch, U.S. cities everywhere were facing a growing shortage in rental housing. The crisis had been building for the previous ten years, slowly but inexorably, as vacancy rates had fallen from nearly 8% nationwide in 1970 to an average level of less than 3% in 1980. In some cities, such as Boston, it reached the 1% level in 1981.

Unfortunately, in most cities the construction of privately financed new rental housing all but stopped in the 1970s. In fact, in many urban areas there is now a negative rate of rental housing availability, as more and more landlords are taking the condo-route and getting out of the rental-housing business altogether. Virtually all new urban housing construction is now condo. Understandably, tenants, particularly elderly tenants, are reacting noisily and demanding protection from city halls and state houses across the country. The danger, of course, is that such "protection" is taking the form of laws (rent control, condo-freezes, etc.) that will only make the long-term rental-housing picture worse than it is. As James Ring Adams observed of this process in Santa Monica, California, where tough and arbitrary new rent controls are now stifling the new housing industry,

> The Santa Monica experiment may wind up forcing the "mom-and-pop" owners to sell out to anyone with the cash reserves to wait out the legal challenge. The ironic result would be that the policies of "economic democracy" would bring about a further concentration of Santa Monica property in the hands of speculators and large corporations.

The basic problem is not (as the Santa Monica zealots would have us believe) greedy or profiteering landlords and investors, but faulty government

TABLE 6-2

RENTS VS. OWNERSHIP COSTS
(100 = 1967)

Year	CPI	Rents	Home purchase	Home owner-ship	Home maintenance	Fuel and utilities
1970	116.3	110.1	118.3	128.5	124.0	107.6
1974	147.7	130.6	142.7	163.2	171.6	150.2
1978	195.4	164.0	196.7	227.2	233.0	216.0
1979	217.4	176.0	223.1	262.4	256.4	239.3
% change	87%	60%	89%	104%	107%	122%

SOURCE: U.S. Bureau of Labor Statistics.

policy, both in Washington and locally, that has made it more and more difficult for landlords to make a fair profit in a high-inflation, high-interest-rate situation. In fact, no other segment of the business community has been in worse financial shape over the last five years than rental-property owners, who now have one of the highest rates of business failure.

Obviously, if rental housing really were profitable, condominiums would not be so popular, and the rental supply would be larger. But, as Table 6-2 demonstrates, rents have steadily fallen not only behind the basic rate of inflation, but also behind the inflation in home-purchase prices; and in terms of maintaining residential property, costs and values have risen almost twice as fast as rental income. Conversely, the returns on home ownership have risen, on average, nearly 70% faster than the returns on rental housing. To put it another way, owners of rental housing, because they have not been able to command even the basic inflation rate in their gross income, have in effect been subsidizing tenants for the last decade.

The effect on overall rental income has been marked. In the period 1970–79, rental income, in real dollars (after allowance for capital consumption), actually fell by 18%, the worst performance of any business-income sector in the nation. Small wonder that even as the total housing market fell behind rising public demand, rental-housing construction fell even further, from 35% of all new starts in 1965 to 27% in 1977. Estimates are that it was below 23% in 1981. With the rapid boom in condominium conversions, it is now estimated that by 1985 rental-housing units will represent less than 10% of all new construction.

At the heart of the problem is the federal tax policy that subsidizes single-family ownership. The new federal income tax provides complete deductions of property taxes and mortgage interest for property owners but not for tenants. The effect of this tax policy was dramatically to reduce the relative cost of home ownership and increase the relative pain of renting, thus forcing renters to demand lower rents to compensate and encouraging home buyers to pay exorbitant housing prices and mortgage interest rates.

In a research paper for the National Bureau of Economic Research, Patric Hendershott shows that because of tax policies that favor individual home ownership and punish corporate capital, the actual "effective" interest costs on owner-occupied (single-family) housing have fallen dramatically, while the effective interest costs on corporate structures (plants, offices, etc.) have soared. For the average taxpayer (at the 30% marginal tax rate), effective interest on homes fell from 8% in 1964 to less than 2% in 1978, and to less than 0% in 1980! In the same period, the effective interest on corporate structures rose from 15% to 27%.

Because of the rapid rise in house values (due to inflation), coupled with rapidly rising marginal income-tax rates being paid by all of us, the real cost of home ownership has steadily declined. With inflation of home prices exceeding 10% a year, the 30% tax bracket means that even a 15% mortgage rate winds up at an effective user cost of capital of 0%–2%. By inversion, Hendershott argues, this acts as a tremendous force for the "mis-allocation" of capital, with too much money going into individual housing and too little either into corporate plant or into rental multifamily housing. His research suggests that in 1978 alone, corporate capital investment markets lost about $12 billion to the individual housing market.

Since rental-housing investors are also dealing in these same corporate financial markets, they too have been savaged by the individual-homeowner tax subsidies. They also have been hurt by the growing availability of subsidized public housing and individual government rent subsidies (under Section 8) which have tended to put a brake on private, unsubsidized rents. The percentage of rental housing under public subsidy has doubled since 1970. Landlords catering to elderly tenants now find themselves competing for these tenants with Section 8-subsidized buildings where rents are held artificially below costs. This forces them to accept a far lower rate of return on their own property—until they inevitably find it necessary to convert to condominiums, just to extricate themselves from an impossible economic situation.

Rent controls, in many cities, seriously aggravate this situation by locking rental income to preinflationary rates. Under these controls, landlords are usually forced to get negative rates of earnings (after inflation) year after year, until they condo-ize in self-defense.

Since there will always be more consumers than producers, more employees than employers, more customers than sellers, more tenants than landlords, politicians, if given the chance, will almost always decide on the side of numbers—and, in the process, favor the demand (consumer) side of the equation and punish the supply (producer or investor) side. That is why such political economics as rent control always leads to shortages and scarcity.

The detailed 54-page study of rent control in New York City by that city's own Temporary Commission on City Finances documents the loss of more than 250,000 units of rental housing in New York in just ten years, traceable directly to the impact of rent control. The authors of the report concluded that the effect (though not the purpose) of rent control was to subsidize renters at the expense of owners, and that this subsidy in New York had reached the cumulative total of more than $20 billion. They found that most of this amount had gone to upper-income groups living in rent-controlled apartments. Furthermore, they found that "rent control and rent stabilization have already facilitated the destruction, beyond repair, of a significant portion of the housing inventory of New York," as owners were forced to abandon marginal properties.

In turn, this massive destruction of marginal rental properties depressed total property-tax assessments and reduced the city's potential property-tax receipts by more than $100 million annually. This shortfall, in turn, was passed right back to the average taxpayer in the form of higher sales and use taxes.

In short, the report (which was prepared by the city's own financial watchdog agency, not by landlords) found that rent control was actively subsidizing the renting rich at the expense of both the homeless poor and the small landlord, even as it promoted widespread abandonment and arson.

Why then, doesn't New York get rid of this scourge of rent control which is slowly destroying it? Politics.

Politics is also the reason why Mayor Kevin White hangs on to rent control in Boston, even though he knows the harm it is doing and the degree to which it is pushing the city toward an unhealthy class split between high-income condominium owners and low-income subsidized tenants. Mayor White admitted as much in a surprisingly candid interview in *Barron's* in which he told the editors that it was only his lack of political courage that made him retain a modified (vacancy decontrol) rent-control program in 1977–78 instead of following the expert advice to fully decontrol rental housing by his own housing adviser, Andrew Olins, whose detailed committee study showed that in Boston:

- Since rent control, privately financed new rental housing had fallen from 68% of the market to 6%, in just eight years.
- More than 90% of all new rental housing development now had to be subsidized—and financed publicly.
- There was a loss of more than 7,000 private nonsubsidized (tax-paying) apartments since 1969.
- Of the 6,700 apartments ripped down since 1970, 90% were under rent control.
- The city's total real-property tax base was now lower than at any time since 1972.
- Among those apartments that were vacancy decontrolled since 1976, more than 17% were rerented at lower prices, over half were increased less than 15%, only one third were rented at more than they would have brought with rent control—and there was no evidence of gouging.

The committee concluded: "The 1977 housing crisis was not brought on by a tight market, uncurbed speculation, rapidly spiraling rents and displacement, as was the case in the sixties. Rather it is one characterized by disinvestment, deferred maintenance, erosion of housing stock and the tax base; and it is one aggravated by keeping the lid on investors' revenue while rising operating costs push up cash outlays."

Predictably, since Mayor Kevin White's failure to end rent control in

1977, Boston has experienced a massive onslaught of condominium conversion, as landlords, frustrated by rent controls that were allowing less than half of the real inflation rate to be recouped, sought the only way out—so the city's rental-housing shortage grew steadily worse.

When White reneged on his pledge to drop rent controls in 1977, the city still had a vacancy rate of close to 10%. Since then, the rate has dropped to 1%–2%, and many lower- and middle-income people have no way to find rental housing, at any price, because none of it is being built, while the present stock is either being condoized in some areas of the city or torched and bulldozed, after deliberate neglect. As a result, Boston has become a clear-cut case history of the destructive effect of rent control—with low- and middle-income residents being driven out even as large corporations are building new office structures downtown and luxury condominiums are in hot demand. The city continues to lose population even as its skyline is regenerated and its business economy is booming.

The Natural-Gas Fiasco

As Milton Friedman has said, "Economists may not know how to run the economy, but they do know how to create shortages or gluts simply by regulating prices below the market, or artificially supporting them above it."

There may well be no more perfect illustration than natural gas.

Energy economists on both sides of the ideological spectrum now agree that the seeds of this nation's energy crisis were sown in the 1954 Supreme Court decision in the Phillips Petroleum case, when the majority ruled that the Federal Power Commission had the right to regulate not only the costs of the interstate pipeline but the gas that flowed through it. The dissenting opinion in that case was written by the eminent civil libertarian William O. Douglas, who warned that such price controls over the gas would ultimately affect the supply of gas at the wellhead.

As it turned out, he could not have been more prophetic, as a decade of artificially low prices caused the annual demand for natural gas to far outstrip new discoveries by 1968, nearly five years before the first enormous OPEC oil price rise. The chief reason was not a shortage of gas in the ground but the artificial stimulation of low prices to the consumer (still 17 cents per MCF in 1967, less than half the oil price equivalent at that time) and low returns to the producers. Despite obvious evidence of massive new natural-gas fields still to be tapped, natural-gas well-drilling actually declined all through the 1960s and early 1970s.

As Lester Thurow explains it, "When [controls] are used to hold prices down for long periods of time they cause perverse effects on both the supply and demand sides of the market." On the supply side the incentives to go after and discover new sources of gas are held down, and on the demand side the consumers are not encouraged to conserve fuel. So low were the Federal Power Commission's price controls on gas that American consumers were literally driven to massive fuel consumption levels. As a result, from 1971 through 1978, we began to experience periodic "crises" in natural-gas supplies at the same time that the supply of crude oil was beginning to tighten. In fact, most economists agree that one of the forces that ultimately helped make OPEC successful was the unrealistic low ceiling on natural-gas prices, which, in turn held down the competitive price of liquid petroleum, subsidized its excessive use, and generated an unnaturally "tight" energy market. Every natural gas crisis immediately sent industrial users looking for more oil in an already-crowded market.

These natural-gas shortages had nothing to do with the actual supply of reserves. In 1981, three years after the price of gas was at least partially decontrolled, potential reserves were estimated to be at least 30 to 50 years—and the exploration and development of new gas fields was once more back above the 1960 levels. On 28 December 1980 CBS's "60 Minutes" did a special feature on the growing evidence of America's "natural-gas riches," pointing out that "as a result of higher prices, natural-gas discoveries are now growing so fast, they could provide the long-term answer to our energy crisis."

Yet two weeks after that broadcast, on 13 January 1981, Massachusetts Governor Edward J. King had to declare a statewide energy emergency because of a serious shortage of natural gas, and half the state went cold.

Consumers had a right to be confused. How could there be a crisis-shortage in New England three weeks after CBS reported a growing glut of natural gas at the drilling sources throughout the Southwest?

Although at least part of the blame had to be laid on bad planning by the utilities in Massachusetts, most of it belonged to Congress and the U.S. Department of Energy, which, until 1978, kept maintaining that natural gas was running out and that even with deregulation there wouldn't be much more gas produced. This long-term head-in-the-sand regulatory approach to one of the nation's most plentiful potential energy sources not only delayed the drilling and discovery boom by at least a decade, but it also significantly delayed the adequate development of more pipeline capacity to consumers, which was the source of the Massachusetts freeze-out.

As a result, too much of the Northeast was, in 1981, still dependent on very expensive supplementary sources (such as imported LNG and SNG) for gas, even though by 1980 there had been ample pipeline gas available in the interstate market at much lower controlled prices.

Situations like this show why, since 1974, energy economists have almost unanimously endorsed the quick deregulation of natural gas and the active development of increased interstate pipeline capacity in order to use this gas to offset up to 4 million barrels per day of oil imports. Even the U.S. Department of Energy now admits that the experience of just the first two years since the slow-deregulation process started in early 1979 showed that we have a likely 40-to-50 year supply of natural gas and that complete deregulation could quickly expand that figure.

One energy maverick, Dr. Paul Hastings Jones, told the *National Geographic* in 1978 that "We could have [natural gas] running out of our ears." Jones is an expert on "geo-pressured methane," gas that is dissolved in brine at depths of from 20,000 to 50,000 feet in the Gulf Coast region. He contends that "this brine could contain as much as 50,000 trillion cubic feet of gas (TCF)," which is about 2,500 times as much as our present annual production, or more than enough to make the "energy shortage" a distant memory of a superstitious past.

Even if he is only 10% right the good news is that this nation is sitting on more than enough natural gas to increase our annual production by 50%–100% over the next ten years. Since less than half of the crude oil we now use has to be in liquid form, this gas potential would enable us to cut our oil use by 4–6 million barrels a day, effectively wiping out our dependence on imported oil by 1990.

The bad news is that when we were debating the energy crisis, neither President Carter nor the Congress believed this good news. Their 1977–78 "energy plans" almost completely ignored it, setting us back years in our quest for energy independence. As this book was written, we were still over three years away from full decontrol. The Reagan administration was still reluctant to risk it politically, despite the success of crude-oil decontrol.

The situation goes back to Carter's first energy speech to the nation on 8 April 1977, when, in an effort to whip up a crisis spirit, he warned: "This nation is rapidly running out of natural gas. At present rates of production and consumption we have only 10–12 years' supply left." He warned that "not even substantial price increases could do much more than arrest the decline in natural gas production."

He failed to tell the nation that two days before, on 6 April 1977, a team of natural-gas specialists from the Energy Research and Development Administration (ERDA) had presented him with the (now-famous) MOPPS study which showed that if the price of new natural gas were simply deregulated, the nation would be awash with natural gas. The study told President Carter that as the price of natural gas rose toward the $3/MCF mark ($18/bbl of oil equivalent), there would be enormous increases in conventionally tapped gas and that, as it rose toward the $4–$5/MCF mark, the nation could have hundreds, even thousands, of years of supply from unconventional sources such as geopressured methane.

The implications of the study were clear: The only thing holding down the expansion of U. S. reserves and the discovery and production of new gas was the artificially low ceiling on its price at that time ($1.43/MCF). Not only was that price well below the uncontrolled intrastate price of gas in Texas at that time ($1.95), but it was 80 cents below the price we were then paying to import gas from Canada. Most important, it was 40% below the then prevailing prices of new crude oil—for which it could substitute. That's why Professor Paul MacAvoy had told Congress in 1976 that controls on natural-gas prices alone had created a shortfall of 1.8 million barrels of oil per day. Today that figure is more than double.

In 1981, for example, the average spot price of oil was about $31/bbl, the equivalent of $5.16 per MCF of gas. Yet the average controlled U.S. price of gas was about $2.80/MCF, or about half the price of oil. This not only

TABLE 6-3   (Gas data in trillion cubic feet [TCF])
U.S. NATURAL-GAS RESOURCE POTENTIAL AT VARYING PRICE LEVELS (CUMULATIVE)

Oil price levels/bbl	Equivalent gas price per MCF	Conventional gas sources	Unconventional gas, including geo-pressured	Total	Supply‡ in years
Old oil $9.65 (1976)	1.61	200-250 TCF†	_____	200-250	10-12
Average domestic price $16.80 (1978)	2.80	250-400 TCF	_____	250-400	12-20
Top U.S. oil price $21.60 (1979)	3.60	400-600 TCF	750 TCF	1150-1350	57-70
Mexican gas price $26.80 (1979)	4.47	600-800 TCF	900 TCF	1500-1700	75-85
Saudi oil price $32.00 (1980)	5.35	900 TCF	1100-1400 TCF	1000-2400	100-120
Top OPEC $40.00 (1980)	6.65	900 TCF	1600-2200 TCF	2500-3100	125-155
Oil shale (syn-fuel) $35.00 (1980)	5.83	900 TCF	2700-3500 TCF	3600-4400*	180-220

SOURCES: ERDA-MOPPS Study, April 1977; Colorado School of Mines Study, May 1977; Commission on Critical Choices. 1975; U.S. Geological Survey Study, 1975-76.

* Cumulative totals of 3600-4400 TCF are equivalent of 600-730 billion barrels of oil — triple all the oil ever used so far by the United States. † Present gas reserves (1980): 201 TCF. ‡ Present gas production per year (1980): 20 TCF.

amounts to a subsidy by oil consumers to gas consumers, but it artificially maintains a high price for oil by holding down the production of new gas.

Yet, as the ERDA–MOPPS study showed, at prices of $3.50/MCF and above ($21/bbl), the United States could have from 120 to 150 years of natural-gas reserves, easily enough to increase present production from 20 TCF to 30 TCF. Since each additional 2.2 TCF of annual gas production is the equivalent of 1 million barrels of oil per day, it is easy to see that the ERDA–MOPPS study showed that the way to wipe out all OPEC imports (and, incidentally, nuclear power as well) was by an all-out assault on natural-gas development plus Mexican imports. This would then force oil prices down.

Naturally, this study presented a serious obstacle to President Carter's whole complex 1977 energy program and its basic premise that decontrol would not raise gas supplies. So he proceeded first to have the study rewritten with lower estimates, and then, when its conclusions still wouldn't go away, in March 1978 he ordered the U.S. Government Printing Office to send out a notice to all libraries to remove the MOPPS study from their shelves. In a kind of Orwellian no-think approach, he asked the GPO to put the study "down the memory hole," even though another public study by the Colorado School of Mines had already verified its findings.

Unfortunately, President Carter didn't bargain on Dr. Vincent McKelvey, the director of the U.S. Geological Survey, who told a Boston audience in June 1977 that the MOPPS study "vastly underestimated" the amount of natural gas available just from the geopressured zones—that "at least 60 to 80 thousand trillion cubic feet (TCF) may be available from the Gulf Coast alone. This represents about ten times the energy value of all oil, gas, and coal reserves of the United States," Dr. McKelvey added.

Predictably, shortly after he made this public statement, Dr. McKelvey was asked to resign. At the same time, the author of the original ERDA–MOPPS study, Dr. Christian Knudsen, was demoted from his position as chairman of the natural-gas supply study committee.

By that time, however, the cat was well out of the Carter bag. On 14 June 1977, in an editorial entitled "Carter on the Run," *The Wall Street Journal* published its own synthesis of all three studies and told its readers that the Carter administration was involved in a peculiar kind of "economic revisionism." The *Journal* pointed out that "Even at the worst the good people of ERDA have found us 55 years' worth of natural gas at a reasonable price." It also pointed out that two of ERDA's top people, Harry Johnson and Philip White, had both told *The Washington Post* that the original first study figures developed by Dr. Knudsen were "probably correct."

Dr. Knudsen was then asked to testify before Senator Henry Jackson's Energy and Natural Resource Committee on 23 June. He was asked point blank whether he thought he had lost his chairmanship of the supply committee because his first study didn't agree with President Carter's own thinking. He cautiously admitted there "might have been some connection."

Dr. Knudsen was far less cautious in a lengthy telephone interview with me in which he effectively confirmed the danger of political control over basic commodity resources. I asked him, "Doesn't your study suggest that with deregulation this nation might well have a real surplus of natural gas?" He replied, "You could infer that, but I am not at liberty to do so at this time for obvious reasons. One thing seems clear. As the price goes up, it will become more and more economic to recover more and more gas. That is clear from our graphs." In other words, the 1977–80 natural-gas shortage was strictly a problem of politics and price, not of supply.

Dr. Knudsen's conclusions were amply supported by sophisticated energy economists and petroleum experts from coast to coast. Professor Robert S. Pindyck of MIT, in *The Public Interest* in April 1977, wrote, "It is of primary importance to move quickly toward the deregulation of natural-gas prices. . . . Past and present controls have resulted in shortages, increased imports, and higher than necessary prices. Policies in effect today depress the domestic price of energy, on the average, by 30% below the world price. Consumption then is 8% higher than it would be otherwise and supply is 6% lower." The effect of deregulation, according to Dr. Pindyck, would be to open up for exploration tremendous new reserves that were then being blocked out by price-control policies. The Canadian experience, 1974–77, proved his point.

In 1974 Canada was so worried about natural gas shortages that it had put an embargo on shipments to the United States. Then it deregulated new gas, and the combination of much higher prices and rising U.S. demand sent the Canadian gas producers into an exploration spree into areas formerly considered too costly to yield. So while price controls depressed U.S. production, decontrol incentives were spurring Canadian discovery. Within two years, they completely transformed and galvanized western Canada's leisurely petroleum industry. The result was that by 1977 Canada was piling up a 1–2 TCF surplus of natural gas every 12 months—a surplus that Canada was happy to sell to us at nearly double the regulated price of new gas in the United States.

At that time (1977), one independent Houston producer told me that he could cite at least 300 major prospective fields he could drill and open at a price of from \$3 to \$4 and could be in full production within six to 14 months. But in 1977–78 it was not worth his while to go after these reserves because all of them were at depths of from 9,000 to 16,000 feet, and the wells would cost over \$1.5 million each, requiring a price well above the controlled price.

It was an outrageous situation, and its implications went far beyond just natural gas, *The Wall Street Journal* observed. "Deregulation of natural gas would bring in so much of the stuff that it would soon force down the price of its nearest substitute, Number 2 fuel oil, which now sells at the equivalent of about \$3 per MCF for natural gas. Which is to say that deregulation of natural gas could very well break the OPEC cartel." That was the opportunity we lost in 1977. It was still a not-fully-realized opportunity in 1981.

That is the theme of a 1980 book entitled *Natural Gas: The New Energy Leader,* in which Dr. Ernest J. Oppenheimer writes: "Natural gas is the most likely candidate to replace oil as the leading source of energy. The emergence of commercial drilling for deep gas on a significant scale in the late 1970s may be considered the beginning of a new era, one in which gas is emerging as the dominant fuel."

The deep-gas boom to which Dr. Oppenheimer refers was the direct outgrowth of the so-called Natural Gas Deregulation Act of 1978—a seven-year tortured phase-down of most gas-price controls, but which also recontrolled intra-state gas and set up perhaps the most complex and tangled price-control mechanisms ever devised for any commodity, with more than 160,000 separate prices established so far, or one for every natural-gas well.

The one place where this act is really working, though, is in the category of wells below 15,000 feet, which have been totally decontrolled. Predictably, wildcatters and investors are completely ignoring the vast potentials of new gas in wells of 5,000 to 15,000 feet and are plunging forward with deep gas, which is now selling at prices of \$8/MCF to as much as \$12/MCF.

Within six months of the passage of the 1978 act, the press was reporting "boomtown conditions" in the previously quiet natural-gas fields. In one of these, the Anadarko Basin, more than 50 drilling companies were sinking 15,000-foot-and-deeper wells into a region which many now think could contain over 100 TCF in new gas reserves, or half of the nation's present resource base.

As Robert Hefner told the *National Geographic* in 1978, "This [Anadarko] basin has 22,000 cubic miles of sediments below 15,000 feet and only 1% of it has ever been touched by a drill." Hefner placed the potential in this one basin at up to 360 TCF, and told the magazine that it would take only 600 producing wells in this one rich basin to produce the equivalent of 2 million barrels of oil a day, or about half of our total imports in 1982.

To put this in perspective, under the Carter synthetic-fuels plan it would have cost, conservatively, \$80 billion to as much as \$300 billion to build the plants to produce this much fuel. Yet the capital costs of drilling 600 deep wells for natural gas would be less than \$6 billion, with none of the vast environmental harm.

Thus just three years of only partial decontrol of gas has already scuttled the syn-fuels boondoggle—and one can only imagine what full decontrol would accomplish to end energy dependency. Although the full decontrol of crude oil has already produced a crushing glut in the world market, the release of all U.S. natural gas from market restrictions would bring OPEC and its inflated prices crashing down completely and wipe out most of our import bill. As William Tucker of *Harper's* put it, "Without the foreign oil needed to make up for the natural gas shortage, OPEC would be about as important to the American economy as a Turkish bazaar."

But What About Safety Regulations?

Although the case for deregulation is very clear in the economic areas of wages and prices, the issue of safety is much more complex. Given the growing hazards of a highly technological environment, Americans are understandably more interested in government protection of their safety than ever before—and much of what has already been done in this area has been both socially and economically desirable, indeed essential.

No one wants a repeat of Love Canal—yet even there, homeowners would never have built over Love Canal had the company's original warnings been heeded by the local politicians, who chose through tax greed to allow development over a well-known hazardous waste dump and then proceeded to blame the fallout entirely on industry.

But the massive and occasionally hysterical publicity of even one Love Canal incident simply compounds what can best be described as a growing national paranoia over the dangers of a technological society—a fear which has at times engendered excessive and often counterproductive regulations of safety.

For the past decade or more, federal regulation of safety issues has been governed by two questionable premises: First, safety regulations always save lives and preserve health. Second, when it comes to safety, it is simply immoral to question the costs versus the benefits.

Now if the first premise were true, then we could get into a heated philosophical and economic argument about the second. Unfortunately, the first premise again and again has proven fallacious. The most frustrating aspect of safety regulation these past 10–15 years is the difficulty in actually demonstrating any measurable results in reducing real risks, real human damage, or fatalities.

Take, for example, the case of mandatory auto inspections, now going on in some 22 states. Every six months some 2.9 million Massachusetts drivers fume and fuss through their semiannual vehicle safety–inspection charade and shell out some $11.6 million for the exercise. In the process they spend some $10 million in lost work or leisure time and, in order to get their stickers, pay for at least $60 million in often unnecessary repairs.

Now, it would all be worthwhile if the whole process actually saved lives or reduced injuries. But in fact, it doesn't do either. It may in fact actually reduce safety and increase the possibility of accident and injury. That is the inescapable conclusion of a 1980 study for the American Enterprise Institute by economist Mark Crain of the Virginia Polytechnic Institute, who found that "vehicle inspection programs have no detectable impact on highway safety." His research proved that when other factors are taken into account, states which employ mandatory inspection programs do not have lower accident rates than states without such requirements. Which may explain why five states have repealed their inspection programs in the last several years and some 23 do not have any mandatory inspection program at all. Crain discovered that even when states had twice-yearly inspections, safety did not improve. But the most interesting aspect of his findings is that "higher than expected death rates are associated with the existence of inspection programs." One reason for this is that the very presence of such an inspection system tends to inculcate in the drivers' minds a false sense of security. Furthermore, statistics show that no more than 4% of all highway accidents can be attributed to vehicle failure, and even the National Highway Traffic Safety Administration admits that in order for a vehicle inspection program to be cost effective it would have to eliminate from 14% to 39% of all such accidents—and apparently it doesn't eliminate any of them.

When this 4% figure is compared with the 74% of all vehicle accidents associated directly with excessive speed and the more than 50% of all highway deaths directly associated with alcohol use, the whole notion that many lives can be saved by periodic vehicle inspections comes into more realistic perspective.

Even the most efficient vehicle-inspection programs seldom discover more than 25%–40% of the most flagrantly obvious and planted defects. A 1975 study, by the Carnegie-Mellon University School of Urban and Public Affairs using a 1969 Chevrolet Bel Air in which 13 defects were intentionally created, found that the average service station would catch only 25%–30% of them but that they did catch at least one or two defects that were not even there. These nonexistent defects escalated rapidly when new car dealers were included in the vehicle-inspection program.

The same study found that in 1975 the average cost of repairing these nonexistent defects was about $35 per car, which at today's prices would be over $80. This means that not only do Massachusetts drivers spend nearly $24 million a year on fees for useless inspections, but that they pile up another $120 million or so in the cost of often unnecessary repairs for essentially nonexistent defects.

To put it in context, the average inspection station in Massachusetts not only picks up some $7,200 in inspection fees but also gets another $30,000 a year or more for unnecessary repairs. Now we see why we have an auto vehicle-inspection program. It has little to do with safety, but it has everything to do with keeping the special interests busy and well paid.

OSHA Follies

This is even more true of the Occupational Safety and Health Administration (OSHA), which in the past decade has spent some $1.6 billion of

TABLE 6-4

OCCUPATIONAL INJURIES AND ILLNESSES, 1973-79

(per 100 workers)

Lost work days	1973	1979	% change
All workplaces	55.3	64.1	16%
Manufacturing	68.2	86.1	26%
Construction	98.1	116.1	18%
Mining	119.6	136.4	14%
Cases involving lost days			
All workplaces	3.4	4.3	26%
Manufacturing	4.5	5.6	24%
Construction	6.1	6.8	11%
Mining	5.8	6.9	19%

SOURCE: U.S. Bureau of Labor Statistics.

taxpayers' money issuing tens of thousands of new regulations. Those in turn have caused employers, mostly small ones, to spend some $25 billion in compliance.

Now an expenditure of $25 billion over a decade should have produced some improvement in the safety record in the workplace, shouldn't it? Well, it hasn't. In fact, just the opposite is true, if we are to believe Bureau of Labor Statistics data. Between 1973 and 1979, the period of OSHA's most intense regulation, lost workdays due to injuries and illnesses in workplaces per one hundred workers actually *increased* by 16%. The increase was worst in the two areas where OSHA concentrated its attention: manufacturing (26%) and construction (18%). Of course, there may well be other factors at work, such as the larger limits on sick time in union contracts and the more generous application of disability standards. Yet that does not account for the number of accidents involving lost work time increasing by 26% over the same period.

It is self-evident that, so far, OSHA has been a huge bust, not merely in its enormous cost and harassment of employers (especially small ones), but in its failure to demonstrate a higher level of safety. Instead, safety has apparently declined since OSHA began meddling in the workplace.

This in no way suggests that there are not many cases of highly effective government safety regulation, both on products and in the workplace. The experience with hazardous wastes and chemicals, not to mention mines and oil drilling, indicates that we cannot ignore clear and obvious dangers. The vast majority of OSHA regulations, however, have not dealt with "clear and present dangers" but with established production and workplace procedures and, more often than not, have generated even more costly and more labor-intensive methods of production, in the name of safety.

In the construction industry, for example, whenever some new labor-saving method of construction was being challenged by the unions, OSHA would immediately step in and raise the safety issue, even where no such issue existed. In this way, OSHA became a tool used by unions to resist legitimate productivity measures.

Thus, the Antonelli Iron Works Company, a steel-erection firm in Massachusetts, was challenged by a local OSHA inspector about the safety of tandem erection, one of the industry's most tried and true methods of putting up steel girders. At hearings forced on the company by OSHA, the only witness for OSHA was its own local compliance officer, Douglas Russell, a former business agent for the Boston Iron Workers Local. In his testimony Russell was unable to cite a single incident of injury or even near-injury caused by the construction method he was challenging. As one reads the case file one cannot help but realize that the real purpose, as in so many other OSHA actions during the past decade, was not the promotion of safety but the feathering of more labor beds. Fortunately, as in most OSHA tort actions, the courts threw the case out, but the costs to the company and the taxpayer were high.

Technology and Danger

There are of course endless examples of such regulatory overkill. Hardly a day goes by that we are not treated to some fresh government revelation of danger—whether from toxic wastes and radiation or from asbestos from hair dryers. More fundamentally, we are being told almost constantly that the price of technology is being paid for in dangers too great to be tolerated— dangers that threaten our survival and damage the quality and longevity of life itself. Jacques Ellul, for example, declares that "History shows that every technical application from its beginning presents certain unforeseeable secondary effects which are more disastrous than the lack of the technique would have been."

Like so many other fears, however, this one is statistically baseless. After all, one of the most serious economic and social challenges facing America today is rising longevity. The population in the age group over 65 is growing four times as fast as the population as a whole. Life expectancy at age 50 is nearly 18% higher today than 30 years ago and has *risen* as our society has urbanized and technified.

In 1900 the life expectancy of Americans was 48, and more than 70% of the people lived in rural areas, on farms, far away from industry, technology, and pollution. Today, the life expectancy of Americans is over 73 years—and our farm population comprises less than 5% of the nation. In other words, the more industrialized and technological we have become, the longer we are living, and our lives are substantially freer of the grinding hardship that characterized life in the 19th and early 20th centuries. This experience is confirmed in Table 6-5, which shows the life expectancy and mortality rates in the most industrialized nations in the world and in some of the largest Third World nonindustrialized societies. The average life expectancy in nonindustrial Africa is about 45, in South America about 55, and in the affluent industrial West 73. Japan, the most heavily industrialized nation in the world, now has the greatest life expectancy and the lowest mortality rates from all causes.

TABLE 6-5

MORTALITY AND LIFE EXPECTANCY RATES,
INDUSTRIAL VS. UNDEVELOPED NATIONS

High-technology nations	Life expectancy (years)	Mortality rates (per 1,000)
United States	73	9
Canada	73	7
France	73	11
Germany	72	12
Italy	72	11
Netherlands	75	8
Sweden	75	11
USSR	70	9
United Kingdom	72	12
Japan	75	6
Low-technology nations		
Algeria	53	16
Angola	41	22
Brazil	56	10
Egypt	55	14
Ghana	49	15
Iran	52	16
India	48	15
Indonesia	43	16
Kenya	49	15
Mozambique	44	18
Nigeria	39	21
Peru	56	13
Sudan	41	18
Tanzania	47	17
Zaire	42	17

SOURCE: U.S. Statistical Abstract, 1979.

Plainly, many other factors affect these rates, including culture, diet, and lifestyle. At the same time, there is no evidence to support the notion that technology endangers the quality of life. Quite the contrary would seem to be true.

There are sensible ways and highly developed methodologies to evaluate the risks of new technologies against their benefits that would, if permitted, enable us to avoid the kind of self-defeating paranoia of many of today's more extreme environmentalists and health faddists. Unfortunately the major broadcast networks greet every attempt to apply such techniques with emotional and pejorative contentions (through rigged interviews) that in some way Americans are being asked to "endanger their lives for the profits of corporations," when in reality we may be about to save needed jobs and protect the survival of needed products and industries that provide infinitely more help then harm.

As Dr. Elizabeth Whelan, one of America's most distinguished health advocates (and the author of 11 books on the subject of environmental hazards) argues:

When a pesticide is banned, it may make the environmentalists feel good, make them think they are doing something. But as an epidemiologist, I know it is not preventing cancer. And as a consumer it makes me angry that even though the banning has no medical benefits, it means that I will pay more for strawberries and corn next year. Such bannings also serve as a disincentive to an industry that could eventually come up with an even better pesticide—which would help us produce more food, for ourselves and the world.

When a food additive is banned, it makes some of the Naderite groups happy, and the government content. But as a scientist I know that, too, will not prevent cancer, but will only serve to remove useful products from the shelves, such as diet soft drinks.

What we need, of course, is a new breed of consumer advocate, one who can effectively explode the myth that we have to choose between modern technology and good health. We can have both. Of course we need to keep health-threatening chemicals out of our food, air, and water. However, with today's consumer advocates leading the show, we are heading toward not only zero risk, but zero food, zero jobs, zero energy, and zero growth.

That, of course, is the guiding motivation of large chunks of the so-called consumer movement who have joined increasingly with the environmentalists to push the "no-growth" agenda through the whole entropic process of spiraling regulation, bureaucratization, and litigation, not so much to protect us as to reorient our society's basic goals from spontaneous free-market unfoldment toward rigid redistribution.

Fortunately, the economy in mind, like the ecology of matter, naturally resists this deadly process by reacting to its more intrusional controls with painful distortions and disruptions which periodically remind us that Father Economy does not like to be "messed with" any more than Mother Nature— and that every regulation has unseen economic costs that all too frequently outweigh its presumed benefits.

Above all, it is not coincidental that physical well-being has followed economic growth wherever it has taken place and that life is infinitely more cruel and hazardous wherever it has not. Economic stagnation is the greatest danger of regulatory excess. As a *Wall Street Journal* editorial put it, what the poor of this world need most is not more government protection but far more economic growth, "and economic growth means *using* the world's resources of minerals, fuels, capital, manpower and land. There can be no return to Walden Pond without mass poverty." There is nothing more "hazardous to your health" than poverty.

Not too long ago I watched a panel discussion on television, in which some prominent physicians were discussing the alarming growth of "iatrogenic disorders"—illnesses caused not by disease but by medical treatment itself. Today, it seems, a growing number of patients are in hospitals not for treatment of a serious disease but for reactions to medical treatment. What concerned these physicians was that, in all too many cases, the medical treatment might never have been given if the patients themselves had not pushed for it and demanded it, even for minor or imaginary illnesses.

As one of the panelists put it, "We have become a nation of hypochondriacs, all too willing and eager to subject ourselves to the most complex and sophisticated medical care and drugs, even for disorders which doctors can't find or trace, or for minor aberrations in our healthy routines." Another panelist agreed. "I find a growing number of patients who arrive in hospitals, whose only need is to be dried out from excessive medication so that their natural healthy functioning can reassert itself."

As it is with the body physical, so it has become with the body economic. During the last 15 years or so, our growing national preoccupation with every monthly economic statistic or indicator has become so intense as to border on a kind of economic hypochondria. The slightest aberration of the Gross National Product, the Consumer Price Index, the money supply, or the unemployment rate sends us scurrying like frightened children to our witch doctors, the economists, demanding some instant cure, some new economic wonder drug, or some new regulation.

Unfortunately, our economists, and especially our politicians, have been all too willing to comply with our every request, even though no such economic wonder drugs exist, and new economic policies almost always make things worse. Growth rate a little sluggish? Let's try a quick shot of deficit spending or easy money to tone up the unemployment rate. Housing starts not high enough? How about a quick tax incentive for the construction industry—or a federal loan-guarantee program—or a new rent subsidy—or a new shot of FHA mortgage money? Or rent control. Capital investment lagging? Let's give the corporations a little needleful of accelerated depreciation, or an investment-tax-credit pill, or some credit allocation.

Over the past two decades or so, this nation's otherwise healthy economy has been fed so many quick fixes, multicolored economic pills, and shots of "fiscal dope," it has become a kind of iatrogenic basket case, so full of conflicting medicines we can't tell which disorder to treat first and which medicine is causing which problem. As one prominent and well-intentioned liberal economist said on public television, "We have so many different structural problems in our economy today, it is hard to know which one to attack first!" He failed to mention that most of these structural disorders are iatrogenic.

It seems ironic yet fitting that Milton Friedman won the 1976 Nobel Prize in Economics in particular for his work showing the total inability of central governments to manage economies. As he pointed out, "About the only thing we can be sure of is that government does not know how to manage economies—and that it shouldn't be so very eager to try."

The Free Market in Jeopardy

At least part of the reason for government's "eagerness" to try to plan and regulate our economy is the enthusiasm of so-called free-enterprise business executives for the safety and stability of the regulated market. As Edith Efron puts it:

The so-called American capitalist, today, usually does not know what genuine free enterprise is. It means the total exclusion of the state from the economic realm, leaving producers free to compete, subject to the risks and hazards of the law of supply and demand alone. But the contemporary businessman's working definition of "free enterprise" is bribing specific government officials for favors—for contracts, for subsidies, for monopolies, for protective tariffs . . . for shelter against competition at home and abroad.

A few years back, I watched, fascinated, a hard-hitting TV debate between Senator Edward M. Kennedy and Frank Borman, president of Eastern Airlines, in which Kennedy, that old big-government liberal, was advocating more competition by doing away with the Civil Aeronautics Board regulation process, while Borman, a free-enterprise mogul, was frantically defending the value of "the orderly regulated marketplace," a position he later was forced to admit was wrong.

Unfortunately, over the past 20–30 years, and very largely as a result of the best intentions, government has shifted from an honest adversary position vis-à-vis business to what is now referred to as the "mixed" economy—the idea that business and government should work together for mutual as well as public advantage. This has meant that the trust-busting populism of Teddy Roosevelt has been traded in for something even worse, a kind of economic fascism in which regulation and tax policy combine with regulatory bureaucracies in both government and industry to promote more and more corporate concentration and oligopoly. The latest guise this process has assumed is "reindustrialization," in which proponents now propose to pour billions in tax money and federally guaranteed and sponsored credit into rescuing the nation's heavy industrial base from needed disinvestment.

Yet it is precisely this mixed or planned economy approach that is the greatest invitation to socialization and ultimate government takeover of industry. France is but the latest model for this process. As industry and government grow more and more interdependent through regulation and tax subsidies, it becomes only a matter of time before they are merged in all but name and the private sector gradually disappears in a vast and loosely coordinated bureacratic monopoly, where it is difficult to find the line of demarcation between government and industry and where the resulting mixed economy ceases to be responsive to anyone or anything except its own bureacratic needs. At this point real freedom is lost.

After all, when we lose our economic freedoms, our civil rights don't mean much any more either. As F. A. Hayek reminds us: "Freedom of action, even in humble things, is as important as freedom of thought. To extol the value of intellectual liberties at the expense of the value of the liberty of doing things would be like treating the crowning part of an edifice as the whole."

One of the great ironies and contradictions of our time is that even as Congress and the courts were preoccupied with the extension of civil rights and the protection of free speech under the 1st and 14th Amendments, government at all levels was taking more and more of our economic freedoms and property rights away, with the benign acquiescence of the Supreme Court itself. This is the theme of a 1981 book by Professor Bernard Siegan, *Economic Liberties and the Constitution*, in which he writes:

> Probably no change has been so drastic as that which occurred in the early 1940s, when the Supreme Court abandoned judicial review of economic and social legislation, review which it had carried out during much of its existence. Laws fixing prices, entry and output, or otherwise restricting the production and distribution of goods and services which could not have passed constitutional muster under the prior standard, have little difficulty surviving under the contemporary court's rulings.

Perhaps the greatest failure of both liberals and conservatives has been in not recognizing that civil rights and economic rights are essentially indivisible. On the one hand, conservatives, who have always aggressively defended property and economic rights, have nearly always dragged their feet on civil and human rights. On the other hand, liberals, who have championed civil rights so successfully, have turned around and routinely legislated away the most fundamental economic rights, destroying due process in the whole area of property with almost casual abandon.

As a result, even as the country was making strides toward greater civil liberties for minorities, these same minorities were discovering their economic opportunities and rights progressively curtailed by the growing welter of government regulations and government-sanctioned monopolies. Fortunately, there is now a broad-based consensus developing among liberals and conservatives that much economic regulation has produced more problems than it has solved and has usually worked to favor special interests over general interests.

The most powerful buzz-word in Washington now is *deregulation*, and one of the leading exponents of it is Senator Edward M. Kennedy (no free-market zealot), who on 1 March 1978 told the Senate that "the problems of our economy have occurred, not as an outgrowth of laissez-faire, unbridled competition. They have occurred under the guidance of federal agencies, and under the umbrella of federal regulations." As a result of Kennedy's early leadership in this area and Ronald Reagan's commitment to it, we are now embarked on the essential course of trying to undo a vast amount of the anticompetitive damage that excessive federal regulation has done to the free markets and especially to the small businesses of the country.

Yet Professor Siegan argues that this process of deregulation would never have been necessary if the U.S. Supreme Court had been doing its job of challenging the lawmakers and protecting economic rights all along. To make his case, Siegan examines the large body of economic cases between 1890 and 1930, when the high court repeatedly threw out federal and state laws and regulations whose ultimate effect was to reduce competition, and thereby hurt the consumer. He suggests that it was no accident that this was the period of the nation's fastest economic growth. Since then, Siegan says, "Both federal and state regulation have often resulted in a reduction of economic efficiency, a misallocation of resources, and the redistribution of income from consumers to the regulated group (industry or commerce)." Ironically, we find that the people who are always harmed by regulation are the poor, the very people whose interests regulations are theoretically designed to help.

Prior to 1940 the high court understood this all very well. A prime example was the case of *New State Ice Co.* v. *Liebman* (1923), in which an Oklahoma state statute had declared that the manufacture and sale of ice is a "public business." It made it a misdemeanor to engage in the business without a "certificate of public convenience." The bill had, not surprisingly, been backed by the existing ice-making industry to keep out new competitors. When Liebman began selling ice out of his own new plant, he was taken to court by his competitor, New York Ice, and enjoined from operating his business. The Supreme Court properly threw out this anticompetitive statute by a 6–2 decision, in which Justice Sutherland observed, "The aim [of the statute] is not to encourage competition, but to prevent it, not to regulate business, but to preclude persons from engaging in it."

Justice Sutherland's perceptive observation of 1923 still applies to most state and federal economic regulations. They are almost invariably designed to protect the interests of the regulated industry at the expense of competition and the consumer.

Unfortunately, more than 40 years of solid judicial defense of competition and the economic rights of due process came to an abrupt halt, beginning with the ominous *Nebbia* v. *New York* decision of 1934, when the high court upheld a minimum-price-fixing arrangement on milk designed by the New York Legislature and the milk producers to prevent competition. Nebbia, a small store in Rochester, wanted to sell milk below the nine-cent legal minimum, but he lost his appeal by a 5–4 decision, which Siegan calls "historically significant, in that it signaled the approaching end of economic due process." It also paved the way for such government inequities as "fair-trade laws," food price supports, minimum wages, and the destructive price controls on energy which directly led to OPEC and the energy crisis of the 1970s.

Unfortunately, the majority opinion in *Nebbia* was that "due process demands only that the law be not unreasonable or arbitrary." As a result of this seminal judicial abdication of economic rights, Congress and legislatures ever since have been passing laws and regulations that violate our economic liberties on everything from right-to-work to legalized price-fixing, all with constitutional impunity and with *Nebbia* as a precedent.

Siegan argues, "There is little pragmatic basis for denying the Framers' intentions to secure economic liberties by restraining governmental author-ity." Yet governmental authority in economic matters is even now increas-ingly sanctioned, and the courts are encouraged to regard property rights as less important, less "inalienable," than civil rights, when in fact the two must be regarded as inseparable.

Certainly, Karl Marx understood that the greatest threat to his own totalitarian utopia was the basic idea of economic and property rights: "The theory of communism may be summed up in one sentence: Abolish all private property."

Even as we recoil from Marxist absolutes of this kind, we realize that the whole process of government regulation can quickly become a thinly veiled pretext for abolishing private property, from forced energy conservation in homes to forced expropriation of factories through costly rules written in Washington, to the spurious argument that tax exemptions are in fact government subsidies.

The danger, as Milton Friedman has pointed out, is that Americans are much too complacent about their basic freedoms. They think they will always have them, that liberty is a natural state of mankind. But, he warns:

That is very far from being the natural state of mankind. On the contrary, it is an extremely unusual situation. If one looks back through history, in any place on the globe, one finds that the natural state of mankind in most periods in history has been tyranny and misery . . . the periods and places in which there has been something approaching a free society have been few and far between.

Friedman blames this complacence about liberty on the academic community: "We have been in the forefront of persuading the public at large that the doctrine of individual responsibility is a false doctrine, that the source of all good is Big Brother in Washington."

Because such utopian dreams start from a collective view of mankind, they utterly fail to account for the most outstanding characteristic of both nature and mankind—individuality—that is behind the innate drive for liberty. No two leaves are identical, no two grains of sand or drops of water are the same, no two atoms are precisely alike. And in all this incredibly diverse and infinitely variegated creation of ours, there are no more individualistic entities than human beings.

This infinite individuality absolutely defies the possibility of ever creating a successful collective human utopia. What makes one man supremely happy drives another to distraction. One man's heaven is another man's hell. Yet it is precisely this drive of individuality that is the real source of our nation's prosperity, the genuine capital of an economy that is progressively moving from the physical to the metaphysical, from matter to mind.

For more than 20 years now, the annual proliferation of new economic regulations has had the effect of taking more and more of our property and economic rights away and, in the process, destroying that initiative that is so basic to economic growth and individual development. As Professor Hayek argues: The freedom to do things is as important as the freedom to think or speak things.

If we give up the free ability to do things, we will soon, as we have observed in Russia, stop thinking things as well. That means the end of true economy, in spirit as well as in mind.

7

Social Spending, Subsidies, and the Pursuit of Poverty

The wisdom of Solomon warns us that "As [a man] thinketh in his heart, so is he." Psychologists contend that our models of thought tend to become our life experience. Individuals oriented to thoughts of success tend to succeed. Individuals oriented to thoughts of failure and self-doubt tend to fail.

As it is with individuals, so it is with nations—which are aggregates of individual thinking. National moods and national preoccupations tend to become national experience and direction. If this is so, the United States may be headed slowly but surely for the poorhouse. In just a few years, national preoccupation with poverty—indeed, the glorification of it—to a surprising degree has replaced Horatio Alger and individual achievement as the national model.

While we should certainly welcome a shift in emphasis from purely material success to compassion for the less fortunate, it seems increasingly clear, both in politics and in the media, that we are now far too preoccupied with poverty and far too scornful of abundance. It must be clear that a nation that becomes preoccupied with lack will inevitably lack.

What also troubles even the social planners (not to mention taxpayers) is the tendency of the most well-intentioned government social programs to institutionalize the problems they are supposed to solve. For example, despite steadily rising rates of employment, we always seem to come out of recessions with much higher levels of income support than when we went into them, and even economic recovery doesn't seem to reduce this load, as it once did.

Take the case of food stamps. In 1973 we *sold* them to some 8.2 million recipients at a total net cost of $2.4 billion. In 1975, at the depth of our worst recession, the number of recipients understandably soared to 15 million and the cost to $5.6 billion. But by 1979, four years into a booming recovery, with employment ratios at record highs, food stamps were being *given* to 18.2 million recipients, at a cost of $6.8 billion—and in 1980 the food stamp program cost $9.2 billion for an estimated 22 million recipients. Some 40% more people were receiving them at the height of economic recovery than at the depth of the 1974–75 recession. Yet when President Reagan attempted even modestly to reverse the spiral, by cutting a million of the recipients off the roster and by limiting food stamps to those earning less than $11,800 per year, he was roundly accused of "cruelty to the poor." This attack was politically powerful and effective even though the level of social spending in 1982 was more than double (as a share of GNP) what it was in the Kennedy-Johnson administrations.

Although many social programs now seem desirable, indeed essential, for the truly helpless, the evidence is mounting that we are moving more and more of our total population into a psychological attitude of dependency and away from self-reliance. The effect of this is not only to change our national psyche but to promote economic and social policies that breed more poverty.

From 1960 to 1981 the nation's spending on human services and social-welfare programs grew from $30 billion a year to more than $500 billion—a sixteenfold increase. Yet during the years 1970–80, for the first time in our nation's postwar history, 4 million more people slipped below the poverty line than climbed above it. And since 1970, largely because of this rapid growth in social-welfare spending—and the taxation and inflation that have gone with it—the average individual worker's after-tax wages have actually declined about 8%—another dubious first. The war on poverty seems now to be impoverishing us!

There can be little doubt that Americans are compassionate and generous people. Every opinion poll shows that the vast majority of Americans still strongly support the goal of eliminating poverty. Yet these same polls now indicate a growing doubt as to the ability of massive government social-spending programs to accomplish this goal. The steady erosion of public support for government social spending over the last four or five years was reflected in the willingness of the 1981 Congress to make significant cuts in social spending—even as the defense budget was increased. Polls showed that over two thirds of Americans supported these cuts and nearly half "strongly" supported them. Over 75% favored "basic changes" or cutbacks in food stamps, for example. Nearly 60% favored changing or dropping CETA altogether.

Does this erosion indicate a decline of public compassion and sensitivity in the "me" generation, or, as one religious program panelist suggested recently, "an immoral attitude about the needs of the poor"? Or is it rather a growing perception that government social programs may be doing more to confirm poverty than to heal it—that the best solution for poverty lies in a strong, growing economy? This perception is more than selfishness, as some have suggested. It is well supported in fact.

Table 7-1 shows that the greatest percentage of progess in the reduction of U. S. poverty took place before 1966, before the Johnson Great Society antipoverty programs took effect and when social spending at all government levels still took less than 13% of our total GNP. During that period (1950–66) the total poverty population was cut by 17 million persons—from 30% of the population to 14.7%, a 50% drop.

As Table 7-2 and Chart 7-A show, the acceleration of the Great Society programs in the late 1960s marked the end of America's dramatic progress

TABLE 7-1

SOCIAL SPENDING AND POVERTY, 1950-80

(in percentages)

	% of population living below poverty line	Social spending as % of GNP	Total tax burden on GNP	Federal spending burden on GNP
1950	30.1	8.9	21.3	15.4
1955	25.9	9.6	25.3	17.4
1960	22.2	10.5	27.6	18.7
1966	14.7	12.7	28.4	19.4
1970	12.6	15.2	31.7	20.6
1974	11.2	17.6	32.4	21.5
1977	11.6	19.6	33.0	21.0
1980	13.0	19.8	33.1	22.5

SOURCES: U.S. Social Security Administration; President's Economic Message, 1981.

From 1950 to 1966 each point of added social spending produced 4 points of poverty reduction.

From 1966 to 1977 each point of added social spending produced only 0.4 point of poverty reduction.

against poverty. The Census Bureau may have written the final epitaph to this social experiment when it reported that the 1980 median family income "suffered the biggest drop for any year since just after World War II"—after inflation, a loss of 5.5%. The same report showed that 13% of Americans now live below the poverty line, *up* from 12.6% in 1970, with 29.2 million poor, compared with 25.4 million in 1970.

This capped a decade during which federal social spending soared from 7.6% of GNP to 13%. Despite (or because of) this massive growth in social spending,

- 4 million more Americans fell below the poverty line;
- 2 million more black Americans fell below the poverty line;
- the median income of black families declined by 8%;
- the median income of white families grew only 1.3% *before* taxes.

It was the worst performance against poverty of any decade in U. S. history except for the Great Depression, and was in sharp contrast with the decade of the 1960s, when, despite social spending that averaged *half* the level of the 1970s,

- 14 million Americans climbed out of poverty, including 4 million blacks;
- the rate of poverty dropped from 22% to 12% for all Americans and from 56% to 32% for blacks;
- the median family income in constant dollars rose by 34% for all Americans and 54% for black Americans.

Thus the social agenda that had as its main purpose the reduction of poverty, particularly for minorities, succeeded only in making it worse.

One can look at this record and wonder why most black Americans, and their leadership, still regard the end of the Great Society era as dangerous to their economic health. Particularly when, as the dotted trend line on the chart shows, had we only continued the progress and policies of the 1960s,

TABLE 7-2

PROGRESS AGAINST POVERTY

(population in millions; income in constant 1979 dollars)

	Number below poverty line		Median family income	
	Total	Blacks	Whites	Blacks
1960	39.5	11.1	$14,301	$ 7,917
1970	25.4	7.1	19,134	12,180
1980	29.2	9.2	19,449	11,252
Percentage change 1960-70	−36%	−36%	+34%	+54%
Percentage change 1970-80	+15%	+30%	+2%	−8%

SOURCES: U.S. Bureau of the Census; U.S. Bureau of Labor Statistics.

another 15 million could have been lifted out of poverty in the 1970s, including 4 million blacks.

What makes this interesting is to note that the steepest reduction in poverty coincided (1963-67) with the across-the-board tax-rate cuts and business tax-cuts enacted during the Kennedy-Johnson administration. Chart 7-A demonstrates vividly the contrasting results of the two different economic policies.

Rising Tide vs. Canal Locks

We have apparently reached the point where government social spending may actually be generating poverty instead of reducing it, by slowing down overall economic growth (through taxation and inflation) and by reducing the relative size of the total economic pie. John F. Kennedy's "rising tide" of the 1960s has apparently been turned into the stagnant "canal locks" of the 1970s and early 1980s.

The inefficiency of our War on Poverty becomes self-evident when we consider that:

- Between 1950 and 1955 we added only $7,165 in new annual social spending for each additional person lifted out of poverty.
- Between 1955 and 1960 that incremental cost dropped to $4,143; and between 1960 and 1966 it dropped again to only $2,920. Very modest growth in social spending accompanied massive improvements in the poverty situation.
- But after the War on Poverty started, the social cost per person raised out of poverty suddenly jumped to $16,491 in 1966–70 and to $167,939 per year in 1970–77; and by 1980 that increment had turned negative as total poverty rose by over 4 million.

To put it another way, prior to the War on Poverty (1950–66) each additional percentage point of social spending "produced" (coincided with) a full 4 percentage points of poverty reduction. (At that time most social

CHART 7-A

PROGRESS AGAINST POVERTY

(in millions)

Number
below
poverty line

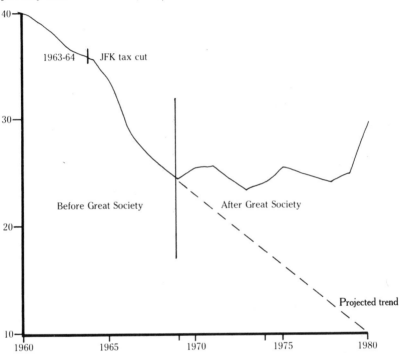

SOURCE: U.S. Bureau of the Census.

spending was on education or retirement.) But after 1966 this "efficiency" fell dramatically, to less than four tenths of a point in poverty reduction for every percentage point increase in social spending. And after 1975 social spending actually turned counterproductive, with poverty population levels rising while social spending soared. (During this latter period, most social spending was in the form of income-transfer payments.)

When we look at the actual economic record, it is increasingly clear that the worst thing that has ever happened to the poor in America (as well as to everyone else) has been the excessive rise in social spending, taxation, and inflation since the Great Society was legislated in 1967–68, because it apparently aborted the real progress being made in poverty reduction, which the Kennedy tax cuts had accelerated.

Without suggesting that we now abolish all of those antipoverty programs, I believe that there is powerful economic evidence that judicious reduction in the high-growth rates of social spending, plus reductions in marginal tax rates, may be the very best thing we can do, not only for the nation's economy, productivity, and inflation, but for its poor population, as well. This, of course, is the exact opposite of the "conventional wisdom" with which the Reagan budget cuts were assaulted in 1981–82.

The Compassion Trap

In 1980 *The Boston Globe* carried an editorial whose principal thrust was "the need, in these times of tax-cutting, for a compassionate approach to welfare spending." It was a liberal response to the mounting conservative fervor for the Massachusetts Proposition 2½ property-tax-cutting referendum. "Compassion" in this particular case was further defined as support for a significant rise in the basic welfare-benefit levels—a rise which undeniably would add several thousand more families to the Aid to Families with Dependent Children (AFDC) program roster in a state that had already had one of the highest such caseloads in the nation.

At about the same time, in another edition, a *Globe* columnist, Mike Barnicle, told the heartrending story of a 101-year-old man living in a Boston housing project, afraid to go out, or let others come in, because he was still recovering from a brutal assault by a gang of teenagers living in the project. Barnicle described the byzantine skills of these child-hoodlums as they found ingenious ways to terrorize and despoil the paltry funds of the elderly, turning their lives into a long nightmare of barricaded terror. In this milieu one wonders whether "compassion" and welfare are as synonymous as the liberal press would suggest.

Table 7-3 shows the astonishing correlation between the spiraling rise in the number of welfare families in this country and the equally rapid rise in teenage crime, teenage unemployment, and the percentage of children born to unmarried mothers. Although we clearly cannot infer direct causality, we are obliged to note its ugly coincidence.

In 1950, when about 1% of all American families were on welfare (AFDC), U.S. teenage unemployment averaged about 12% and among blacks about 13%. At that time, the under-18 groups accounted for less than 12% of all crime and the nation's illegitimacy rate was under 4% (under 17% for blacks).

By 1976 nearly 6% of all families were on welfare (AFDC)—a rise of 500%. And in the midst of one of the highest overall employment ratios in our nation's history (58%), teenage unemployment had risen to nearly 20% and was well above 40% for young blacks in most urban areas. With that level of unemployment, is it really any wonder that teenage crime (under 18) had shot up to 26% of all crime and nearly 47% of all violent crime? Nor is this level of crime any surprise when we look at what has happened to the U.S. family and to the illegitimacy rates. By 1982 over 55% of all black children were being born out of wedlock, in fatherless homes.

TABLE 7-3

SOCIOLOGICAL DESTRUCTION AND WELFARE

(in percentages; families in thousands)

	AFDC families	Illegitimate births		Teenage unemploy- ment		Crime by youths under 18
		White	Black	White	Black	
1950	651	1.7	16.8	10.8	12.9	11.8
1960	803	2.3	21.6	14.7	24.0	14.4
1965	1,054	3.9	25.5	12.9	23.3	18.9
1970	2,552	5.7	34.9	13.7	25.0	24.8
1975	3,553	6.8	43.6	18.9	35.4	25.7
1976	3,571	7.7	45.2	17.3	36.0	26.2
% change	449%	353%	170%	60%	179%	122%

SOURCES: U.S. Bureau of the Census; Statistical Abstract, 1977.

When we look at these figures, we can reasonably conclude that the present welfare system has been almost as destructive to the black American family as slavery itself. It is apparently equally destructive to the more than 50% of all welfare families who are white, and this, in turn, is promoting poverty and declining income.

The best proof of this is cited by George Gilder in *Wealth and Poverty*, where he points out that "divorced, separated and single men of all races work 20% fewer hours than married men, and even with the same age and [professional] credentials bachelors earn less than 60% as much money as husbands. . . ." In other words, being married spurs greater work, more achievement, and more economic productivity. It should therefore not be surprising that as the American family has begun to break down over the last decade, the nation's real income and productivity have fallen with it.

Since female-headed households, like unrelated single men, earn on average about half as much income as traditional male-female married families, it is not surprising that median family income, after growing a whopping 37% in the 1960s, grew only 2% in the 1970s—as the nation's divorce rate shot up from 10% of all women in 1965 to nearly 23% in 1980.

This family breakdown has been particularly devastating for black Americans, whose traditional family formation, after rushing forward in the 1960s, fell apart in the last decade, declining from 64% married in 1970 to only 52% in 1980. This shocking breakdown in traditional black families is probably the primary reason for the 2-million-person rise in black poverty in the 1970s, after such excellent progress in the 1960s.

It may come as a surprise to both blacks and whites to know that when one compares traditional families (husband-wife-children), blacks in 1980 earned 90% of the median income of comparable whites, up dramatically from 71% in 1970. This means that black nuclear families made far more real economic progress in the 1970s than their white counterparts, with real incomes rising nearly 30%. But because of the enormous rise of female-headed black households, the average black household steadily lost ground in the 1970s, with overall median black family income actually falling by 5%.

Both George Gilder and Thomas Sowell now argue that the biggest reason for black poverty today is not discrimination, but sociological breakdown in family life—too many single men and female-headed households. Gilder says, "There are proportionately twice as many black as white *single* men. If the differences between blacks and whites are corrected for marital status, the gap between the earnings of black and white males of truly comparable family background and credentials completely disappears."

As Harvard Professor Martin Kilson (himself a black) argues in *The Public Interest* (Summer 1981), the most important factor in black poverty is "the seemingly endemic incapacity of [female-headed families] to foster social mobility comparable to husband-wife and male-headed families." He points to the "enormous expansion of female-headed households during the past two decades," from about 25% of black families to more than 40% today, as the principal reason for persistent black poverty.

Even so, economist Morton Paglin argues that raw-income figures mask the fact that when one includes the "in-kind" benefits (including food stamps and Medicaid), the number actually living below the U.S. poverty line declines to less than 6% of the population, a figure now supported by the Census Bureau in a study released in the spring of 1982. This means that with only modest improvements in the basic family structure in our society, so-called financial poverty would all but disappear as a serious social issue.

Paglin's research caused Irving Kristol to ask, "Since we have all but eliminated financial poverty, why hasn't anyone noticed?" Why, he asks further, does poverty seem so much more pervasive and cruel today than it did 25 or 30 years ago?

The vast burned-out sections of the South Bronx in New York, the block after block of deserted buildings and blight in Detroit, the boarded store-fronts of Roxbury in Boston, the sweep of desolation on West Madison Street in Chicago, the ravages of Liberty City in Miami, tell us that while the exigencies of financial poverty may have been softened by the so-called compassion of welfare, the poverty of the spirit has risen to epidemic proportions. It now threatens to engulf us and permanently destroy the legitimate upward aspirations of the poor, particularly those of blacks and other minorities.

The Message from Miami

Anyone who wrote off the 1980 Miami riots in Liberty City as merely an isolated expression of rage at a particular case of racial injustice was missing the point. Although the evidence of police brutality and justice denied was the flashpoint, the $200-million destructive spree was, in fact, a highly selective expression of outrage at both the white and the black power structures. While white-owned businesses took the severest beating, prosperous black businesses also were hit hard. When black leaders Andrew Young and Jesse Jackson came to Miami to commiserate, they, too, were treated to a cold, even hostile reception by their own people.

The message from Miami seemed clear: "Whatever you're doing for us (or to us), it isn't working. Things are getting worse for blacks, not better."

TABLE 7-4
IMPACT OF WELFARE ON EMPLOYMENT, 1955-78
(in percentages)

	Employment ratios		Unemployment ratios		Welfare (AFDC) ratios	
	Blacks	Whites	Blacks	Whites	Blacks	Whites
1955	58.6	55.1	8.0	4.0	5.4	0.9
1960	57.9	54.9	10.2	4.9	7.4	1.1
1965	56.8	54.8	8.1	4.1	9.8	1.4
1970	55.5	56.2	8.2	4.5	20.8	2.9
1974	53.0	57.5	9.9	5.0	21.4	3.3
1978	53.3	59.3	11.9	5.2	19.8	2.7
% change	−9	+8	+49	+30	+267	+200

SOURCES: U.S. Department of Health and Human Services; U.S. Bureau of Labor Statistics.

Their perception was accurate. From 1968 to 1980 the number of black families living below the poverty line actually increased by nearly 25%, and the total percentage of blacks under the poverty level rose somewhat from 32% to 33%. By contrast, in the same period, the percentage of whites living below the poverty line dropped from 9% to less than 7%. The War on Poverty was not color-blind. Although affirmative action helped push the percentage of blacks earning over $25,000 from 14% in 1968 to nearly 20% in 1980, the real median income of all black families declined by 10% in the same period. Relative to median white family income, it actually slipped, from 60% in 1968 to less than 58% in 1980. This deterioration took place during a period when government spending on specific urban poverty programs, job programs, and income support (welfare, health care, food stamps) soared to dramatic heights—from $30 billion in 1968 to $190 billion in 1980.

Unfortunately, the major impact of this social spending has apparently been to encourage black Americans to trade in admittedly dead-end jobs for equally dead-end welfare. Prior to 1968, for example, a higher percentage of blacks than whites actually held jobs (employment ratio). Since 1970, however, this has been completely reversed. By the end of 1978 white employment had reached a record level of nearly 60% of the adult population, while the black employment ratio had fallen to a postwar low of 53.3%. Until 1970 black unemployment held steady at about double that of white unemployment; by 1981 it was 130% higher, a 25% deterioration.

A primary reason for this dramatic decline in the black employment ratios seems evident from the welfare ratios, which have risen from only one black family in 20, prior to 1960, to one black family in five in 1978. Given the appallingly low income levels, meniality and drudgery of most black employment in the 1950s and 1960s, it is not surprising that a growing share of the black population simply traded in that rut for welfare. With their income potentials still far below those of whites, they have been able to achieve much better income parity with poor whites by getting and staying on welfare than by facing marginal tax rates of 100%–150% to get off or stay off. Thus, for most poor black Americans, the Great Society was simply a form of "hush money" and not genuine economic development.

The problem is that as welfare benefits have risen, while black earning and job potential have not, the system has become a more and more deadly trap, and, so long as black pay scales remain only 58% of whites,' it is going to be doubly costly for blacks to escape that depressing system, since they will face 40% higher marginal costs (in lost income) in leaving it.

This economic racism explains why poor blacks today are twice as likely as poor whites to be on welfare. In 1978 black AFDC recipients made up about 65% of the total black poverty population, while white AFDC recipients comprised only 22% of the total white poverty population. Poor whites can find and afford low-pay work; poor blacks cannot.

The Need for Real Jobs

There may now be no more dangerous social time-bomb than the egregiously high unemployment rates among black and other minority youths, despite the extraordinary youth employment explosion that actually took place in the 1960s and 1970s.

Contrary to perceptions, total youth employment has actually risen twice as fast as adult employment. In spite of the recent population bulge of the 16-to-19 age group, the ratio of youth employment increased throughout the troubled 1970s to over 48% by the end of 1979—the highest youth employment ratio in U.S. history. This was accomplished while the percentage of this young age group engaged in full-time schooling (college and high school) rose dramatically. In fact, of the 1.52 million unemployed teenagers in 1979, over 720,000—almost half—were students, unavailable for anything but part-time work. So even though the unemployment rate for 16-to-19-year-olds kept rising (because of the baby-boom bulge) to an all-time high (apart from recessions) of 16% in 1979, only 4.9% of all teenagers 16 to 19 were both unemployed and not in school.

In a 1980 summary report on youth employment for the National Bureau of Economic Research (NBER), Professors Richard Freeman and John Wise concluded: "Many commonly held views about youth employment problems are erroneous and . . . have been inadequately understood. Youth unemployment, rather than being widespread among a large proportion of youths is, in fact, concentrated among a small group of youths" (most of them blacks or of other minorities). Or, as Professor Martin Feldstein points out elsewhere, less than 10% of the youth population (16 to 24) now account for more than 50% of all the total youth unemployment.

According to the NBER study, "This relatively small group of youths who are chronically without work . . . are disproportionately black, disproportionately high-school dropouts, and disproportionately residents of poverty areas." In other words, unemployment is not a problem for 90% of young people; but for the 10% in the urban ghettos it is a calamity—and one that developed in the last two decades. In 1977, for example, 44.3% of all white male youths of 16 and 17 had jobs, compared with only 18.9% of black youths of the same ages. For whites this was a 10% improvement over 1954; for blacks it was a 53% *loss*. "This disturbing trend," said the NBER, "is even more troublesome in light of the fact that it is a relatively recent one." Most of it had taken place since the Great Society went into effect in 1967.

Since 1969 employment ratios have plummeted an average of more than 23% for every age and sex grouping of black youths, while unemployment ratios have soared an average of more than 110%; and for the 20-to-24-year-olds, over 150%. Yet since 1968, under a variety of programs, the federal government has invested a cumulative total of more than $80 billion in trying to alleviate high urban unemployment, through job training and public service employment. Over $30 billion of this total has been spent entirely on youth training and employment programs, aimed, in particular, at urban black teenagers, whose unemployment rates have been 40%–50% in some areas. The more we have spent, the worse the unemployment situation for black teenagers has become, with unemployment ratios for black male youths actually rising by an average of 116%—to levels more than triple their white male youth counterparts.

It would appear from these dismal results that not only is social spending not producing gains for black youth employment—it may actually be making things worse. A variety of studies now demonstrate that unemployment is usually more a function of lifestyle and family structure than of family income.

The NBER studies by Freeman and Wise tend to support this conclusion, because they show that family background, as measured by income, "shows little relationship to [youth] employment." In other words, they say, "the children of the working poor seem to go out and get jobs just as effectively as the children of the working well-to-do, black or white." The big difference comes with welfare: "Youths in households on welfare tend to have jobs less often than youths from other families, as do youths in households headed by females. Role models have more to do with youth unemployment than poor income." Thus, it is not surprising that the spectacular rise of welfare dependency among blacks has exactly coincided with an equally devastating rise in black teenage unemployment, a rise which has not been matched among white youths.

Not that welfare is exclusively black—far from it. But blacks still account for more than 46% of all AFDC families, even though they account for less than 12% of the population.

The Marginal Tax of Welfare

It is also unfortunately true that every move to raise welfare benefit levels, no matter how humane the motivation, invariably raises the number of those who become eligible for such aid and increases the disincentive (marginal tax) to choose full-time work over welfare.

From 1973 to 1977 Massachusetts AFDC benefits rose about 7% more than the after-tax income of hourly-paid employees (nationwide). It is therefore no surprise that during that period the state's welfare rolls rose 46%, or four times the national growth rate of 11%. However, since 1977, Massachusetts's AFDC benefits have risen far less than gross weekly wages and much less than the rate of inflation. As a result, the AFDC rolls abruptly leveled off at 121,000, and then fell to 115,000, as the squeeze of inflation, coupled with record-high Massachusetts help-wanted advertising, made even marginal employment steadily more attractive and preferable to welfare. The direct result of this was not only more people who dropped out of welfare for full-time work, but a dramatic increase in those who augmented their welfare benefits by full- or part-time work, as 20% of them now do. By the end of 1982, with the help of the Reagan budget cuts, total AFDC case loads in Massachusetts had been reduced to 96,000, as AFDC benefits had fallen from third in the nation to twelfth. Massachusetts discovered what states with already-low welfare benefits had learned, that low benefits act as a stimulus to work, while high benefits act as disincentives to work.

There is nothing mysterious about this. Elaborate HEW studies in Trenton, Denver, and Seattle, from 1975 to 1977, proved that whenever benefits were guaranteed at levels approximating the poverty line, the total hours worked in those cities dropped by 10%–12% because such benefit levels act as disincentives to work. Conversely, whenever benefits are lowered, hours worked rise in direct proportion.

In part, this is because people on welfare, in general, tend to be low skilled, commanding only modest levels of pay in the work force. Massachusetts found that in 1978 some 86% of all new AFDC recipients had averaged $3.34 per hour in private employment. That amounted to about $8,110 per year, before taxes, or about $7,100 after taxes, but before child care, commutation, and additional clothing expenses—for a net at-home income of below $6,500. Since the 1978 average Massachusetts AFDC family benefits (including food stamps and Medicaid) amounted to nearly $7,000, AFDC household heads were being asked to take a loss in effective income just to work 40 hours a week at a low-level job. Who can blame anyone for resisting that forbidding option and choosing welfare?

That is why experts on welfare benefits say that in most of the top-benefit states the effective "marginal tax" rates on welfare household heads of going back to work range from 80% to 150%. The net cash gains from working (as opposed to not working) range from tiny to negative. That also helps to explain why, in 1980, of the 34.7% new cases opened each year in Massachusetts, 23% (or two thirds) are cases being reopened after a lapse of six months or less. In other words, welfare mothers do want to get off and stay off welfare, but often they just can't afford to because the marginal costs in lost income of doing so are much too steep—and the higher the benefits go, no matter how humane the reasons for raising them, the more difficult it becomes to reduce welfare case loads permanently, even in a strong economy. Welfare then becomes a block to employment and economic growth.

An analysis of the 15 highest-benefit states versus the 15 lowest-benefit states in 1978 found that there is a surprisingly strong connection between levels of unemployment and levels of welfare benefits. The 15 highest AFDC-benefit states not only had a 20% higher share on welfare (5.7% versus 4.7% for the nation), but they had a higher level of unemployment (7% versus 6% for the nation). Conversely, the states with the lowest benefit levels had much lower levels of both welfare dependency and unemployment. These 15

TABLE 7-5

WELFARE VS. EMPLOYMENT, 1970-78

(in percentages and in weighted averages)

	15 highest benefit states	15 lowest benefit states	U.S. averages
% on welfare (1978)	5.7	3.6	4.7
% unemployed (1978)	7.0	5.5	6.0
% minority unemployment (1978)	12.3	10.6	1.9
Average job growth (1970-78)	10.6	46.6	21.0
Average personal income growth (1970-78)	17.1	57.5	32.1

SOURCES: U.S. Department of Health and Human Services; U.S. Bureau of Labor Statistics; U.S. Bureau of the Census.

lowest welfare-benefit states were providing double the level of economic growth (jobs and personal income) of the nation and more than triple the economic growth in the highest-benefit states. During the 1981–82 recession Texas had both the lowest unemployment rate (5.8%) and the lowest welfare benefits. That is why any move to raise welfare benefits, or to standardize them nationally, no matter how humanely intended, must be viewed in the light of what it will certainly do to increase welfare rolls, to raise unemployment, and to curtail real economic progress, individual and collective, not to mention what the "welfare option" does to institutionalize the very poverty and family breakdown we say we are trying to arrest.

Disincentives, Disabilities, and Social Security

The Golden Rule has been interpreted in recent times almost solely as requiring those who have done well to help others from their own largess; and that is the primary meaning of this moral law. But too often it has been perverted into a justification for imposing one's dependency on others by law, thus bringing both down to a lower level. Should not the Golden Rule also imply that one of our primary duties to our fellow human beings is *not* to become a burden to another, just as we would not have another become a burden on us?

For example, one of the most heartening developments in our time is the growing realization that people with physical handicaps can and want to learn not only to pull their own weight but to make valuable contributions to society in many forms of productive activity. Even as this is going on, however, the rapidly rising benefits to the disabled (and for early retirement under Social Security) have been luring vast numbers of good workers aged 50 and over into the ranks of the pensioned-disabled or prematurely retired.

It was this situation that underlay the Reagan administration's politically unpopular proposal in 1981 to cut Social Security benefits for early retirees and to tighten up on disability eligibility. Instead of reneging on basic benefits by raising the retirement age three years, the administration intended to make early retirement less appealing by cutting prospective benefits from 80% at age 62 to 55%—delaying the 80% rate by 20 months.

Not only would this reduce outlays and their rate of growth, it would attack one of the most serious problems in the nation's work force—productivity.

Over the past 20 years there has been a dramatic drop in one of the most productive work-force age groups. Males from ages 55 to 64 went from a labor-force participation rate of 85% in 1960 to less than 70% in 1980. This was the single most dramatic change in work-force composition in U.S. history; and it is no accident that it began to take place after 1962 and accelerated after 1965.

It was in 1962 that Congress first authorized early retirement at 80% of benefit levels at age 62, and it was in 1964–65 that Congress began the long process of accelerating both the benefits and the eligibility ease for Social Security disability pensions. The effect of these actions was stunning. Disability retirements soared from 455,000 in 1960 to 2.9 million in 1978 and the number of disability beneficiaries increased from 543,000 in 1960 to nearly 5.8 million in 1978, a nearly 1,000% rise.

The total rise in disability beneficiaries alone between 1970 and 1980 was 128%, during a period when the total population in the 45–64 age range rose less than 7%. This is not surprising since the average benefit payment for disability rose by 180%, almost double the inflation rise of 111%. In fact, between 1970 and 1980 no other income-recipient group in America did better in keeping pace with inflation than Social Security retirees. Their average benefits rose by 184%, against an inflation of 111%, while the average pay of the American worker rose 96%. Put another way, during a decade when the average American worker lost a full 8% in real wages, the average Social Security retiree actually gained 35% in real income. That's why, by the last half of the 1970s, more and more workers from age 45 to 64 were choosing either disability benefits or early retirement augmented by underground cash earnings.

Vital statistics suggest that Americans are living longer and more healthy lives every year. Thus there would seem to be no medical premise to support a 980% increase in disability and early retirements over the past two decades. Taxpayers may be surprised to learn that in 1982 the federal government spent over $50 billion on all disability pensions for persons under the age of 65 (including veterans' and other programs).

What makes this figure scary is not its sheer size (7% of the total federal budget) but its trend, up over 40% in three years alone (1978–81)—and more than 2400% since 1960. The sad truth is that a rapidly growing number of Americans are being encouraged to accept permanent disability as an economically advantageous way of life. The Government Accounting Office (GAO) found in 1981 that over 20% of all Social Security disabled pensioners were not actually medically disabled. Proof of this was contained in a CBS documentary on "60 Minutes," on 13 February 1977, which tracked down the prodigious growth in disability retirements on the part of federal employees.

According to the Office of Management and Budget, the number of disabled federal employees rose over 43% in three years (1978–81), during a time when federal employment actually declined. And in 1982 American taxpayers were expected to pay out over $800 million for federal civilian employees' disability benefits for individuals under the age of 55, and over $4 billion for all civil service disability retirements. As "60 Minutes" documented, a surprising number of these recipients are not actually disabled. Many are using stress, anxiety, pressure, and mental tensions as the basis for their pension benefits, and, as the GAO report confirmed, 20%–30% of these claims don't wash.

At the heart of this disability explosion is the fact that the federal government now pays its employees from 40% to as much as 75% of their full-time salary in tax-exempt disability pensions. Back in 1977 CBS located a $25,000-a-year 35-year-old air controller who had somehow managed to retire on a disability pension of $18,750 a year, tax free. This meant that, as CBS found, some of these "disabled" people were receiving a larger net income, at home, than they could earn at their jobs, and with cost-of-living increases their pensions were rising faster than their on-the-job wages.

Understandably, in many federal agencies the rate of disability more than tripled in the four years 1977–81, with many departments reporting as high as 15%–20% of their total staff living on full-time disability pensions. In 1980 there were over 400,000 federal civilian employees living on disability pensions, over 13% of the total federal work force. Any fair analysis of these figures suggests that either the nation's physical health is suddenly going downhill at an alarming rate or we are changing our society's whole notion about what constitutes real disability, even as the physically handicapped are reaching out for new dominion and new productivity.

There have in fact been major changes in the tightness and the policing of disability rules and eligibility in both the Social Security and federal pension systems, removing the age requirement in 1960, reducing disability from lifetime to 12 months in 1965, and adding widows in 1965. As a consequence, although there were only four disabled workers per 1,000 in 1965, by 1980 there were eight per 1,000. But both Martin Feldstein and William Hsaio of Harvard believe that it goes beyond eligibility. They suggest that the major reason for the colossal growth in this program is that tax-free benefits have risen nearly twice as fast in real dollars as average weekly pay.

In a very real sense, the experience of the Social Security and federal disability programs like those of our welfare complex has been a paradigm of the way in which this nation has gradually shifted its goals from the pursuit of independence and freedom to the pursuit of security and, ultimately, has moved in the direction of impoverishment and dependence.

In the welter of heated public debate over social spending and the "cruelty" of reducing its future trends, Americans might do well to remember that in the period when the United States made its greatest economic progress in lifting its citizens out of poverty, its welfare burden (as a percentage of GNP) was less than half of its present level—and its economic growth was three times as great.

Breaking the Subsidy Mentality

Our failure to alleviate urban poverty through traditional spending programs reinforces the historical reality that subsidies almost always tend to do more harm than good—especially those given to failing private businesses. The reason is simple: Subsidies are invariably demanded to rescue failing enterprise. If we subsidize failure, we will assuredly get more of it. Every U.S. industry that has had direct subsidies from the government has ultimately been weakened by them. The list is long: shipbuilding, railroads, small farmers, mining, housing, and construction. All are industries that have come to rely too heavily on subsidy for survival, and all are industries in continuous trouble.

Businesses, like people, seldom if ever fail solely because of lack of money. They fail because of lack of ability, judgment, wisdom, ideas, organization, leadership. When these qualities are present, money is seldom a problem. Legitimate private credit can nearly always be obtained. But when these qualities are lacking, money may be hard to come by, as it should be.

There is nothing inherent in money itself—no intelligence, no ideas, no skills, no leadership, no vision—that can solve the fundamental problem. So the money goes down the drain, and everyone loses, including the company (or the individual) being subsidized.

Ray Eppert, former president of Burroughs Corporation, once said: "It is not possible to separate the freedom to fail from the freedom to succeed." The freedom to succeed necessarily *requires* the freedom to fail. If one takes away the freedom to fail, through subsidy or bailout (or other forms of "government security"), one automatically limits the freedom to succeed.

To bail out or subsidize those companies and individuals who fail, we must tax, and therefore punish, those who succeed. As Michael Novak puts it, "The system does not guarantee success. It does guarantee opportunity. It multiplies occasions for luck and good fortune. It is an open, porous, highly mobile system. Downward mobility is as characteristic of it as upward mobility." When government begins bailing out corporate failures, big or small, it is subtly removing the necessity to succeed, and thus ensuring more and more failures and less and less success.

That is why largely government-owned and -managed economies such as Britain's invariably produce less growth and success than those where necessity and incentive, combined with the freedom to fail, encourage success.

As this book was being written, Chrysler Corporation was well into the second billion dollars of government-guaranteed credit. Although the structure of this bailout imposed some useful discipline on the company, its future remains in deep doubt, and the precedent this has set is dangerous, to say the least. The one thing we did not want to do was to reward Chrysler for years of its own (and its unions') misdirecton by punishing the rest of the economy which is, itself, struggling to prosper. Not only does such a bailout unfairly penalize the success of others, but it might just prevent Chrysler from doing the kind of reorganization and rethinking that it must do to become healthy again. That is why bankruptcy and receivership laws are so useful—they often provide a humane way to force basic reforms.

That is not to say we should have been unmindful of the troubles that faced 140,000 Chrysler employees and the larger Chrysler family. But we must ask ourselves: What about the 10,000–20,000 smaller businesses that fail every year, businesses whose total annual lost employment is nearly 200,000? Should we not bail them out, too? Are they really less important, simply because they are smaller?

Of course, if we did bail out all business failures would it be very long before we'd have hundreds of thousands of business junkies living on government handouts and producing goods and services the market doesn't want or need? As Milton Friedman suggested, if we had been bailing out every business that failed because of economic change or mismanagement, we would still have a very large horse-carriage industry.

Lester Thurow argues that failure is more often than not the process through which individuals and companies ultimately achieve success. It's called trial and error—and if investors and creators were not allowed to make mistakes, they could never profit from them. Why then should government interfere with this natural process?

To understand, concretely, why it should *not*, let us look at America's oldest fully subsidized industry, the maritime and shipbuilding (owning) industry. In 1979 taxpayers shelled some $2.3 billion in direct cash subsidies to the U.S. maritime industry, plus another $150 million in direct tax credits. We have been doing this ever since 1946—primarily because the maritime unions have had terrific clout with the Congress. (They were, incidentally, among the largest contributors to Walter Mondale as a U.S. senator—and to President Carter, from whom they extracted direct pledges of support for future tax breaks and subsidies, before they subsequently joined the Reagan bandwagon and began to extract support from the Reagan administration.)

What have these subsidies really done for (or to) the U.S. maritime industry? The record is devastating.

- In 1950, 30% of all waterborne U.S. commerce was under the U.S. flag. Today only 5% is carried in U.S. ships.
- In 1960 the United States owned 19% of all world merchant tonnage. In 1980 we owned less than 4%, and 80% of that was in petroleum tankers.
- In 1950 the U.S. built more than 12% of the world merchant tonnage. In 1981 we built less than 2% of it.

For all intents and purposes, the U.S. maritime and shipbuilding industry is now a permanent welfare client, totally washed up in the world market. Federal subsidies have grown over 600% (from $300 million in 1965 to $2.2 billion in 1979), and as fast as they have grown the industry has fallen apart.

By insulating this industry from failure, we have insured it thoroughly against success. Are we now in danger of doing the same to automobiles? We certainly should have learned enough from our experience with American

TABLE 7-6

WHY FARM SUBSIDIES DON'T WORK

(in billions of dollars)

	Subsidies	Net farm income in current dollars	Net farm income in 1969 constant dollars
1969	$5.3	$14.3	$14.3
1970	4.6	14.2	13.4
1971	3.7	14.6	13.2
1972	4.6	18.7	16.4
1973	4.1	33.3	27.4
1974	1.5	26.1	19.4
1975	0.8	24.3	16.6
1976	1.6	20.0	12.9
1977	4.5	20.4	12.4
1978	6.6	25.8	14.4

SOURCE: U.S. Department of Agriculture 1979 Budget Report.

In 1969-75 net constant farm income went up by 16%, and subsidies went down by 85%.

In 1975-78 net constant farm income went down by 14%, and subsidies went up by 725%.

agriculture where subsidies have been provided for more than 40 years, presumably "to rescue the small family farms." During that period more small farms failed than ever before, as the nation's farm population has dwindled from 9 million in 1950 to less than 4 million today. Massive improvements in technological productivity overwhelmed the subsidy programs. The only thing that subsidies ever accomplished was to hasten the demise of the small farmer and speed up the concentration of the farm conglomerates (which ultimately made the most use of them). But subsidies have never done very much for real farm income. Thus, Table 7-6 shows that as subsidies dropped (as they did from 1969 to 1975), farm income soared; but when subsidies soared (from 1975 to 1978), real farm income actually declined.

Despite serious personal shortcomings, Earl Butz had proved to be an effective Agriculture Secretary. Under his guidance, farmers were gradually weaned away from costly tax subsidies, which dropped from $5.3 billion in 1969 to only $800 million in 1975, the lowest subsidy total in 30 years. Concurrent with this decline—perhaps because of it—net farm income during that period rose from $14.3 billion to $24.3 billion, the best six-year performance in modern American agricultural history.

Unfortunately, ever since Earl Butz put his foot in his mouth and left office unceremoniously, things at the U.S. Department of Agriculture have also been going the wrong way for both farmers and consumers—but most especially for the taxpayers. Under President Carter subsidies again soared to record heights, reaching past the $7-billion mark in the 1981 fiscal year, the last Carter budget, and even after budget cuts they are now running over $10 billion in 1982, the highest in history. Since 1975 farm income has remained virtually at a standstill and, considering inflation, has actually dropped substantially. Both farmers and taxpayers were unhappy and, of course, so were consumers who watched food prices soar in 1977-79 as never before. From 1975 to 1978 farm subsidies went up over 725%, while net real farm income actually dropped by 16%. In 1980 farm income reached its lowest level in two decades and subsidies their highest level.

In the first year of the Carter administration the prices of dairy products were arbitrarily jacked up from 8 to 10 cents a pound by price supports alone, a direct 1977 payoff to the election-generous milk producers. Fortunately, in the spring of 1981 one of the new Reagan administration's first real victories was the withholding of still another round of such dairy price-support hikes, but the basic subsidy still remains, and some commodities (notably sugar) have received new support.

Table 7-6 demonstrates that farm subsidies are the wrong way to go from every standpoint—farmers, consumers, and taxpayers—and that there is a pressing need for the Reagan administration to put together a farm policy that continues to cut farm subsidies as fast as humanely possible and that pushes for a freer market in food, internationally as well as domestically.

If that doesn't happen we might soon see double-digit inflation in food prices again, as well as double-digit subsidies, plus an accelerated flight from the farms by small farmers who don't really benefit from this federal largess. Most subsidies will continue to go (as they always have) to the large corporate farms which have the bureaucratic expertise to make the complex agricultural subsidy programs work for them—and against the rest of us.

In his call for the reindustrialization of America, Columbia sociologist Amitai Etzioni warns that we must not prop up failing industries and companies, a process which he dubs "lemon socialism." And Lester Thurow echoes this warning in his *Zero-Sum Society*: "Disinvestment is what our economy does worst," he declares. "Instead of adopting public policies to speed up the process of disinvestment, we act to slow it down with protection and subsidies for the inefficient." From a conservative economist this would be regarded as heartless, but from liberal Thurow it is perceived as good sense.

Yet both President Carter and President Reagan chose to ignore this good sense completely. In Carter's cosmetically political "economic revitalization" plan in 1980, he fully embraced "lemon socialism" by an unprecedented call to give investment tax credits to companies and industries that were losing money—that is, cash grants from the Treasury. Surprisingly, this "corporate bail-out" plan drew significant support from the liberal press—the same press which correctly condemned Ronald Reagan a year or so later for the "tax-leasing" portion of his 1981 business tax cut—under which losing companies can essentially "sell" their accelerated depreciation allowances to profitable (tax-paying) companies who then use them (in a lease-back arrangement) to reduce their own tax burden.

The effect of such policies is obvious: Companies and industries that are expanding are indirectly taxed to prop up older industries and companies that are failing (such as steel, autos, and textiles), which, instead of making necessary adjustments to their marketing and product strategies, merely use such tax credits or leasing arrangements to provide short-term cash flow, and thereby postpone economic reality.

As Thurow warns, "All of these actions (protections, subsidies, etc.) are designed to provide economic security for someone. Yet each of them imprisons us in a low-productivity area. If we cannot learn to *disinvest*, we cannot compete in the modern growth race."

In a sense, the 1980 Carter tax plan and parts of the Reagan business tax package were sort of a Chrysler-type bailout for the whole U.S. economy—at least the portion of the economy in trouble. That it was seriously entertained and partially enacted should trouble us more. Even as we write, the federal government is still deeply involved in massive lemon socialism, not only through the tax code, but especially through the credit process.

For example, the bailouts of New York City and Chrysler were accomplished by loan guarantees, but the effect of those guarantees was to make it more attractive for investors to put money into failing propositions than into successful ones. Bailing out New York made it more costly for Chicago to borrow money. Bailing out Chrysler made it more expensive for GM and Ford.

That is precisely what the federal government has been doing on a massive scale for the past 30 to 40 years—pouring both subsidies and loan guarantees into otherwise uneconomic activities (especially housing) to the point where the federal government now siphons off nearly 50% of all the new credit available to our economy each year.

It may come as a shock to most Americans to realize that by the end of 1981 the federal government had in force a total of more than $400 billion in guaranteed loans to the private sector and that we are adding to this total at the rate of more than $80 billion a year. This is in addition to the more than $100 billion that the federal government will borrow for itself.

The major share of this federally assisted borrowing goes to the one industry that is in as much trouble as automobiles—housing—yet one of the major reasons for housing's troubles is the inability to get private credit at sensible interest rates. Just as price controls on natural gas led to higher prices for oil, so the subsidized credit for some segments of the housing industry are today being paid for by 16%–18% mortgage money for the private builders and buyers—while the open-ended Section 8 housing-subsidy program (also the recipient of federal credit subsidies) is undermining the entire private rental-housing market.

It is in this way that a kind of creeping lemon socialism is corroding the market viability of every industry it touches, moving them away from the necessity to perform and toward the political barter place of favor and counter favor, lobby and counter lobby, in very much the same way America's poor and minority groups have become the pawns of the federal budget process.

Protectionism

Direct subsidies are by no means the most devastating way in which we pursue poverty in U.S. industry. Tariffs and other forms of protectionism are indirect subsidies by consumers and taxpayers. By restricting competition from more efficient producers abroad, we now protect inefficiency and obsolescence at home. Not only does this ultimately cost the consumer, but instead of protecting jobs it ultimately destroys more of them, because it penalizes the efficient exporter of goods in order to save or protect the overcosted domestic producer.

As Lester Thurow warns, "One man's security [protection] is another man's lack of opportunity. The demands for protection have grown up because, in a real sense, we have abandoned our belief in the virtues of a competitive, unplanned economy . . . At the first sign of trouble, everyone runs to the government looking for protection."

Not long ago a retired Brockton, Massachusetts, industrialist, Harold Geilich, took me to task for being "a free trader," that is, an opponent of the protectionism, quotas, and tariffs designed to save American industries such as autos and steel. Geilich, a pioneer and leader in the now nearly extinct U.S. leather-goods industry, argued: "If free trade, unrestricted on manufactured goods, is followed to its final destination, then what will follow in a highly industrialized society is the complete destruction of every single industry. No other outcome is possible. It took 20 years for steel and autos to bite the dust." Superficially, Geilich has a point. Japan and Germany are both doing a number on the U.S. auto and steel industries, in much the same way the Spanish, Italians, and Asians had done a job on the leather-goods industry. And Japan is hardly a model of reciprocal free trade, with one of the most impenetrable barriers to imports in the free world.

The problem with Geilich's argument is that it deals only with what economists call "first effects." It doesn't look at the longer-term analysis of secondary impacts. We need to understand that when we import a product from abroad, we are paying out U.S. dollars for it. The overseas seller in accepting those dollars has also accepted the obligation either to spend that money on something that we will sell him or to find someone else who will. So long as any overseas sellers are willing to accept U.S. dollars, we don't have to worry, because they will come back to us in the form of orders for U.S. goods.

The basic law of international trade is that the more you import, the more you can and must export; and the more you export, the more you must ultimately import, unless your country goes bankrupt and your currency is no longer worth anything. Those who think this is just theory should look at Table 7-7, which shows that in spite of the massive increase in U.S. imports of automobiles and TV sets from Japan and Germany, our own manufactured exports have risen just as fast. More important, the U.S. manufacturing exports business has grown in direct proportion to our expanded imports of everything, including OPEC oil. Indeed, in some ways, OPEC did our export

TABLE 7-7

THE BOOMING U.S. MANUFACTURED EXPORTS

(all data in current billions of dollars)

Year	Manufactured exports	% of total GNP	Manufactured imports	Balance
1970	$ 29.3	12.3%	$ 25.9	+3.4
1973	44.7	13.5%	45.0	−0.3
1974	63.5	18.8%	56.2	+7.3
1975	70.9	20.2%	51.1	+19.8
1976	77.2	19.1%	64.8	+12.4
1977	80.2	17.4%	76.6	+3.6
1978	94.5	18.3%	100.4	−5.9
1979	116.3	20.6%	112.3	+4.0

SOURCE: U.S. Department of Commerce.

industries a huge favor, by flooding the world market with U.S. currency demand.

In 1973, for example, prior to the full impact of the OPEC price hikes, the U.S. exported only 13.5% of all of its manufactured goods. By 1975 this had grown to 20.2%, and in 1979 reached 20.6%. The faster we increased our imports, the faster we also increased our manufacturing exports. During the 1970s, except for 1973 and 1978, the value of our manufactured exports exceeded the value of our manufactured imports—Japanese cars included. Were it not for the unusual 1979–80 rise in OPEC prices, it is very possible that we would now be running a substantial trade surplus. In fact, we had a substantial trade surplus in 1975, and a modest one in 1976, even after the first increase in OPEC prices.

More important, as economist Paul McCracken points out, 20% of manufacturing jobs in the United States now depend on our export business—up from 6.6% in 1955 to 9.2% in 1970 and 15.5% in 1975. "The United States," he writes, "has been doing surprisingly well as an exporter in recent years, a success story that has been as dramatic as it has been unnoticed." And he notes that our total manufactured-goods exports, as a percentage of "goods GNP," surged from less than 5% in the 1950s to nearly 14% in 1980—a huge bonus from free world trade.

McCracken argues that free trade is as important to economic progress for the nation as it is for the world. "The most important feature of a liberal, market-organized economy's industrial policy is that it has an effective and objective way to sort out winners and losers. If something new brought to the marketplace is preferred by customers, it prevails, and the old fades out," he said. "The dynamics of the liberal economies, therefore, mean that productive resources are continuously being shifted from older to more efficient ones." Through this process disinvestment is accelerated and productivity is encouraged. Unfortunately, protectionism resists this process by artificially subsidizing unproductive domestic industries at the expense of the consumer and, more particularly, at the expense of shifting our domestic capital to new and more productive U.S. industries, which could export much more.

When an American customer is prevented by quotas from buying a

Japanese car and forced to buy a higher-priced domestic one, not only is he subsidizing the highest labor cost in the world (at Ford, more than $22 per hour including fringe costs, compared with less than $13 in Japan and Germany and in the rest of U.S. industry), but he is not being allowed to encourage the more rapid export sales and development of other more efficient U.S. industries, such as high technology, chemicals, and minerals. Tariffs not only raise domestic auto prices, they kill off jobs in export industries. As Japan's exports to the United States are artifically reduced, the dollar demand for our exports is automatically depressed.

My friend Mr. Geilich also forgets that most of the original demise of New England leather and textile industries came not from imports, but from the Sunbelt, with its lower labor costs and more capital-intensive, efficient new factories and mills, not to mention its much lower rate of tax burden. I doubt whether Geilich would want us to erect tariff barriers between U.S. economic regions; although there are now some liberal legislators who want to do precisely that, with artificial plant-closing regulations that would make it too costly for U.S. capital to shift to more efficient markets and locations within the country.

The greatest challenge facing the U.S. economy today is not to subsidize failing regions, companies, or industries, but to stimulate more productivity and more innovation in both labor and capital investment by "explicitly focusing national policies away from programs that keep productive resources in obsolete and inefficient uses."

At their core, subsidies and welfare derive from a mistaken concept of the real nature of wealth. If wealth really were primarily physical, we could achieve some kind of justice simply by redistribution, but since it is not, the real metaphysical capital embodied in individual human capacities is not developed—it is destroyed.

The badly managed company is no more rescued by cash subsidies than the uneducated or unmotivated welfare recipient. Instead, their potential to survive and to regenerate themselves is always sapped, even as the cash dissipates. That is precisely why welfare-state policies carried to their logical extreme inevitably destroy the real wealth potential of any country that tries them—and lead only to still more widespread impoverishment and lost opportunity.

8

Massachusetts on
the Laffer Curve

Surprise, surprise.

Massachusetts, with an economy scorched in the 1970s now blossoms—at least compared with the rest of the United States. In fact, a hidden message lies in the Bay State's unexpected departure from the national economic recession: "Follow me."

In 1980, the Commonwealth recorded the lowest unemployment among the top industrial states, and remains a full two percentage points below the national joblessness average. . . .

In three areas, Massachusetts is setting a pace for the nation: tax-cuts, energy conservation and high technology. "No state has changed as much or gone as far as Massachusetts since the mid-1970s," states economist Thomas A. Barocci. . . .

If the "Laffer Curve" theory of cut-taxes-and-end-stagnation works, it will be shown here.

—*The Christian Science Monitor, 10 March 1981*

As the reader may have guessed, Massachusetts is the paradigm for my vision of "an economy in mind." No other major industrial state is more abundantly stocked with mental wealth capacities. If, then, my argument that the real capital of our future economy lies in individual imagination, inventive and creative potential, and technological development, then Massachusetts with its now declining tax burden and rising level of economic freedom should be performing well. It is.

As this book was being edited for final publication, Massachusetts, despite recession, enjoyed the second-lowest unemployment rate of any major industrial state, nearly 20% below the nation, the lowest CPI year-to-year inflation rate (2.9% versus 6.5% for the nation), and an above-average rate of growth in real personal income, with tax revenues coming in at one of the fastest rates in history. Yet it was performing this miracle not with massive infusions of industrial capital (where its share has actually continued to decline), but with the vitality of its high-growth, low-capital, high-technology economy, an economy that has been rejuvenated since 1978, at least in part, by a declining rate of taxation.

Both before and after the now infamous David Stockman interview in *Atlantic Monthly* (November 1981), supply-side economics, and especially the Laffer Curve with its thesis that lower tax rates lead to more rapid economic growth, was coming under scornful attack.

It is no coincidence that among the leaders of this attack were prominent Massachusetts politicians Senators Edward M. Kennedy and Paul Tsongas and House Speaker Thomas P. O'Neill, and economists such as John Kenneth Galbraith and Lester Thurow, all of whom had been vigorous partisans in trying to stop the Bay State from pursuing similar tax-cutting policies since 1978.

Fortunately for Massachusetts taxpayers and their economy, they failed, and if the nation and President Reagan are still looking for vivid reassurance that the Laffer Curve "lives," the Bay State provides a solid proof of this curve in action.

Chart 8-A illustrates the fact that the economic fortunes of Massachusetts residents have fallen and risen again in precisely inverse proportion to the tax burden they have carried. As the burden rose, pre-tax income fell, and as the tax burden declined, both pre-tax personal income and employment began to rise sharply again.

Exactly in proportion as the state followed the high-tax, high-spend, welfare-state policies of contemporary American liberalism (1968–78), its economy fell apart; and after it electorally rejected those policies in 1978 its economy was rejuvenated dramatically.

Between 1970 and 1978 the state's total tax burden rose from less than 13% of income to 17.6%, from 3% below the national state average to 11% above it, from twenty-second in the nation to fifth. The primary reason for this fastest-in-the-nation tax-burden rise was a 137% increase in real dollars of welfare costs, lifting the state to number-one ranking in that category.

Exactly as the Laffer Curve predicts, the inevitable result of such a rapid increase in tax burden and welfare disincentives (which are a form of marginal tax rates) was a corresponding decrease in the state's economic output and personal income—as the per capita pre-tax income fell from almost 10% above the nation's to only 3% above in eight years, and from one of the fastest-growing personal incomes in the country to almost the slowest (forty-seventh) in 1977. In the same period, unemployment, which had been 1–2 points below the national figure in 1965–72, rose sharply to 2–3 points *above* it throughout the middle 1970s.

Small wonder that the political fallout of Proposition 13 in California (in June of 1978) hit Massachusetts with such gale force. Even as Governor Michael Dukakis was assuring the public that "Massachusetts voters are much too smart to fall for something like that," the Legislature passed a huge $340-million local-aid property-tax-relief program for fiscal 1979—the largest in

CHART 8-A

MASSACHUSETTS PER CAPITA PERSONAL INCOME AND TOTAL STATE AND LOCAL TAX BURDEN COMPARED TO NATIONAL AVERAGE

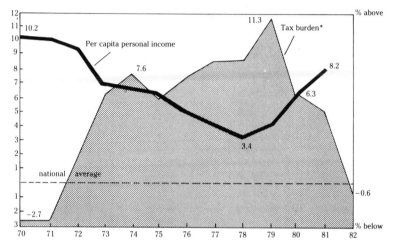

SOURCES: U.S. Department of Commerce; 1981/82 estimates by Associated Industries of Massachusetts.

* Tax burden equals total state and local revenues as a percentage of total personal income.

history, and nearly $200 million more than Governor Dukakis had asked for—and it politically forced the governor to sign it, even though in May of that year (before the passage of Proposition 13) he had threatened to veto anything over $150 million. By then, however, the political damage had been done, and conservative Democrat Edward J. King was swept into office on a $500-million tax-cutting platform. Although Governor King fell far short of his promises, his 4% spending cap in fiscal 1980 led to the first property-tax reduction in state history and, coupled with state spending restraints and ultimately "Proposition 2½," began immediately to push the tax burden down and the state's economy up.

Between 1979 and 1982 the state's tax burden dropped a full 3 percentage points, from 17.5% of total income down to 14.5%, a nearly 20% drop and the largest such reduction of any state in modern history, taking Massachusetts from fifth highest back down to below the national average in fiscal 1982 for the first time in nearly a decade.

At least part of this drop was due to the fact that, as a result of the fact that Massachusetts unemployment was once more significantly below the U.S. rate, by 1980 Massachusetts personal income once again began to grow faster than the nation's. It rose from only 3% above the nation in 1979 to a projected 8% above in fiscal 1982—the most dramatic income upsurge in the nation's history for any state. Massachusetts had finally gotten on the right side of the Laffer curve, both economically and politically. It was an extraordinary political and economic transformation.

When I started my conservative, supply-side economics column in the *Boston Herald American* in October 1975, it was received with all the local enthusiasm of a snake at a picnic lunch. After all, Massachusetts was the classically liberal state, the only one that voted for George McGovern in 1972.

The voters had just exchanged a very liberal Republican governor, Frank Sargent, for an equally liberal Democratic governor, Michael Dukakis, who spent most of his first year raising taxes to record levels and floating a huge bond issue to rescue the Commonwealth from almost certain bankruptcy. The capital city of Boston was (and still is) under the lavishly imperial mayoralty of Kevin White, whose flirtations with bankruptcy were to take place in the fall of 1976 and again in 1981.

In 1975 Massachusetts was a microcosmic preview for the nation as a whole, a welfare state run amok, a tax burden soaring to choking heights, and an economy that had fallen apart at the seams. Soaring welfare costs and taxes acted as double-pumped brakes on the entire economy. (See Chart 8-B.)

This deadly combination of excessive welfare and tax burdens produced the most striking evidence of economic deterioration of any state or national governmental entity one could ever find. In every category—population, employment, personal income—the Massachusetts economic performance, which had been close to the national average in the previous decade (1957-67), had dropped to the bottom five or ten states in the nation during the 1967-77 period.

As economist Arthur Laffer reported to the Massachusetets Business Roundtable in 1981, this huge expansion in tax burden and welfare expenditures had cost the state about 11.5% in lower economic growth (than it should have had, relative to the nation) for a loss of nearly 300,000 jobs and about $5.4 billion in 1979 personal income. Laffer suggested that this loss fell most heavily on the poor and disadvantaged for whom the welfare programs had theoretically been designed. The state had thus become (as James Ring Adams was to remind me), a modern illustration of the very old supply-side thesis enunciated by Adam Smith's Scottish colleague David Hume, who wrote: "Taxes, like necessity, . . . when carried too far, destroy industry by engendering despair; and even before they reach this pitch, they raise the wage of the laborer and manufacturer, and heighten the price of all commodities. An attentive disinterested legislature will observe the point when the emolument ceases and the prejudice begins." Hume's "prejudice" had taken such a toll from the state's economy that Massachusetts had become, by 1975, the perfect laboratory to prove Arthur Laffer's thesis that cutting taxes could reverse this economic downturn.

CHART 8-B

STATE AND LOCAL WELFARE PER CAPITA EXPENDITURES

(in 1979 dollars)

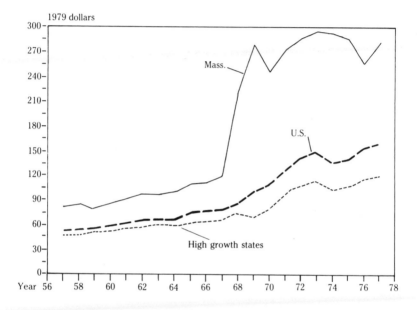

SOURCE: A. B. Laffer Associates.
——————Massachusetts per capita welfare expenditures (1979 dollars).
--------- High growth states average per capita welfare
     expenditures (1979 dollars).
— — — Source: U.S. Bureau of the Census; *State Government Finances.*

A Tale of Two States

I had not even heard of Arthur Laffer when, as a budding journalist, on 11 January 1976, six weeks before the New Hampshire primary, I wrote:

> In a few weeks the helpless voters of Massachusetts and New Hampshire will be besieged by an invasion of presidential candidates with a barrage of rhetoric ranging from the liberal populism of Fred Harris and Morris Udall on the left to the social and fiscal conservatism of George Wallace and Ronald Reagan on the right. . . .

Candidates on the liberal left will argue that the best way to improve the economy will be to strengthen government's role in the management of economy and the creation of jobs. Candidates on the right will be arguing that the key to high employment and jobs is to get government out of the economy and to cut government spending and interference.

As they argued those viewpoints, I suggested that the candidates would have a virtually unprecedented opportunity to weigh their theories and promises against the actual performance of both liberal and conservative viewpoints.

Taken together, Massachusetts and New Hampshire offered the sharpest direct contrast available in this country in both the style and substance of their approach to government and in the relationship of government to the people and their economy.

In 1976 Massachusetts was the textbook example of American liberalism in action. It also just happened to have, in that January of 1976, the nation's worst unemployment figure, over 13%—70% higher than the national figure of 8.3%. (See Table 8-1.)

New Hampshire, by contrast, was a classically conservative state, in both its Republican and Democratic politics. Its governor was far to the right of Ronald Reagan. Its leading newspaper was owned and operated by a Democrat who made even George Wallace seem mildly left wing. Its human and social services, while complete, were modest. It had consistently had among the lowest rates of total human-services expenditures in the New England area. It had done relatively little in either business regulation or consumer protection. In short, New Hampshire was anything but a social-welfare state, and its politics in both parties was strongly conservative, tending to favor local government and somewhat suspicious of big central government and its programs. It was downright friendly to business. In 1976 it also had one of the lowest unemployment levels in the country, less than half that of Massachusetts and 25% less than the nation as a whole. In fact, New Hampshire's unemployment levels for the previous five years had consistently been 35% to 40% below those in Massachusetts, and it had maintained this low unemployment despite the fact that its population had risen, over the period 1960–73, by 29.3%, nearly twice the rate of the nation as a whole (16.6%) and two and one half times as fast as that of Massachusetts (12.7%).

So, while New Hampshire had been gaining in population share, Massachusetts was actually losing its share of the total U.S. population. Since birth rates in both states had declined more than 40% in 12 years alone, the only explanation was that people were moving into New Hampshire at a substantial rate, "voting with their feet." More important, the record showed that most of them were moving there from Massachusetts. The biggest population growth area in New Hampshire was just across the border from Massachusetts in the Nashua-Manchester area.

There were two reasons why this migration was taking place. The most important was employment opportunity. While Massachusetts's employment growth (23% in the period 1960–73) had fallen far behind that of the nation

TABLE 8-1

A TALE OF TWO STATES, January 1976

	Massachusetts	New Hampshire
Unemployment	14.1%	6.2%
Population, 1960-73	+12.7%	+29.8%
Employment, 1960-73	+23 %	+46 %
Manufacturing jobs, 1960-73	−11 %	+11 %
State and local taxes as a percentage of personal income	17.8%	12 %

SOURCES: U.S. Bureau of the Census; U.S. Bureau of Labor Statistics; U.S. Department of Commerce; Statistical Abstract, 1974.

as a whole (39%), New Hampshire's employment growth (46%) had been nearly 20% faster than the nation's and twice as fast as that of Massachusetts. It was apparent in 1976 that Massachusetts was exporting jobs to New Hampshire, and people were apparently quite willing to go, even though wage rates in New Hampshire were still about 8%–10% lower than in Massachusetts.

The other main reason for this willingness to migrate, of course, was taxes. Massachusetts then had one of the highest individual tax rates in the nation as a whole, while New Hampshire had one of the ten lowest. In Massachusetts, in 1976, the average family paid out nearly 18% of its income in state and local taxes, a total of nearly $2,400 a year per family. The Bay State government had a full range of taxes, including a 5% sales tax, an average of 6% personal income tax, and a comprehensive range of excise taxes including 8% on meals, 6.6% on automobiles, and a host of other nuisance taxes. In New Hampshire, however, the average family paid out less than $1,400 a year in state and local taxes, or about 12% of income, and most of that was in the form of local property taxes. The state government had no general sales tax, and its income tax applied only to dividends and interest.

While the state budget of New Hampshire had increased about 300% in the period 1960–75, the Massachusetts state budget had grown more than 900%, or three times as fast. This huge disparity made New Hampshire the consistent target of stinging and scornful attacks, especially by *The Boston Globe,* the leading liberal newspaper, which routinely criticized New Hampshire's conservative governor and what the *Globe* perceived as his failure to fund social services on an adequate scale.

New Hampshire Cries All the Way to the Bank

Governor Meldrim Thomson was of course a delightfully inviting target— with his homiletic right-wing preachments on everything from the Panama Canal to the dangers of pot. But somehow the whole tenor of the media discourse seemed tinged with more than a little touch of the grape—sour grape, that is.

The few fiscal problems then facing New Hampshire were born out of economic prosperity—too-rapid growth—while the problems then facing Massachusetts were entirely from economic stagnation. This may have accounted for the intemperate and sometimes gloating nature of the attacks on the Granite State's lack of elaborate social services. But there was one service that most Northeastern state governments did not then provide which New Hampshire did. It was called *jobs*, and it's the one service that kept New Hampshire glowing with health in the fall of 1977.

From 1970 to 1980 New Hampshire led all of the New England states, and the nation, in the growth of jobs and industry. Year after year its job growth was double and triple that of the nation and Massachusetts. Of the total of 112,000 new jobs created in New England between July 1976 and July 1977, for example, 22,200 were in New Hampshire, which meant that the state with 6.6% of the population of the region was responsible for creating 20% of its total new jobs. That was an impressive performance.

For all of his annoying tendency to make simplistic pronouncements about complex issues, Governor Thomson did understand two simple concepts which had apparently escaped the more sophisticated Massachusetts opinion-makers: First, the primary need of any economy is to provide work—jobs for its people. Without jobs (i.e. taxpayers), there can be no government service. Second, Governor Thomson had grasped a simple economic fact: The money (investment and savings) that provides jobs comes from precisely the same source that taxes do, namely disposable, or discretionary, income. It automatically follows that the higher the taxes, the less money available for new jobs. Thus, states that tax the most will have the lowest job growth, while states that tax the least will have the highest job growth.

Taxes vs. Employment

This premise was confirmed by David Wendell, then editor of the Babson weekly letter, who made a study in 1976 of the actual taxation and employment levels of all 50 states over the six-year period 1969–74. First, he ranked the states in the order of the rate of increase in state and local taxes over the period, from lowest to highest, arranging the states into five different groups of ten, and found a median increase for each group of ten. Then he listed the actual growth in employment (jobs) in each of these states during this period and again found a median increase rate for each group of ten.

He found that the states whose taxes grew the least had the greatest increase in employment and that the states whose taxes grew the most had employment increases well below the national figure of 12%. During this period, Massachusetts taxes grew by 71%, a higher growth rate than 32 other states, while its employment grew only 3%, 75% below the national rate. Wendell also found a striking correlation between the individual tax burden in each state and the unemployment rate. In this analysis, only two states (Rhode Island and Michigan) had higher average unemployment than Massachusetts (10.3%), and only seven states had higher average tax-burden levels than Massachusetts (17%).

TABLE 8-2

TAXES AND EMPLOYMENT GROWTH

(in percentages)

States	1969-74 median increase in state and local taxes	1969-74 median increase in employment
Best group	50	28
Next best	58	19
Middle group	66	15
Next worst (Massachusetts)	72	11
Worst group	85	9

SOURCE: *David L. Babson Company Weekly Staff Letter,* 26 February 1976.

TABLE 8-3

UNEMPLOYMENT AND TAX BURDEN

(in percentages)

State	Median unemployment rate 1974-75	Median tax burden 1974
Best	4.7	14.1
Next best	6	14.3
Middle group	7	14.2
Next worst	8	15.5
Worst group	8.9	16.6
(Massachusetts)		

SOURCE: *David L. Babson Company Weekly Staff Letter,* 26 February 1976.

As Wendell pointed out, taxes are not the only variable in any economic equation; but they are an important component, particularly when industry faces a variety of tax situations and can choose the most attractive situation in which to invest and create new jobs.

Of course, the Massachusetts labor unions immediately rebutted Wendell's conclusions with the argument that it was low wage rates in nonunion right-to-work states that really accounted for the state's economic problems.

I debunked that myth in a column on 4 May 1976, where I pointed out that Massachusetts' wage rates were actually no better than their Sunbelt counterparts, and in many cases were worse. The wage differential between the North and the South had, in the last decade, been washed away, primarily because many of the companies in the South also have plants in other Northern states and they have to pay roughly equivalent salaries, even though most of their Southern plants are not closed union shops while their Northern plants are. A series of studies by Lynne Browne of the Boston Federal Reserve in 1977–79 verified the fact that over the previous decade Massachusetts and New England had rapidly shed their high-wage position, and by 1980 those states were offering labor costs (not counting union work rules) very competitive with even the poorest of the Sunbelt region.

When this "low-wage" accusation failed, the unions and their liberal political allies argued ⁺hat there was a direct connection between taxes and services.

Taxes and Services

We were told that high taxes simply meant high services and that states with lower tax rates weren't providing the services that people want and need. I was rescued in this debate in the summer of 1976 by a scholarly comparison of New Hampshire with another heavily taxed state—a study done by two Dartmouth College researchers, Professor Colin Campbell and his wife Rosemary, who looked at the fiscal systems of Vermont and New Hampshire from 1940 to 1974. What made this study ideal was that not only were the two states roughly similar in population, physical size, climate, and general socioeconomic makeup, but the two presented sharp contrasts in basic fiscal and governmental policy.

Vermont was the third most heavily taxed state in the nation (even higher than Massachusetts), taking 19.2% of total personal income in state and local revenues. New Hampshire was the forty-seventh, taking only 13.4%. Vermont had both a statewide graduated income tax and a sales tax. New Hampshire had neither. Property taxes took 6.2% in Vermont and 5.7% in New Hampshire. In short, Vermonters paid 50% more taxes than did the people of New Hampshire.

So the question arose: What did the Vermonters get in services that their neighbors in New Hampshire did not? The answer was nothing—at least nothing one could measure.

The Campbells found that New Hampshire's education performance was as good or better than that of Vermont, and its teachers earned more. New Hampshire's welfare-payments schedules were as high as Vermont's, but it had fewer unemployed and fewer on the welfare rolls. New Hampshire's roads were as good—and as well cared for—and its parks were as extensive and accessible. Its higher education was more accessible and more available to state students—and cost much less. On all major issues, on all measures of government services, Vermonters were being short changed, paying 50% more for the same or fewer services. Why was that?

The answer: In Vermont the services were being managed and supported by an expensive statewide bureaucracy and a higher-paid and less-efficient state government. Over 60% of the funding and control came from the state. By contrast, in New Hampshire the local governments ran and controlled more than 55% of "the action." All Vermont seemed to have bought for its money was more bureaucracy and not more value.

The conclusions of this study were that people get more for their government dollar when it is spent close to home than when it is spent by distant bureaucracies and full-time politicians.

More important, as Parkinson's Law predicts, politicians tend to spend whatever they can get in revenue whether that spending is worth it or not. The existence of broad-based sales and income taxes in Vermont hadn't decreased its citizens' property-tax load; all it had done was to increase their total spending by giving the politicians and bureaucrats more money to play with.

Conversely, not having either sales or income taxes had not hurt the people of New Hampshire. All it had done was to save them money and give them as good services for 40% less outlay. This applied even to welfare costs. Despite equal welfare-benefit levels, the actual total welfare costs were 50% higher in Vermont than in New Hampshire—and taking 3% of total personal income in that state versus 2% in New Hampshire.

The reason for this, Professor Campbell concluded, was that "the [local] scrutiny of welfare cases in New Hampshire is probably more careful and reduces the number of persons receiving welfare. In New Hampshire welfare families have to reestablish evidence of need monthly, while in Vermont proof is required only every six months."

In Vermont a lot more people were qualified for welfare and Medicaid benefits (by a state bureaucracy) than in New Hampshire, relative to the total population, even though the income levels were the same for both states.

As it was with Vermont, so it was with Massachusetts, where benefit levels were not only higher but total welfare costs were taking the highest share of per capita income of any state in the country (83% above the U.S. median level at that time), a condition that did not arise until welfare was taken over by the state government in 1968. Before that takeover in 1967–68, Boston managed its own welfare efforts entirely for $49.6 million, and with only 1,000 employees. By 1981, under state control, the total welfare costs for Boston alone had reached nearly $940 million, with more than 3,000 bureaucrats. Discounting inflation, that was a 600% increase in constant dollars, as the total welfare rolls of Boston tripled—even as the city lost 12% of its population.

Welfare State vs. Economic Growth and Income

One of the primary lessons from the Massachusetts experience was that heavy social spending seems to make poverty worse, not better, because it not only institutionalizes the poor, it drags down the income and economic performance of the rest of the economy. In exact proportion to Massachusetts's social spending and tax burden, the state's share of total U.S. income dropped (from 3% of U.S. personal income to 2.7% in the period 1970-78 and from 4% of U.S. capital income to 3% in the same period) in every sector of the state economy as its productive population was pushed out to New Hampshire and the Sunbelt.

I first documented this "pursuit-of-poverty" effect in a March 1977 column that showed what the state's tax and economic policies were doing to its citizens:

> Not only do we have the highest welfare spending per capita in the nation, fully 70% above the U.S. median, but in 1975 we passed a major new milestone in the state's economic history. In that year, for the first time, total transfer payments (payments made for welfare and income support) exceeded all the income earned by savings, investment, and capital in the state.

In 1975, according to the Survey of Current Business, transfer payments in Massachusetts were $5.76 billion, fully 11% higher than the $5.2 billion earned by investment (savings, rent, industrial capital, etc.). That meant that the net earnings of its private economy were now 10% smaller than the money being paid out for welfare and income support.

But the full impact of Massachusetts's welfare-state policies could not be measured only in terms of what they had done to reduce the state's gross personal income. It had to be looked at in terms of what it had done to effective income—that is, the cost of maintaining not only individual livelihood but the growing welfare burden. According to the U.S. Department of Labor 1978 Study of Urban Family Budgets, the Boston metropolitan area was the nation's most expensive place to live—18% above the U.S. median for middle-income families. (It was 10% higher for lowest-income families and 21% higher for upper-income families.)

Not surprisingly, the main reasons for this extraordinary 18% differential in the cost of living were not food or clothing, or even fuel, but income taxes (45% higher than the U.S. median) and property taxes (80% above the U.S. median).

So while Boston's total gross per capita income in 1977 was about 3.5% above the national median, its cost of living was 18% above. This meant, in cold terms, that effective income in 1978 was only 88% of the U.S. median—fully 12% below the nation, and the lowest of any urban area in the United States.

In 1977 Dr. Alan Reynolds, then chief economist of the First National Bank of Chicago, made a detailed comparison of the actual living standards of some 30 states and found that Massachusetts was by then one of the poorest in terms of net adjusted (for the cost of living) disposable income per capita, whereas a decade before it had been one of the richest. In 1975 only two states, Vermont and Mississippi, had lower net disposable income than Massachusetts did. The single biggest reason for this was the excessively high state and local taxes. In that year, the average resident of Texas, for example, earned 36% more, after taxes, than the average resident of Massachusetts, even though the pre-tax income of the average Commonwealth resident was 8% higher than that of his Texas counterpart.

Massachusetts's Federal Dependency

In 1976–77, sensing a growing tide of fiscal conservatism, Massachusetts politicians, using the so-called outflow argument, began to blame the state's poor economic performance on its being shortchanged on federal funds. However, an analysis I made in a six-part series in December 1976 showed that Massachusetts, in fact, had long since become a net dependent on federal largess, receiving far more in spending than it paid out in taxes. But despite this inflow, the economy was still stagnant—demonstrating that welfare of any kind seldom does much to generate real prosperity. This series was subsequently validated in December 1977 in a 64-page study issued by the Comptroller General of the General Accounting Office (GAO) of the United States entitled "Changing Patterns of Federal Aid to State and Local Governments." It showed that Massachusetts got back in federal aid about $1.08 for every tax dollar it sent to the federal government—a profit of 8 cents on the dollar—a complete denial of the propaganda about outflow. The GAO study made the following additional points:

- During 1969–75 per capita federal aid increased more rapidly in the Northeast than in other sections of the country.

- The Northeast, during this period, began to receive a greater percentage of federal aid than it paid in federal taxes.
- New England stood third among all regions in per capita federal assistance in 1975, and its 1969–75 increase exceeded the national average by 21%.
- The primary reason for this tax inflow was welfare. Although New England had the least poverty, the proportion of its population receiving AFDC (and Medicaid) increased 42% faster than the nation's between 1969 and 1975.
- Massachusetts, which rose from 90 cents on the dollar in 1969 to $1.08 in 1975, did so primarily because a higher percentage of its expenditures (18%) went for welfare than in any other state in the nation, even though its poverty rate (at 8%) was one of the nation's lowest.

Yet this rising tide of federal aid to Massachusetts had been of no help to the state's real economic health. The GAO study showed that in 1970 unemployment in Massachusetts was 4.6%—below the national figure of 5%, but by 1975 it had risen to 9.6%, well above the national figure of 8.5%, even though federal aid had soared. While the nation's total personal income grew 60% from 1969 to 1975, Massachusetts's growth was only 52%. And although in 1969 its personal income per capita was 10% above the national average, by 1975 that margin had fallen to 3.5%.

Plainly, the GAO study demonstrated that the effect of rising federal aid on most Northeastern states was not positive but negative. It also showed that those states that had the greatest net "loss" in federal funds, Illinois, Ohio, Iowa, and Indiana, all did far better economically than Massachusetts did in the same period, and all spent much less on welfare and public assistance than did Massachusetts.

The Tax-Limitation Debate of 1978

When Michael Dukakis came to office as governor in 1975 he showed signs of understanding this and trying to wean the state away from excessive social spending. The recession of 1975, with Massachusetts close to bankruptcy, supplied the perfect rationale for his tight-spending concepts, which initially infuriated his liberal supporters. But after three years of relative fiscal restraint, in early 1978 the Dukakis administration, stung by liberal criticism in an election year, suddenly turned loose a fiscal 1979 budget showing a 15% increase in spending, even as property-tax relief continued to lag.

While the flush social budget drew predictably rave reviews from The Boston Globe, it got quick and biting rebukes from the state's leading economists, who were worried about its declining economic position. "Compared to the U.S. and the rest of New England, the Massachusetts economy is in very poor shape indeed, and getting worse," warned James Howell, chief economist for the First National Bank of Boston, in response to the Dukakis budget for fiscal 1979. What troubled Dr. Howell was that since 1974 Massachusetts had experienced a 39% drop in real capital spending for new plant and equipment, while during the same period such spending in the United States and New England as a whole rose almost 14%.

In 1977, while capital spending in Massachusetts declined 7%, it had risen more than 12% in the rest of New England. Investment plans for 1978 called for another 12% drop for Massachusetts. During a period when U.S. capital spending on new plant and equipment was recovering modestly, if nervously, the Massachusetts economy had witnessed a steep nosedive in investment. Writing in the February 1978 issue of *Industry* magazine, Dr. Howell warned, "The expectations for Massachusetts manufacturing capital spending must be considered negative when compared with the national outlook," and he called for a sharp reduction in taxes and public spending.

Naturally, the liberal politicians and pundits rejected this gloomy assessment with the premise that even though Massachusetts was still losing low-pay and low-technology industry to the Sunbelt, it was leading that region in high technology. Whereupon Howell put out a study that showed that investment trends for high technology in Massachusetts actually lagged far behind the burgeoning regions of the "growth belt," where high-technology investment had grown nearly six times as fast as in Massachusetts from 1963 to 1975.

"Any way you slice it," James Howell warned, "this is an exceedingly poor performance for what is supposed to be our very best economic activity." What it suggested, he continued, was that companies like Digital and Data General had already decided to spend most of their new investment money outside of Massachusetts. So while Massachusetts was a nice place to have a headquarters, it was turning out to be a very poor place for companies to build their plants.

On 15 March 1978, with lucky prescience, I warned that while the Massachusetts Legislature was wrestling with bottle bills and other assorted scandals, a real 1978 election issue was developing right under its nose. "It is called the Massachusetts economy." And I declared that, by every possible measure, the performance of the Masschusetts economy over the past four years had been nothing short of scandalous.

This was confirmed in a March 1978 report by the U.S. Department of Commerce which showed that over the period 1973–77 the incomes of Massachusetts workers were growing more slowly than those in all but three other states. The real reason, of course, was the sagging Massachusetts economy—and, particularly, declining capital investment. I predicted: "The 'bottom line' of any political administration must be its impact on the economic health of the state or nation it is governing. By this measurement, the voters of Massachusetts should be making a very harsh judgment this fall."

Proposition 13 Awakens Massachusetts Voters

Until the election night of 6 June 1978 when Proposition 13 was passed in California, it seemed apparent that both the governor and the Legislature were going to resist the growing business pressure for tax relief. But, following the stunning passage of Proposition 13 in California, both were forced to "get the message," as the possibility of a similar measure in Massachusetts suddenly came into focus. In a last-minute scramble in August 1978, some $340 million in additional property-tax relief was approved by a still-reluctant Governor Dukakis (who had wanted only $150 million).

As it turned out, Dukakis's early insensitivity on this issue cost him his job in a dramatic primary upset in September, as I came close to predicting:

> What happened in California can, and many think, should happen right here. After all, the tax burden in Massachusetts is as bad as it is in California—and over the last four years it has grown faster here than it has there. . . . Against this grotesque reality, Governor Dukakis had the · miraculous chutzpah yesterday to say: "I think the Massachusetts voters are too smart to fall for such a simplistic proposal."

The voters had some news for him. If California had a right to be furious over their taxes, the people of Massachusetts had far more right. Whereas property taxes in California had reached an average of about 2.8% of market value, in Massachusetts they had reached nearly 4.5%, or 61% above even the California level before the passage of Proposition 13. Whereas property taxes had been providing about 28% of total California revenues, they were now raising almost 46% of total revenues in Massachusetts, the highest proportion in the nation.

Ironically—and this was the message that both the governor and the Legislature ultimately didn't heed—the California politicians could have averted the meat-axe approach of Proposition 13 entirely if they hadn't successfully stonewalled and defeated Ronald Reagan's pioneering but moderate Tax Limitation Amendment in 1974.

A similar situation prevailed on Beacon Hill in the summer of 1978, when legislative leadership, with the tacit support of the governor, successfully destroyed (with last-minute loopholes created behind closed doors) a proposed tax-limitation amendment petitioned for by 90,000 citizens under the leadership of Citizens for Limited Taxation (CLT). That action prompted me to suggest that:

> While this column has generally favored the concept of tax limitation as a reasonable step in at least flattening out the growth curve in Masschusetts public spending (which has grown 8% faster than personal income over the last 10 years) we would be even more delighted by a real tax-cut proposal, in the same vein as Jarvis-Gann [i.e., Proposition 13], though not as radical. Instead of the Jarvis-Gann 1% figure, a cut to 2% or 2.5% of fair-market value would have wondrously salutary impact on this state's staggering economy—and a disciplinary impact on our politicians, bureaucrats, and big business.

Out of this almost innocuous paragraph (buried on page 8) Proposition 2½ was born into the political arena. The public response was immediate, with almost 14,000 letters to the *Herald American* endorsing this Proposition 2½ concept and a *Boston Globe* poll confirming its support by a 70–30 margin just two weeks later. With his primary campaign floundering, Dukakis's Democratic opponent Edward J. King took up the Proposition 13 theme and rode it to a stunning political upset in September.

Early on Tuesday morning, 19 September 1978, Michael Dukakis, the state's popular and confident governor, was awaiting what the media predicted would be a sure renomination in the primary. By 10:30 that evening, he was forced to concede defeat, in one of the most startling political reversals in state history. In the state with the second-highest property tax in the nation, in the year of Jarvis—and with an opponent promising a "$500-million property tax rollback"—anything turned out to be possible.

I studied the election results carefully and found an astonishing correlation between high property-tax rates and a strong anti-Dukakis, pro-King vote. For example, among the 75 most heavily taxed cities and towns, with FCV (fair cash value) property tax rates of $42 per thousand and up, Dukakis lost to King 45% to 55%, a landslide. King won handily in 60 of those 75 cities and towns, and frequently by two- and three-to-one margins. Exactly the opposite took place in the 50 lowest-taxed cities and towns, where Dukakis won by 52% to 42%. One could have forecast King's margin of victory in each town by the relative size of its property-tax burden.

Ironically, at about the same time, a new economic analysis by Robert Genetski of the Harris Research Department (Harris Bank, Chicago) showed that future economic growth could be predicted in much the same way. The essential finding of his analysis was that while the *average* tax burden is not significant to economic growth, the *trends* in tax burden, up or down, for any state, relative to the rest of the nation, are absolutely crucial. "Between 1969 and 1976," wrote Dr. Genetski, "a state's relative economic growth was related to the *change* in the state's relative tax burden, with those states displaying above-average increases in their tax burden tending to show below-average economic growth and vice versa":

- Of the 37 states with lower-than-average tax-burden growth, all but three, or 90%, had above-average economic growth.
- Of the 14 states (including the District of Columbia) with high-tax growth, all but three had substantially below-average economic growth, a nearly 80% correlation.

The study showed, for example, that Massachusetts, with the ninth-fastest growth in tax burden, had the third-lowest growth in personal income and economy, while New York, with the fifth-fastest growing tax burden, had the worst economic performance of all. Conversely, Colorado, with the fortieth ranking in tax-burden growth, had the eleventh-fastest-growing state economy. Florida, with the thirty-eighth growth in tax burden, had the fourth-fastest-growing personal income.

So total was the inverse correlation between tax growth and economic

TABLE 8-4

KING AND DUKAKIS: A FIRST-YEAR COMPARISON

(in percentages)

	Dukakis (1975-76)	King (1979-80)
Taxes		
State	+26	+7
Property	+6	−1.2
Total	+16	+3.2
Tax burden on personal income	+7.8	−7.4
Spending		
Total (actual)	+11.4	+9.8
Local aid	+4.2	+15.7
Net state	+13.6	+7.5
State debt burden		
Total debt	+37	−3
Debt service	+169	−1

SOURCES: Massachusetts State Comptroller; Massachusetts Department of Administration and Finance; Massachusetts Senate Ways and Means Committee; U.S. Department of Commerce data on personal income.

growth that the study concluded that "those states which are successful in cutting relative tax burdens will experience higher economic growth than the nation as a whole, while those states which do not reduce their relative tax burdens are likely to suffer below-average economic growth."

Governor King took this basic message to heart and tried to implement it. Although his accomplishments fell far short of his election promises, they nevertheless were significant as, for the first time, in fiscal 1980 the Massachusetts tax burden began to go down modestly, in sharp contrast to the experience of his predecessor.

By early 1980 *The Wall Street Journal* recognized this change in economic direction in Massachusetts. In an article called "Taxachusetts Turns Around" (a piece that did wonders to change the state's unfortunate national image), James Ring Adams told the national audience that the new King administration was "heavily influenced by the 'Laffer Curve' argument that high rates of taxation can cause economic stagnation," and credited King with the "first significant tax reduction in nearly two decades," which had brought on a "nascent economic boom."

"It's the economic thinking of the '80s," said Howard P. Foley, president of the aggressive new Massachusetts High Technology Council, a business group representing companies in high-technology fields. In 1979 the Council signed a "social contract" with the governor, pledging to create 150,000 new jobs for Massachusetts by 1982 if he brought the state tax burden down to the average of 17 competing industrial states. This drop from a burden of 17.6% of state personal income to a goal of 15.3% would allow an extra $2 billion of state economic growth. The result would be a fresh $300 million in state and local tax revenues to support worthy social goals.

Despite Governor King's many political fumbles and hostility from the liberal press, the first two years of the "social contract" worked out surprisingly well, as the Legislature in 1979 agreed to a 60% reduction in the state's highest-in-the-nation capital-gains tax, to be phased in over three years.

Governor King also pushed through a 4% cap on local government spending. Although far short of the zero-growth cap of his campaign promise, it caused 199 of the Commonwealth's 351 cities and towns to reduce property-tax rates and 33 to hold them steady, for a total reduction of more than $36 million. For their part, the state's entrepreneurs more than kept to their schedule. State Commerce Department Commissioner James F. Carlin reported that the economy made a net gain of 12,000 new manufacturing jobs through plant expansion in 1979, nearly restoring the state to its peak before the sharp losses of the early 1970s.

By April 1980, for the first time in a decade, Massachusetts was outperforming the nation in both personal-income growth and job growth and was successfully reducing its tax burden as a result. Even as the national economy was falling apart, the Massachusetts private sector was humming. The state's unemployment rate was down to 4.9% (compared with the nation's 6.2%)—the lowest among the ten largest industrial states. (In 1981's recession it was still the second lowest.) During 1980, 215 companies expanded their production facilities in Massachusetts, the largest number in history.

Proposition 2½ and the Massachusetts Budget

Unfortunately for him, Governor King decided in 1980, after his early economic success, to turn a deaf ear to the rising property-tax-limitation movement, which was then in the process of placing Proposition 2½ on the November ballot. Instead of embracing this issue, he chose unaccountably to speak against it—something that would eventually greatly reduce his standing in the political polls and put him on the opposite side from the Massachusetts High Technology Council. The Council supported Proposition 2½ as the only way to cope with the growing challenge of attracting professional people to the state with the second-highest property taxes in the nation.

In fact, the passage of Proposition 13 in California in 1978 had put even more pressure on Massachusetts's high-technology industry from a recruiting standpoint. In one fell swoop, that high-technology state had taken its property taxes from third highest in the nation (behind Massachusetts) to one of the lowest—from 6% of income to less than 3%. And since the passage of Proposition 13, California's unemployment rate had gone from an average of 1.5 percentage points above the national average to 0.5 percentage point below it. And while public-sector employment did fall by some 20,000 jobs (1.2%), private-sector total employment leaped ahead in the next 24 months by 720,000, the largest and fastest growth in total jobs of any major industrial state in the nation.

Using Arthur Laffer's regression-analysis curve, economist David Ranson predicted publicly that should Proposition 2½ pass in Massachusetts, the total tax burden of the state would go down between 1 and 2 percentage points and the state could expect a 10%–20% increase in its basic economic growth rate relative to the nation. On the dark side, he also predicted that if it did *not* pass, the much-touted boom in high-technology growth could well be aborted in the 1980s, since other high-technology states (such as California, Florida, North Carolina, Texas, and Colorado) were all lowering their tax burdens compared to Massachusetts.

This was significant because in 1980, largely because of the high property taxes in Massachusetts, a professional engineer thinking of moving to Massachusetts from a Sunbelt state (especially from Texas or North Carolina) faced an automatic rise in the cost of living of $4,000 or more per year. Yet that engineer was basic to the hiring of 12 other people in direct high-technology employment and another 18 people in outside services that would be generated, since each successful recruitment of a professional engineer to Massachusetts automatically added from 25 to 30 jobs to the state's economy and tax-revenue base. That is why Proposition 2½ was so very high on the high-tech agenda and why the future of the Massachusetts economy was absolutely dependent upon its passage.

After Proposition 2½

The measure was passed overwhelmingly in November 1980 by a 59–41 margin, despite massive scare propaganda by public employee unions and surprisingly close pre-election polls. As it turned out, the public employees had reason to be frightened of the measure. Not counting losses from CETA termination, some 17,000 public workers lost their jobs out of a total municipal employment base of 243,000 (again not counting CETA personnel), a cut of about 7%. Most of that cut came in the public schools, and more than half of that was really overdue response to drastically declining enrollments, which had left Massachusetts some 15%–20% more highly staffed (pupil-to-teacher ratio) than the national average.

Aside from Boston, whose mayor tried to sabotage Proposition 2½ by laying off policemen, firemen, and other providers of essential services before trimming his political machine, the rest of the state adjusted to the new tax cap with surprising smoothness, largely because the Legislature generated a substantial $265 million in new "local aid," which effectively removed some of the pain of the total cuts forced on the communities (some $335 million in property taxes and $256 million in excise taxes the first 18 months).

As a result, total spending by the municipalities declined by a modest 2.4%, while taxpayers pocketed over $590 million in tax savings in fiscal 1982. At the same time, the strain of generating new local aid forced the state to cut its spending outlays on its own programs, which caused the total outlays of the state and local governments to drop about 1%. In a year when inflation still averaged 10% and personal income in the state rose by more than 10%, this meant a "real cut" in tax burden of 10% and finally drove the

TABLE 8-5

MASSACHUSETTS'S DECLINING TAX BURDEN
(as percentage of personal income*)

Fiscal year	Total revenue burden Mass.	U.S.	Taxes only Mass.	U.S.	Property tax burden Mass.	U.S.
1975	16.6	15.7	14.2	12.3	7.5	4.4
1976	17.3	16.0	14.7	12.5	7.3	4.5
1977	17.7	16.3	15.1	12.8	7.4	4.6
1978	17.6	16.2	15.1	12.8	7.2	4.4
1979	17.5	15.7	14.8	12.0	6.9	3.8
1980	16.5	15.5	13.9	11.6	6.2	3.5
1981	15.9	15.1	13.3	11.4	6.0	3.4
1982 (est.)	14.5	14.6	11.8	11.0	4.6	3.3
Change under Dukakis budgets (1975-79)	+5.4	0	+4.2	−2.5	−8	−14
Change under King budgets (1979-82)	−17.1	−7	−20.3	−8.3	−33	−13

SOURCES: U.S. Bureau of the Census; U.S. Department of Commerce; 1982 estimates by Associated Industries of Massachusetts.

*Actual revenues are from fiscal year factored against prior calendar year personal income (1976 fiscal year revenues against 1975 personal income).

Estimates made using data supplied by Associated Industries of Massachusetts and House Taxation Committee.

Massachusetts tax burden below the national average for the first time in a decade. (See Table 8-5 and Chart 8-C.)

Despite the unrelentingly negative reporting of the implementation of Proposition 2½, public support for it hardly wavered. As the Becker Institute, a public opinion research firm, reported in December 1981, "It is significant that despite all the emotional pronouncements, political maneuvering, threatened and actual layoffs of public employees, the ratio of opposition and support regarding Proposition 2½ remains evenly divided and has not budged one iota during the past nine months." Becker found that among those who actually voted, the measure still got a 53–45 support, not far from its 59–41 margin in November 1980. And the Massachusetts Poll, taken by the University of Massachusetts, also affirmed the voting population's continued commitment, at all levels, to tax reduction, especially of property and income taxes. The public overwhelmingly agreed with the Lafferite premise that lower taxes would help generate more economic growth and jobs—a premise that as of this writing is coming true despite the deadly impact of the 1981-82 deep recession. Massachusetts unemployment, while up, is well below the nation's, a sharp reversal of the 1974–75 experience, when unemployment in the state soared to nearly 4 points above the national figure.

And personal income continues to outpace the nation—so much so that in January 1982 Governor King discovered that instead of a revenue deficit for fiscal 1982, the state was headed for a $100-million surplus, largely because of an unusual increase in income-tax revenues. Cutting the tax burden, it seemed, had been good for the Massachusetts revenue base as well, so much so that the governor was able to propose a cut in the income tax for fiscal 1983. Or, as he bragged in the "economic" preface to his 1983 budget message: "The Massachusetts economy is as strong as any state in America.

It's been a long time since such a bold statement could be made, but in the last three years, the economy of Massachusetts has improved dramatically. Downward trends which developed early in the last decade have been reversed, and the economy has outperformed most expectations."

King took his good news to the Joint Economic Committee (JEC) of the U.S. Congress where, at a hearing on 24 February 1982, he told Senate and House members that "the upward spiraling tax burden [of the early 1970s] had become a deterrent to the growth and expansion of our economy. [Reversing that trend] has achieved an estimated savings of $2.1 billion in 1982 for the taxpayers of the Commonwealth. In 1978 the wage earner paid $177 in taxes out of every $1,000 earned. This year [1982] the wage earner will pay $145 out of every $1,000 earned." King told the hearing that the real benefit of this reduction was in increased employment opportunity. In the first three years of his administration, he said, 200,000 new jobs had been created. "The Commonwealth has been below the national unemployment rate for 28 consecutive months . . . a dramatic change." By May 1982 that string had been extended to 33 months, and the state's inflation rate (Boston–SMSA) had fallen to a year-to-year decade low of 2.9%, half the national figure of 6.5%

Sadly, the state's leading liberal politicians seem to have learned nothing from the experience. Senator Paul Tsongas even told a Lowell audience in December 1981, "In spite of Proposition 2 1/2 the Massachusetts economy is doing surprisingly well"! Senator Edward M. Kennedy was so incensed by King's testimony to the JEC that he first tried to have it canceled, and then boycotted the hearing. In 1982 King faced very tough sledding in his effort to get reelected against the determined opposition of an overwhelmingly liberal Boston media establishment, and it remained to be seen whether the voters would ever give him credit for the state's new-found economic strength—at the moment partially overshadowed by national recession.

Climbing down the Laffer Curve and up the Growth Curve

No one could look at Chart 8-A (at the beginning of this chapter) without recognizing the dramatic change in economic policies and priorities that it represents, or the economic success it has helped to spawn and nourish— not from companies that immigrated to Massachusetts but from those that have been encouraged by its changing tax structure to grow faster within the state.

In just two years (1980–81), for example, 21% of the new entrants on the Fortune 1000 list were from Massachusetts (which has only 2.7% of the nation's population). This compares with 16% from California and 12% from New York. Massachusetts has twice as many, per capita, of the nation's top 100 growing companies as California, New York, and Texas, and three times as many as Florida and Maryland.

In 1976 none of those achievements seemed even possible. Indeed, that

CHART 8-C

MASSACHUSETTS TOTAL TAX BURDEN

Percent

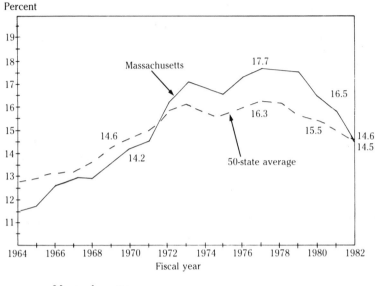

————— Massachusetts

– – – – –50-state average

SOURCES: U.S. Department of Commerce; 1982 estimates by Associate Industries of Massachusetts.

Total tax burden: state and local general revenue from own sources as percentage of total personal income.

year I reported that one of the state's very largest high-tech employers was seriously considering relocating its permanent headquarters to New Hampshire. Today, Boston and Massachusetts have become focal centers for the nation's greatest future potential in high technology.

Without a massive change in the political and tax climate—from the punishment of productivity to incentives for growth, from the total preoccupation with social welfare to a genuine interest in enterprise—much of the turnaround might never have taken place.

Not that taxes alone made the difference. Most of the "seed capital" for Massachusetts's technological economy has been generated by its top private and public educational institutions, Harvard, MIT, Boston University, Boston College, the University of Massachusetts. Through them, the Commonwealth has proved for the nation, as a whole, that it does not require a rich raw-material resource base to generate wealth and that the most important "capital" in the decades to come will consist of creative, trained individuals.

It is no longer possible to pursue economic policies that punish productive human capital through taxation, regulation, and bureaucracy. Either it will stop producing or (as in the case of Massachusetts) it will go elsewhere. The only real limits on the future growth of the Massachusetts economy now lie in the state's ability to attract professional people to come into the state to live—an ability that seems strong if the state continues to ease the taxing burden it places on individuals.

The state that launched the American Revolution by throwing tea in Boston Harbor to protest taxes is once more demonstrating that the most important ingredient in the generation of real economic wealth is still the freedom of the individual human mind to express and develop its ideas.

9

Goodness and the GNP

To the masses of the Western world the news that all men are more than things was proclaimed by the Christian gospel and was celebrated in its central mysteries . . . For in the recognition that there is in each man a final essence—that is to say, an immortal soul—which only God can judge, a limit was set up on the dominion of men over men in the long ascent out of the morass of barbarism. Upon this rock they have built the rude foundations of the Good Society.

—Walter Lippmann

Although liberty is the supreme end of a democratic society, and fundamental to economic development, we must not naively think that more liberty and less government, alone, will solve our economic ills and produce endless wealth, nor should we be beguiled by the more extreme libertarian point of view that morality itself has nothing to do with the common wealth.

This attitude reflects a legitimate rejection of the legislated theocracy of the religious right (as well as the excessive regulations of the left), but it also reflects a failure to understand that, at its roots, economics is a metaphysical rather than a mathematical science, in which intangible spiritual values and attitudes are at least as important as physical assets and morale more fundamental than the money supply. Products, after all, are the assembly of qualities, and their value derives directly from the innate character and ideals of those who create them and the workmanship of those who produce them. Things are, in their final analysis, the expression of thoughts. Quality products derive from quality thoughts, shoddy products from shoddy thoughts.

Plainly, then, a national economy, like an individual business or a specific product, is the sum of the spiritual and mental qualities of its people, and its output of value will be only as strong as the values of society. There are many examples of barbaric societies which practiced the "free market" of the jungle and finally perished in the poverty of hedonism. Without the civilizing force of universal moral standards, particularly honesty, trust, self-respect, integrity, and loyalty, the marketplace quickly degenerates. A society that has no values will not produce much value; a nation whose values are declining should not be surprised at a declining economy. As Ralph Waldo Emerson postulates, "A dollar is not value, but representative of value, and, at last, of moral values."

In this present age of intense libertarianism, we can see that Epicureans and hedonists are not given to work and savings; and in our urban ghettos the freest of Huns and vandals are unlikely to produce many goods and services. It takes serious self-discipline to contribute more than we take. Our national epidemic of crime in both offices and streets is far more indicative of our economic ills than we care to admit—not merely for the direct damage that is done to victims, but for what it says about the values and the morale of a nation. Can we really expect economic revival without spiritual revival? Can economic regeneration be spawned in the soil of moral degeneration?

Take, for example, the appalling breakdown in the family over the past decade or so. Not only is the family the basic social unit, it is the most fundamental economic force in society, the key to work, consumption, savings, investment, and the whole future thrust of any nation. Yet it is also the economic force most vulnerable to deteriorating moral and spiritual values. Marriage itself is after all a moral commitment. So the continuing, ever-mounting assault on traditional family values may well be more destructive to our economic well-being as a nation than any of our faulty fiscal or monetary policies. As William Barrett argues, "The violent dissatisfaction with the prosaic and workable arrangements of society (from the family on up) that permit liberty, is part of the general spiritual sickness of modernity"; and Norman Podhoretz rightly contends, "It cannot be cured by any set of economic or political arrangements."

That was the theme of the 1981 Connecticut Mutual Life "Report on American Values in the 80's," which found that more than half of all Americans now doubt that politics or economic policies alone can solve our basic societal problems such as energy shortages, inflation, and crime; and that, more than we have suspected, Americans are seeking a new level of spiritual and religious commitment as the solution. "Bewildered by the confusion of the present, large numbers of citizens now find solace in the firm conviction of their ancestors." The Report also found that these firm convictions of religious commitment have a direct bearing on *economic* values, particularly work and family:

- "The 'most religious' Americans are more likely [than the 'least religious' to feel a sense of dedication to their work" (97% vs. 66%).
- "The 'most religious' are more likely to feel that their work contributes to society" (91% vs. 53%).
- "The 'most religious' are more likely to find their work interesting and rewarding" (92% vs. 68%).
- "The 'most religious' are more likely to believe financial security can be obtained by hard work" (88% vs. 70%).
- "The 'most religious' are much more likely to say they would reconcile marital problems at all costs rather than seek divorce" (60% vs. 33%).

TABLE 9-1

LEADERS AND PUBLIC ON MORAL ISSUES

(in percentages)

Issues considered morally wrong	Public	Leaders	News media
Abortion	65	36	35
Homosexuality	71	42	38
Lesbianism	70	42	37
Adultery	85	71	72
Premarital sex	40	31	20
Sex before 16	71	55	54
Cohabitation before marriage	47	32	24
Pornographic movies	68	56	46
Hard drugs	84	73	66
Marijuana	57	33	22

SOURCE: *Report on American Values* (Connecticut Mutual Life Insurance Company, April 1981).

In short, the study affirms a growing public recognition that the spiritual and metaphysical are more basic to our economic progress and prosperity than the physical and political; that spiritual values are fundamental to economic values; that goodness does have something to do with the GNP.

Unfortunately, the study also found that on a whole range of specific moral issues, "American leaders are substantially out of tune with the public they are supposed to represent." The moral ethic of our culture, then, is being directed, particularly in the media, by leaders of thought whose personal values are moving against the spiritual and moral currents of the public at large.

The study found that "the reemergence of America's religious strain represents far more than a recent response to national concern about Vietnam and Watergate. It symbolizes nothing less than a determined effort to revitalize American self-confidence in the face of adversity"—and, it would seem, in the face of determined opposition from the movers and shakers of American public debate and conciousness.

During the 1980 election campaign, the distinguished American political commentator David Broder told a Public Television audience, "People have the feeling that the country has lost its greatness," and he observed that "for many, the return to greatness means a return to traditional spiritual values."

More than 150 years before, another great observer of the American scene, Alexis de Tocqueville, recognized the direct connection between this nation's economic strength and its moral ethos, when he wrote in *Democracy in America*:

I searched for America's greatness in her matchless constitution and it was not there.

I searched for America's greatness in her halls of Congress and it was not there.

I searched for America's greatness in her rich and fertile fields and teeming industrial potential and it was not there.

It was not until I went into the heartlands of America and into her churches and met the American people that I discovered what it is that makes America great.

America is great, because America is good, and if America ever ceases to be good, America will cease to be great.

Following Tocqueville's hypothesis to its logical conclusion, the current decline in this nation's economic as well as strategic strength ultimately may have more to do with a decline in our "goodness" than with the failure of specific policies or leaders.

When Moses went up Mount Sinai in search of direction out of the wilderness, he did not come back down with a road map but with a set of moral laws. The central theme of the Old Testament is that when the Hebrew people, the Children of Israel, were obedient to those Ten Commandments, they prospered and found their way. When they departed from them and "worshipped other gods" they failed, and lost their freedom. A clear moral code thus became the foundation of a great, though small, nation and, in turn, the cradle of Western civilization itself. Spiritual values were understood to be precedent to economic and social well-being.

But today most of these Ten Commandments have been regarded by an increasingly permissive and corporate society (particularly its leadership) as slightly outmoded, or at least irrelevant. Most of them are being violated more casually than ever before in our own nation's history. We now seem as a nation far more preoccupied with private sensual fantasies than with dreams of glory, far more prepared to defend the pornographers than to glorify the prophets.

Yet people ask, what do these personal moral and ethical standards have to do with the Gross National Product and a failing economy? I would answer with a number of rhetorical, metaphysical questions of my own:

- When we abandoned the gold standard in 1971, was this simply a faulty economic decision or was it an outward expression of the wholesale abandonment of traditional internal moral standards?
- Is it reasonable to expect a nation absorbed in existential self-gratification to save for the future?
- Can young people routinely "spaced out" on dope really be expected to be productive or to strive for excellence in academic or economic endeavor? Is our productivity falling prey more to "pot" than to policies?
- Is there not some definite connection between moral pollution, the miasma of white-collar crime and greed, and the physical pollution of hazardous wastes and foul air?
- Can business executives who routinely cheat on their spouses be expected not to cheat the consumer, the government, or their competitors?
- Can the 58% of minority children now born out of wedlock be expected

to grow up to lead productive and stable economic lives when 80% of child abuse and teenage crime now can be traced to fatherless homes?

• Can a society where abortions have become a more and more routine form of birth control (and outnumber live births in many major cities) be expected not to throw away its natural resources, too?

• Can we expect people who "want something for nothing" in their private affairs not to get the same thing from their government in the form of inflation?

• Is the steady devaluation of our currency merely the outward expression of the steady devaluation of our lives?

I ask these questions not because I agree with those who would again tie up our nation in a strict Puritan straitjacket. Prohibition didn't work and censorship is abhorrent. Although our laws must be deeply rooted in our moral standards, it is difficult to legislate private behavior without potential totalitarian abuse. On the other hand, when we speak of our economic product, we call it "*goods* and services." We do not call it "*bads* and ripoffs"! Yet that is what it becomes if this product derives from a culture that has lost its moral moorings and its innate sense of goodness. We look at Japan and marvel at its productivity and examine its economic policies, but do we also examine the kind of strict lifestyles, disciplined family values, and work ethic that dominate most Japanese lives?

These concerns are not being raised only by Christian fundamentalists. They are troubling some of this nation's deepest non-Christian thinkers. Irving Kristol told an American Enterprise Institute Conference on "Capitalism and Socialism: A Theological Inquiry":

> Until 20 or 25 years ago, it was thought natural for liberal governments to interfere in matters pertaining to individual morality, and it was thought to be wrong for such governments to interfere too much in economic matters. We have turned these two propositions around. We now think it right for government to intervene in economic matters and wrong for government to intervene in matters of individual morality. This is the great disaster of our age. Government can be productive in interfering with morality, but it is likely to be counterproductive when it interferes with economic affairs.

It is Kristol's concern that capitalism and the free marketplace, without the inspiration and moral framework provided by Judeo-Christian values, will degenerate into ugliness and repression and lose its dynamic character: "To the degree that organized religion has decayed and the attachment to the Judeo-Christian tradition has become weaker, to that degree capitalism has become uglier and less justifiable."

Today it seems self-evident that because of our decline in values, our economy is paying an enormous price in lost productivity and higher social costs—shifting from the production of "goods and services" to the promotion of "bads and ripoffs" in both our public and private sectors. Capitalism without the moral underpinning of the Decalogue and the inspiration of the Beatitudes soon degenerates into self-destructive greed.

Christianity and Capitalism

The unpleasant confrontation between Iran and the United States indicates the degree to which in this nuclear age, human warfare has been shifted from the battlefield to the mind, from the physical to the mental realm. Almost as never before, the Judeo-Christian (and mostly capitalistic) West is engaged in a warfare of ideas, not only with the forces of atheistic Communism in the Warsaw Pact nations but also with the Islamic East.

It is not unduly pessimistic to observe that in this metaphysical arena, the West (including Israel) seems to be losing some ground and finding itself hostage to a world that is increasingly non-Jewish, non-Christian, and noncapitalistic. Superficially, we can blame this loss of leadership on the economics of energy dependence and the erosion of Western military preparedness. Yet most of us realize that dry rot within is always more hazardous than assault from without.

As virtually every public opinion poll still shows, there is also an alarming uncertainty, a malaise, among Americans as to whether there is not a fundamental conflict between our spiritual values on the one hand and our institutional economic arrangements on the other—whether, in fact, capitalism and Christianity can continue successfully to coexist. The evidence suggests that a substantial share, if not the majority, of our academic and religious leadership now believes that it cannot. In a 1981 issue of *Harvard Business Review*, Norman Podhoretz writes, "Most intellectuals have always looked upon capitalism as an evil: a system unsound in itself and the cause of moral and spiritual depredations throughout society as a whole."

It was this pervasive mental uncertainty among American opinion-makers that the Ayatollah Khomeini exploited so skillfully during the hostage siege, calling on the whole nation of Islam to wage "holy war" against what he called "the satanic forces" of the Judeo-Christian world and its "oppressive and exploitive economic system." In the context of the abject poverty of most of Islam today, with its gaping polarization between the ludicrously rich and the incredibly poor, Khomeini's charges certainly had a hollow ring, coming as they did from that part of the world which was the very last to be forced (by the West) to give up slavery, and which still practices unconscionable religious and intellectual persecution and mass political murder.

Yet in the context of the aggressively sensual hedonism and crass commercialism which now drives so much of our own capitalistic system, Khomeini's attack in 1980 touched sensitive nerves. There is, for example, little connection between the purity and simplicity of the Bethlehem babe's appearance on earth and the merchandising madness that annually turns the U.S. Christmas season into a frenzy of frustration and robs us of much of its potential holiness and inspiration. This is a sorry annual reminder that while it is true that capitalism seems to have flourished most from the impetus of the Judeo-Christian ethic of individual self-betterment, its economic afflu-ence and prosperity have not always brought spiritual well-being. Quite often it has generated the opposite. Good Christians may become successful capitalists, but successful capitalists are not necessarily good Christians (in spite of what Dale Carnegie may argue).

This may explain why, in this most capitalistic of all nations, there now seems to be even more theological distrust of capitalism than there is of atheistic socialism and, indirectly, why no other nation in the West, except Great Britain, has more severely punished capitalism's economic lifeblood (savings and profits) than the United States has (at least until 1981). Not surprisingly, no other Western nation saves as little—or is experiencing slower growth in productivity.

Irving Kristol thinks this American "love-hate" relationship with capital-ism is due to the overwhelming dominance of traditional Christianity in our cultural and economic institutions: "Orthodox Jews have never despised business, Christians have. The act of commerce, the existence of a commer-cial society, has always been a problem for Christians." The reason, Kristol contends, is that Judaism and Islam provide mankind with laws which help them adapt to and live in an imperfect human world. Christianity, on the other hand, is more "gnostic," or prophetic, in character, calling on mankind to *change* the world we live in. "It tends to be hostile to all existing laws and all existing institutions . . . to insist that this hell in which we live, this 'unfair' world can be radically corrected."

It is this material utopianism which draws so many Christians to socialism, which seems to rest on the Christian ideal of the essential spiritual brotherhood, equality, goodness, and perfection of man, and which theorizes that it is only the iniquitous and discriminatory economic forces of capitalism that make man behave badly. Remove these forces, the Christian socialist promises, and mankind's inherent goodness will flourish in a kind of kingdom of heaven right here on earth.

Socialist experiments have always enticed Christians, from the ill-fated Brook Farm of the 19th century to the tragic Jonestown of 1978. Almost without exception, these experiments have foundered on the shoals of unredeemed human nature (i.e., sin) and on economic fallacies dominated by distribution, not production—fallacies that succeed only in spreading poverty, not in producing wealth. This utopianism arises from a rather superficial demand-side view both of religion (or metaphysics) and of eco-nomics. Kristol suggests that "Socialist redistribution bears some resemblance to Christian charity," but charity is no more the be-all of Christianity than distribution is the whole of economics. Charity without redemption becomes itself an expression of poverty and futility, as does distribution without production to replenish it.

Moreover, economy itself is the creation and production of *value*. Since, at its root, value is an expression of spiritual qualities with moral implications, religion, which is the teaching and promulgation of values, is intimately connected to the economy. From this perspective religion can be seen as supply-side in nature, because without a strong and flourishing value system, economic output must inevitably languish. Most religions, and especially Christianity and Judaism, also teach that a basic source of our daily supply can be found in the spiritual ideas, inspiration, and qualities of thought and character that come from a relationship to God. From this standpoint, true economy becomes the active expression of God-derived qualities in human endeavour, including the process by which we give raw matter value and purpose, and turn it into economic "goods."

Faith in the Infinite—which St. Paul calls "the substance of things hoped for"—leads directly to the Christian and Judaic teaching that giving is its own reward, since the more one gives the more one has to give. As St. Luke presents Christ's teaching, "Give, and it shall be given unto you; good measure, pressed down, and shaken together, and running over, shall men give unto your bosom. For with the same measure that ye mete withall it shall be measured to you again." The Golden Rule, actively followed, would wholly destroy both individual and collective poverty. And if everyone is busy giving (contributing and producing), then we have the ultimate under-pinning for Say's law that supply generates its own demand and rewards its own effort.

Further, what we have to give, whether in our work lives or our home lives, is, in the last analysis, also qualities of thought and attitudes. Integrity, loyalty, responsibility, trustworthiness, inspiration are powerful economic and social assets in any endeavor. Yet they are not elicited simply by financial incentives. They are the product of spiritual search, self-discipline, and teaching. They are also the positive wealth which millions of religious refugees and immigrants brought with them to America. Spiritual disciplines undergirded the development of our common wealth.

Unfortunately, however, just as the nation has turned away from its first economic and libertarian principles, from supply to demand, so too has the focus of the Church shifted gradually from the teaching of faith to secular political action, from turning men to the search for metaphysical supply—the true wealth of divine ideas—to the reallocation of material demand and apparently limited material resources. Redistribution has replaced contribution as the dominant theme.

God and the Welfare State

Over the past two decades, to the horror of some and the joy of others, the organized Church, Protestant, Catholic, and Jewish, has moved forthrightly into broad areas of economic, political, and social concern, as if in delayed response to Walter Raushenbush's *New Social Gospel,* which in its day (1917) seemed wildly radical but today seems quaintly moderate.

It is no longer unusual to find such venerable organizations as the National Council of Churches and the U.S. Roman Catholics' Campaign for Human Development taking strong leftist stands on such controversial issues as tax reform, rent control, subsidized public housing, welfare, national health insurance, and even vertical divestiture of the oil companies.

The underlying theme of most of this activity seems to boil down to the demand-side premise that income redistribution and the fully socialized welfare state are the highest human expressions of the Judeo-Christian ethic of compassion, that distribution is in some way more Christian than production, that one (distribution) equates with compassion and the other (production) with exploitation. With all due respect to these religious leaders, at best they seem guilty of a shallow interpretation of their own Biblical teachings (not to mention economic reality), and, at worst they appear to have a strange kind of death wish, through the sacrifice of the metaphysical initiative for the frustrations of power politics.

It must be transparently clear to any thinking person that the ultimate effect of the creation of the fully socialized welfare state is not merely the destruction of human liberty (and true economy—the unfoldment of ideas) but the shift of human trust from dependence on God to dependence on the state—the exchange of the worship of Deity for the idolatry and tyranny of Leviathan.

As the theologian Peter Berger admonishes, "Whatever socialism may be as an ideal, its empirical realization removes from the scene yet another limiting factor to the power of the modern state"; and this modern state is fundamentally dangerous because it represents "the most massive concentration of power in human history." "Since the demise of Nazi Germany," he notes, "all totalitarian societies have been socialist."

Even so-called democratically socialist countries annihilate what Michael Novak calls the mediating role of the Church, as the state and its welfare programs become the repositories of an increasingly secular faith.

If religious leaders doubt this, they need only consider what has happened to the Christian Church (both Protestant and Catholic) in Great Britain's democratically socialist welfare state. In 1947, a public opinion poll showed that about 90% of the public claimed to believe in God. But by 1975, after 30 years of welfare-state development, another poll showed that belief in God in Britain had dropped to less than 27% of the population, while in the United States it had remained over 90%. Actual church membership and attendance, which has drifted down to 44% in the United States, is now down to less than 15% in Great Britain. The same decline has taken place in socialist Sweden, where religion has almost ceased to be a serious issue. The same can be said, to a lesser extent, of Roman Catholicism in socialist Italy, France, and Germany.

Why has this taken place? Can it not be because the Church, in stressing human material needs so completely (needs which it has neither the resources nor the mandate to fulfill), has abdicated its unique role as spiritual feeder and focused the thought of the people, instead of on God, even more assiduously on the state (and therefore on material things and relationships) as the source of all good? As William Barrett suggests, the turn to socialism among religious intellectuals "represented a displacement of moral and religious values which had not found their outlet elsewhere, and here came to distorted expression." The distortion, however, lay in failing to understand the essentially spiritual and metaphysical nature of wealth and supply and the consequent drift to humanitarianism.

That could be why, today, we hear so much about "Christian humanism" and "Christian humanitarianism." Yet these very terms seem to be contradictions, since humanism and humanitarianism are ethical beliefs that specifically deny the existence or aid of God. Webster defines "humanitarianism" as "The doctrine that man may perfect his own nature without the aid of divine grace; the doctrine that denies the divinity of Jesus."

James Curry, former president of the American Humanist Association, admitted in 1970 that "Humanism is a polite term for atheism." In other words, humanism is an approach to life (albeit charitable and compassionate) that relieves mankind from the necessity to establish any relationship with God or to look to Him as the fundamental source of all good. It totally denigrates the supply side of faith and spirit. Corliss Lamont, a leader of the humanist movement, declares that "Humanism believes in a naturalistic metaphysics . . . that considers all forms of the supernatural a myth. Humanism is the viewpoint that men have but one life to live, and that human happiness is its own justification and needs no sanction or support from supernatural sources: that, in any case, the supernatural does not exist."

Compare this anti-faith, man-centered humanist (and ultimately entropic) view of the universe with the essential spiritual concept of God and man that permeates both the Old and New Testaments of the Bible, both the Torah and the Gospels. It was Moses, for example, who spurned the comparative comfort and security of the Egyptian "welfare state" (and its bondage) to lead a national tribe out into a cruel and dangerous wilderness to find a "promised land," because he deeply believed God had commanded his way toward greater human freedom and abundance ("milk and honey"). Yet through that tough experience, both Jews and Christians believe, Moses was able to prove for all time that God "could set a table in the wilderness" and that even the most basic human needs could be met by putting God first—that faith indeed is *real substance*.

It was this essential message that permeated the Sermon on the Mount, when Jesus admonished man to "Take no thought, saying what shall we eat, or what shall we drink, or wherewithal shall we be clothed. For your Heavenly Father knoweth that ye have need of these things. But, seek ye first the Kingdom of God and His righteousness, and all these things shall be added unto you."

When the Pharisees came to him, wondering just what kind of "kingdom" (welfare state?) was to be established and where it would appear on earth, Jesus rebuked their materialistic utopianism, saying, "The kingdom of God cometh not with observation. Neither shall ye say lo here, nor lo there, but the kingdom of God is within you," within human consciousness. It was in a way the first formal expression of supply-side thinking. He did not say that first you take care of all human needs, and *then* you will find God. He told them that if they would search for the individual understanding of God, this understanding and resulting inspiration would in turn give them all the "things" they would need. He put spiritual causation in individual consciousness first, and material results second. Thoughts, Jesus taught, were fundamental to things. Emerson put it succinctly: "Great men are they who see that spiritual is stronger than any material force, that thoughts rule the world."

Humanism (a demand-side view) reverses all that, putting man's material needs first as the prerequisite of the good society. It places the pursuit of immediate material comfort and security first, and the search for freedom and spiritual dominion second. Where the Talmudic philosopher argues, "The noblest charity is to prevent a man from accepting charity; and the best alms is to show and enable a man to dispense with alms," the welfare state would encourage even greater tyranny over the human spirit.

As Professor Howard Parsons, a member of the American Humanist Association and a scholar at the University of Bridgeport, declares: "Marxism [socialism] is the most effective and influential form of atheism to appear in history, and the most formidable non-religious challenge to Christianity for the commitment of men." This may explain why the left-leaning "liberal" establishment churches are not benefiting from the current spiritual and religious revival in the United States, which is taking place in the more fundamentalist denominations. In 1979 virtually all of the "liberal" church denominations lost members, while almost all of the "conservative" churches gained. Also in growing numbers, individuals are apparently turning not so much to organized religion, but directly to God and the power of prayer for answers to their human problems—on an individual level rather than through collective religious or political action.

Ironically, just when a growing share of the public sees the direct connection between spiritual and moral values and real economic well-being, the mainstream liberal Christian Church has all but abandoned primary emphasis on moral teaching. Yet without this teaching, capitalism loses its enormous potential to bless. It is no accident that capitalism rose to world economic leadership only as a byproduct of the spread of Judeo-Christian spiritual values and laws; and to the extent that these values dissipate in hedonistic, amoral humanism, capitalism itself will decline. As Kristol charges, "Capitalism is facing today not an economic crisis but a crisis of belief." The same humanist-socialists who hate the market hate Christianity and Judaism with equal intensity, because the God of Israel requires individual spiritual growth and freedom.

Instead of lying down with these "strange bedfellows," the Church liberals should stop their ideological war on democratic capitalism, and instead renew their commitment to the spiritual and moral teaching of metaphysical qualities which have always in the past made capitalism the most effective weapon against the poverty they contend is their chief human concern. The fact that they do not do this suggests that too much of the liberal church is more intent on cultivating the poor than on healing them of poverty. If healing poverty were really their goal, they would support and redeem capitalism with even more enthusiasm than they now seem to show for the dialectics of Marx.

Capitalism and Healing Poverty

One day in 1979 the front pages of many newspapers featured a haunting picture of the frail Mother Theresa receiving the Nobel Peace Prize for her magnificent but frustrating work among the very poorest of Calcutta's impoverished 7 million—where up to 50% are unemployed and hundreds routinely die of starvation in the streets each night, defying the most heroic efforts at relief.

Mother Theresa's saintly life and grand humilities present a clear and implicit rebuke to the opulence of an uncaring West, more concerned for the price of oil and gold than for the cost of human suffering. But that, too, could be a superficial view, since nothing could do more for Calcutta's starving millions than a vital economy, freed from the shackles of centuries of religious superstition and pagan mysticism. Buried deep in the business sections of the same newspapers that carried Mother Theresa's story was the news that despite a much-heralded recession, U.S. unemployment had dropped, once more, to 6%, while the "troubled U.S. economy" was still employing 60% of its adult population, the highest employment percentage of any nation in recorded economic history (and nearly 20 points higher than in India).

In spite of spiraling inflation and energy costs (and after all benefits), less than 7% of all Americans in 1982 live below the comparatively high U.S. poverty line; and even this 7% live better than 80% of the rest of the world's population. As Michael Novak wrote, "No better weapon against poverty, disease, illiteracy, and tyranny has yet been found than capitalism. The techniques, human skills, and changes of cultural habit necessary to expand the productive capacity of the earth have been pioneered by democratic capitalism. Its compassion for the material needs of humankind has not in history, yet, had a peer."

There are, however, no Nobel Peace Prizes for democratic capitalism or for American industry and its fabulously successful assault on poverty. Instead, only brickbats, as the media daily parade industry's more unseemly excesses on page one and bury its successes on page 40, while "profit" has become an ugly epithet and capitalism itself is scorned as "trickle-down" economic theory.

It is ironic that the same Christian Church which was once the strongest apologist for the "Babbittry" of unrestrained 19th-century capitalism and the so-called Protestant work ethic, has now turned with such savage scorn on the affluent society which this "ethic" has produced. Although some of this radical shift in American Christian thought has been spurred by a long-overdue awakening to the real plight of the poor and minorities, it also seems to represent a more fundamental change in today's Christian models.

The "new world" ethic of productivity and industry, which has done so much to alleviate human suffering, has apparently been traded in for the "old world" model of poverty as being synonymous with Christian piety and "no growth" as synonymous with "Christian stewardship." In this new-old model, so graphically and repeatedly presented on the television screen, to be poor (regardless of cause) is automatically to be deserving of social reverence and concern (and absolved of responsibility), while to be well-off (by this same semi-Marxist/pseudo-Christian logic) is to be guilty of exploiting the poor both at home and abroad, or at the very least "destroying the environment"!

In the process, observers now suggest, the Church may have fallen prey to a total reversal of the Christian message. In Dostoevsky's novel *The Brothers Karamazov,* the Grand Inquisitor argues that when the Antichrist comes, his message will be *first* to feed the people and *then* to ask of them virtue—thus abandoning the teaching that spiritual values precede material well-being and giving up the war against sin.

One of the tragedies of our time is that even as U.S. material poverty has been statistically reduced (by more than two thirds since 1963), the evidence of spiritual poverty and human degradation has steadily mounted. Between 1960 and 1979, while social spending soared from 10% of the GNP to 22%, the nation's crime rates more than doubled, the percentage of fatherless homes more than tripled, and whole sections of great cities disappeared in the violent rubble of what passes for "social compassion." Irving Kristol writes, "The conventional Christian wisdom of today is that the poor—what we call underprivileged people—need not be expected to behave virtuously (or rationally) until their material situation has been remedied." Yet this conventional wisdom is a mockery of Christ's teaching, which demands the relinquishment of sin as the precursor to the reception of good, placing primary stress on the metaphysical, rather than the physical, as the source of supply.

Curiously, aside from the fundamentalists, most of the established churches in America have been actively downplaying individual sin as it relates to the overcoming of social ills. Collective victimology seems to have replaced individual salvation as the central message of liberal theology. As a direct result, too many of our social programs have been predicated on the "no-fault" principle that an individual should not have to suffer even for his own irresponsibility. The state must act as protector and insurer against failure regardless of cause. Unfortunately, while the irresponsible benefit, the vast majority who do act responsibly are penalized by rapidly growing taxation and programs, which, in turn, subsidize even more no-fault actions and higher costs for all. Sin succeeds while good purpose is punished by the vast array of no-fault government policies:

- no-fault unemployment compensation available even to those who leave their jobs and stay off them voluntarily, or to employers who "schedule layoffs" simply because compensaton is available;
- no-fault tax-subsidized private health-insurance programs which most economists now agree are unnecessarily promoting exaggerated use of hospital care and are mainly responsible for skyrocketing costs of U.S. medical care and insurance;
- no-fault compulsory car insurance in which the 10% who cause 90%

of the accident losses pay no more for coverage than the 90% who drive responsibly—a program which has driven damage claims and insurance rates to all-time highs—30%–40% higher than in states that do not have this program;

- no-fault criminal justice which tends to blame "society" for crime and, by 1975, reduced the level of punishment to less than 2% of all crimes committed, helping to triple the crime rate in the country in less than ten years, with enormous economic and social costs;

- no-fault divorce laws and "sexual liberation" which have contributed to the highest divorce and family breakup rates in history, an epidemic in venereal disease, and the highest rate of teenage illegitimate pregnancy ever; and

- no-fault education policies which have downplayed individual achievement and performance and discouraged the whole concept of individual moral responsibility and the work ethic.

What worries the social scientists, economists, and political theorists is not only the enormous economic costs of such no-fault living, but its deeper psychological costs to the nation's morale. Dr. Karl Menninger suggests that one of the principal reasons for the rapid rise in mental illness in our society is the decline in a sense of individual responsibility and personal worth—a feeling of helplessness and lack of direction. He argues that people have always learned more from their mistakes than from their success; but when the "price" of mistakes is eliminated, the result is confusion and a loss of motivation to "do better."

What is now being recommended, even by many liberal economists and social scientists, is the introduction into most of our social programs of elements of restraint which put a greater premium on individual responsibility and provide penalties for errant behavior. A good example is the recent decision in several states to withhold unemployment compensation from those who quit work voluntarily and to take individuals off welfare who refuse repeated offers of employment. The intent of these efforts is not to be harsh or merely fiscally prudent, but to take a more reasonable approach to providing generous help to those who really do need it, while restoring the positive economic assets of individual responsibility and worth to the substantial number who really don't—to encourage the satisfaction of work over the degradation of chronic dependence on the state.

In Massachusetts, for example, where 55% of the population in 1980 was directly dependent on government (up from 41% in 1960), and where a nearly $3-billion welfare budget barely kept over 500,000 recipients from starving or freezing, the most serious impediment to the future of the state's economy was not energy but severe and chronic shortages of both skilled and unskilled labor! Yet the strongest opponents of attempts to move individuals from welfare to work have included not only the bureaucracies but the Church.

This institutionalization and subsidization of poverty threatens the very productivity and prosperity that could heal it—and the Christian Church, both Protestant and Catholic, too often looms as the staunchest defender of this system of curious compassion, vigorously opposing even the mildest efforts to reform it or tighten it. This arises, it would seem, not only from a shallow sense of true compassion but from an even more superficial reading of the actual teachings of Christ Jesus.

Although it is plain that the Master ministered to the poor (and urged us to imitate him in this), nowhere can he be found glorifying poverty as an end in itself. Instead, Jesus promised that the very quest for spiritual understanding and faith in God would, itself, bring the increase: "I am come that ye might have life, and that ye might have it more abundantly."

While Jesus lifted up the poor, the halt, and the sick, it was also plain that he did not tolerate the self-pity, helplessness, or ingratitude that would make such conditions worse. "Take up thy bed and walk," he commanded the pitiable invalid, as he healed him. One startling indication of this came when Judas challenged the Master to sell off the bag of provisions and ointments which the disciples carried with them and to give the proceeds to the poor. Jesus rebuked this contrivance of compassion by telling Judas, "The poor ye have always with you, but me, ye have not always with you," thus ascribing more power for healing poverty to the spiritual ideas he presented than to the "petty cash" of temporary charity. He even rebuked the do-gooding Martha, "thou art careful and troubled about many things," while praising the contemplative Mary. Reflection was shown to be more valuable than reaction.

And in his parable of the talents, Jesus taught mankind to use their God-given talents, faith, and understanding to overcome limitation and lack instead of submitting to them, concluding with the disturbing warning: "unto every one that hath [i.e. those who use their talents] shall be given, and he shall have abundance: but from him that hath not [those who do not use their talents] shall be taken away even that which he hath."

That is hardly a model of sentimental Christian compassion or pious poverty. That such a stern but loving supply-side lesson in individual responsibility and productivity should come from the lips of the same Teacher who preached the parable of the Good Samaritan shows that Jesus saw no essential conflict between the Old Testament image of God as Lawgiver or Principle and his own revelation of God as Love. He understood that it is Love's purpose to compel progress and that mankind often learns more from adversity than from success.

Without the demand to strive and grow, implicit in the ideal of God as Father (or divine Principle), would mankind continue its search for a higher human standard and for the perfection the Gospels urge as our birthright? Without God as Principle, would not compassion merely become a self-justifying trap for human stagnation and defeat? Can we really have a genuine sense of God as Love, without a sense of Him as lawgiver?

While each of us, theoretically, has the capacity to be both strongly principled and warmly compassionate, both fatherly and motherly at the same time, the fact is that few of us achieve this balance easily, regardless of gender. Most families still need both a father and a mother, in qualities at least—father qualities which produce, provide, and discipline, and mother qualities which care, love, and nourish. As it is with the family, so it is with nations, which throughout history have tended to swing back and forth between extremes. Whenever they became too captive of any one extreme for too long, the opposite has tended to reassert itself. But balance and completeness have never come without hard work to nations or individuals.

Human beings soon discover that principle without love or compassion ceases to be principle and becomes oppression. Contrariwise, love or compassion without the strength of self-discipline and principle soon ceases to be very loving and becomes the "smotherhood" of domination. There is nothing very loving about a family or a society that fails to discipline its children in order to prepare them to live responsibly on their own. Thus the failure of permissive education and the social-welfare state.

On the other hand, there is nothing very principled about a family or a society that deals out harsh discipline without compassionate and rational support. Thus the failure of the narrow "law-and-order" mentality that practices autocracy and usually generates only more resentment and rebellion. Human political systems are, at their very best, imperfect efforts to find the balance between these two main aspects of Deity—the righteous lawgiver and judge of the Old Testament and the God who is Love in the New—between Moses' Commandments and the Beatitudes of Jesus Christ.

Unfortunately, for too many years Western democracies, in particular, have believed that liberal compassion was all good while conservative restraint and discipline were all bad—that they could forever have unlimited demand and distribution without worrying about production and supply. In the process they have fostered a whole "me" generation of takers and nearly destroyed a generation of producers. The demand side of our country has been eating up the supply side, in religious expression as well as economics. We love to talk about "caring," but we don't like to think about sin or responsibility. The time has come, therefore, not to throw out compassionate liberalism, but to tame it somewhat by reasserting some of the restraints of principled conservatism on the body politic.

But beyond this, it seems to me, Americans need to understand why neither ideological extreme should ever dominate completely as the left has been doing or as the extreme right might like to do in the future. The utopian moral absolutes presented by both left and right are impossible to realize in human experience, unless consciousness is redeemed far beyond its present level.

Government as God?

Above all, we must avoid the worse result of giving godlike powers to any government, left or right. Not only does this lead to arbitrary tyranny, but it undermines our most powerful metaphysical and economic assets—our morale, our individual sense of self-worth, indeed, morality itself. It should not surprise us that in direct proportion as we have traded in our original commitment to individual self-government of law for centralized government of men (bureaucracies), we have seen lawlessness, chaos, and corruption rise.

As Leonard Read warns: "We find in a growing statism the explanation for our double standard of morality. The same person to whom stealing a penny from a millionaire would be unthinkable will, when the state apparatus is put at his disposal, join in taking billions from everybody, including the poor. . . ." The Church itself now runs the risk of publicly admitting its own failure to generate spontaneous sharing, contribution, and giving as acts of faith, inspired by love. It is too gladly subsituting the force of compulsory institutionalized government for spiritual leadership and persuasion. Read continues:

> As this is done, man loses his wholeness; he is dispossessed of responsibility for self, the very essence of his manhood. The more dependent he becomes, the less dependable. . . .
>
> Thus, the state inflicts itself as a dangerous centrifuge on society; man violently spun from the center which is his wholeness, his self-reliance, his integrity, and thrown in fragments onto an ever-widening periphery of unnatural specializations; man disoriented in unnatural surroundings, lost in detail and trivia; man from whom integrity has taken flight; man minus responsibility for self, the state his guardian and master.

It seems no accident that just at this moment of spiritual crisis, Providence should provide the Roman Catholics with a pope, John Paul II, who clearly appreciates this danger and the need to dampen the fires of secular socialism, who knows first hand the failure of government to "stand in" for God. It is no easy task. As he discovered in Puebla, Mexico, in 1979, a growing share of Catholic clergy both here and abroad are falling for the exciting lure of Marxist political activism as the way to better the lot of their parishioners; and given their impoverished lot, the lure is entirely understandable, if not credible, since too often these helpless people find they have merely traded one human tyranny for another.

"We believe we should not be satisfied with just prayer," one of the activist rebels said. To which Pope John Paul II had the courage to respond: "The idea of Christ, as a political figure, does not tally with the Church's catechesis. Clerical involvement in radical politics is counterproductive. You are not social managers, political leaders, or functionaries of a temporal power," he warned his rebel clerics. His recipe for true spiritual activism: "A soul living in habitual contact with God will know how to care for the poor without surrendering to sociopolitical radicalisms, which in the end are shown to be inopportune and counterproductive. Whatever the miseries or suffering that afflict man," he concluded, "it is not through violence, the interplay of power and political systems, but *through the truth concerning man, that he journeys toward a better future.*"

What the new pope so vividly expresses is his clear understanding of the one thing that separates Christianity from both Marxism and materialistic capitalism: the idea of spiritual causation—that the way to human triumph and freedom is not through material systems, but through spiritual and metaphysical understanding; that spiritual ideas do indeed have the power and substance to effect material betterment and peaceful social reformation and revolution. But the notion of world redemption through individual spiritual salvation is anathema to the Marxist humanism beguiling many materialistically minded clergy, who are looking only for an earthly utopia. Not that capitalism has any special claim on Christian virtue. It certainly does not. A greedy capitalist is no more spiritual than an imperious Marxist ideologue. Both have equally materialistic views—and goals. The difference is that while capitalism thrives on the political and religious freedom also essential to Christianity, Marxism relies on tyranny for survival.

"Where the spirit of the Lord is, there is liberty," wrote St. Paul. And wherever there is such spiritually supported liberty, capitalism invariably flourishes; but where Marxist totalitarianism rules, all religious experience is automatically threatened and spiritual inspiration stagnates. As Pope John Paul found out from his experience in Poland, while Christianity can live (albeit critically and disapprovingly) with capitalism, it withers in Communist states, which, he says, "produce only oppression, intimidation, violence, and terrorism."

On the other hand, while Christ Jesus plainly rejected the materialistic utopianism which seems to characterize so much of the rhetoric of present-day populist Christianity, he also rejected the human pursuit of material wealth for its own sake, the "bottom-line" thinking that has become so self-defeating, economically and morally, to present-day capitalism.

The Profit Motive Is Not Enough

Although capitalism may not be essential to the survival of Christianity, the metaphysical insights of Christianity and Judaism are essential if we are to keep capitalism from destroying itself. The troubled state of the American private economy, with slackening productivity, uncertain profitability, and growing public distrust, mandates a fresh vision for capitalists in the 1980s and beyond.

It is in no way to denigrate the essential role of profits in our economy to suggest that the profit motive, alone, is simply no longer enough—indeed, it never was. There is, after all, nothing particularly sacred or inspired about the profit motive. It is as natural to apes and squirrels as it is to human beings—as endemic to unredeemed human nature as raw greed. The most selfish infant often displays as much of it as the largest corporate conglomerate.

Yet, it often escapes the notice of some religionists that both individuals and corporations with the most intense expressions of the profit motive often fail in the long run, while some of the greatest business successes (and profits) have come to men and women with the most generous and unselfishly motivated natures. This would seem to confirm the validity of the Christian teaching that "It is more blessed to give than to receive," more rewarding to contribute than to exploit, and to point to an ideal for the conduct of private enterprise and the true "market economy."

Throughout the economic history of this nation, we can see that those companies survive and succeed the longest which have done the best job of identifying real human needs and filling them—and thereby contributing to our general well-being by responding to the market. Conversely, we observe again and again that those companies which systematically abuse and exploit both workers and consumers (markets) for the sake of short-term gain tend to have very poor survival rates. There is nothing in this that is inconsistent with the fundamental metaphysical principles and laws which permeate most religious doctrines, which teach that evil motives produce their own failures, while good inevitably produces its own generous rewards. Capitalism, then, can survive only if it is leavened by the insights of the spiritual sense which tempers greed and promotes genuine vision.

Among these insights is the realization that profits, while they are the natural and legitimate result of businesses well run to serve the public, cannot be the exclusive goal of business. When the single-minded pursuit of profit dominates corporate thinking, it can tend to exclude vision, hinder true creativity and productivity, debilitate the dynamism of enterprise, and ultimately reduce wealth itself.

In exact proportion as corporate America has in recent years come to be dominated by "profit maximization," its innovation and invention have been inhibited, its productivity sapped, and, curiously enough, its real growth and profitability reduced. It is easy enough to blame this on the impact of rising government regulations and stultifying federal tax, spending, and inflationary policies, which have turned most American business toward "defensive" economic thinking, putting more emphasis on this year's gain than on building for the future.

Although government must share the blame for this situation, so must the boardrooms of corporate America, which have allowed the ethically neutral business-school mentality to substitute its accounting manipulation, cash-flow thinking, and the tax-accounting logistics of mergers for the real vision of growth through the metaphysical process of creativity, invention, and true enterprise. It is this decline in creative vision that has led to the increasing spiritual impoverishment of executive suites.

It has also affected the relative success of the corporations and the country as well. The Preacher's warning that "Where there is no vision the people perish" applies especially to business.

The American economic scene is littered with the wreckage and evident deterioration of companies that for too long have ignored creative thinking and basic research and development, as well as the changing pattern of real human needs, while fixating on this year's balance sheet. Automobile companies, railroads, and the steel industry are examples of how excessive profit orientation has produced not more growth and profits, but less. This could also be said of those labor unions that have overextended their reach beyond productivity.

There is a profound metaphysical reason for this experience. It arises from a failure to understand the real nature of profits as savings and their basic purpose, not as an overarching goal in and of themselves, but as an ethical and moral discipline, a standard of efficient performance, and ultimately the product of self-denial. Savings (including profits) are the result of the willingness to put aside immediate gratification and consumption for the purpose of increasing future good. In this sense, then, profits, like savings, are the economic expression of the spiritual and moral ethic of self-control, the willingness to check our purely animal instincts for short-term pleasure, and to sacrifice our most selfish desires in order to achieve a much larger reward—specifically, more real dominion over our human experience and more secure well-being.

The most successful companies in this country have been built, by and large, out of the self-discipline and creative faith in the future of a comparatively few men and women who, had they been motivated purely by short-term greed or "bottom lines," could never have achieved what they did. I think for example of Bradley Dewey, Sr., who helped give this nation synthetic rubber during World War II when we needed it most, and in the process contributed valuable private inventions for the public good.

Dewey's greatest achievement was the plastic packaging process known as Cryovac, which, along with subsequent imitators, revolutionized the production, distribution, and consumption of meat and poultry in this country. The process has saved consumers literally tens of billions of dollars in reduced waste, distribution costs, and spoilage, and has been the basis of the creation of tens of thousands of new jobs.

It took Dewey nearly 20 difficult years before Cryovac finally became a profitable venture—during which time he continually confounded his accountants and controllers by sacrificing nearly his entire capital investment and life savings to bring this idea through all its technical and marketing problems to fruition. Dewey's long-range vision ultimately produced a major new and profitable business that has blessed millions; yet there never was a man, in my experience, who was less preoccupied with "profit maximization" or more occupied with genuine service to his country. For Dewey, profits were a secondary and disciplinary measure of performance, only a means to the larger end of enabling his company to carry out other new ideas that would improve human welfare.

We should not be surprised that the nation's healthiest industry today, high technology, is one of the few places in American business where one will find lots of visionary Deweys. Real economic growth and vitality depend on this imaginative and courageously trusting type of mentality—the kind that, for a good example, will rise above nearly three years of million-dollar-a-month losses to produce the billion-dollar success that is now Federal Express.

Unfortunately, the corporate-conglomerate scene is all too often dominated by the myopic slide-rule mentality that is interested primarily in the next stockholders meeting, the next merger move, the next hearing in Washington. The substitution of short-term self-gratification for the self-denial of genuine creativity (which is the true compassion of the entrepreneur) is cause for alarm.

The Compassionate Capitalist

In all the sentimental folderol that characterizes so much social and political commentary today, we almost never hear the term "compassionate" applied to a business executive or an entrepreneur. Yet in terms of results in the measurable form of jobs created, lives enriched, communities built, living standards uplifted, and poverty healed, a handful of "compassionate capitalists" have done infinitely more for their fellow men than all the self-serving politicians, academics, social workers, or religionists who claim the adjective "compassionate" for themselves.

I had, for example, the special privilege of coming into direct contact with an obscure Austrian immigrant to this country by the name of Ernst Mahler, who had come to work for Kimberly Clark shortly after World War I. Mahler was an entrepreneurial genius whose innovative ideas and leadership, over a period of about 30 years, transformed this once-small, insular newsprint and tissue manufacturer into one of the largest paper corporations in the world, which gives prosperous employment to more than 100,000 and produces products (which Mahler helped innovate) that are now used by more than 2 billion people. Mahler became enormously wealthy, of course. Yet his personal fortune was insignificant when compared with the permanent prosperity he generated, not only for his own company but for the hundreds of thousands who work for industries which his genius ultimately spawned and which long outlived him—not to mention the revolutionary sanitary products that have liberated two generations of women, or the printing papers that completely transformed international publishing and communications for fifty years.

I can safely predict that you have never heard of him up to this moment. Not one person in 100 million has. Yet his contribution has permanently uplifted the lives of millions and far exceeds in real compassion most of our self-congratulatory politicians and "activists" whose names are known to all. What is so troubling is that those who cloak themselves in this "compassion mantle" are so often the very people who are hedging in the economic freedom that made Ernst Mahler's life and contribution possible.

As Michael Novak so ably expresses it,

> The motive of this system [democratic capitalism] is to concentrate upon improving the material base of humankind; but its higher purpose in doing so is to empower individuals to use their native liberty as they see fit. For democratic capitalism, liberty is at once the means to greater

productivity, and the end thereof. Unlike pretentious socialism, democratic capitalism does not presume to take the place of archbishops,
philosophers, and poets in instructing individuals how to use their
liberty. Instead such a system permits individuals to find, or to lose their
own way.

—or, as St. Paul suggests, to work out their own salvation.

The "liberal" Christian clergy routinely condemns men like Ernst Mahler
and the market they have created as exploitive and selfish and calls for a
"more compassionate society," based on statist regulation and a forced
redivision of wealth that obviates Christian charity. But who among these
theologians has contributed a scintilla as much practical good for their fellow
men? Where is there more effective Christian compassion—in the truly
creative capitalist or in the sympathetic social worker? In the "invisible
hand" that guides the market or in the heavy bureaucratic hand that stifles it?

Theology vs. Entropy

Even more troubling is the utter failure of most of America's spiritual
leadership to challenge the "scientific determinism" that would impose
growing limitations on compassionate capitalism and on the upward hopes
and mobility of the American people. Even as technology itself daily breaks
new ground into the exhilarating realm of the metaphysical and cosmic
sciences, the liberal Church seems more and more earthbound in its outlook
as it embraces what Jeremy Rifkin archly calls "the theology of entropy."

This new liberal-theological "entropic world view" argues that mankind,
having received a material creation as a gift from a spiritual God, must now
redefine its hopes and dreams in the context of finite limits. It must accept all
of the unspiritual premises these limits imply, from environmental extremism
to zero population growth, from abortion to the "right to die"; it must see
itself merely as transitory stewards of an untouchable earth environment.

Not only do such views come perilously close to adopting Rousseau's noble
savage as a model for Christian living, but, in implicitly accepting entropy as
"the supreme governing law," they are denying the immortality of God and
His image, man, and, in particular, the prophets from Moses to Jesus, who
preached and demonstrated the triumph of the metaphysical (or spiritual)
over the physical and material.

The Entropy Law, after all, is the essence of materialism. It posits the case
for growing disorder, destruction, inharmony, disintegration, and death. As
Jeremy Rifkin argues, "We desperately search for immortality in this finite
world, while *knowing there is none*. There is a nihilism in our search." Is it not
precisely that search for immortality that is the central theme and cause of
Christianity and, indeed, of most of the great Hebrew prophets as well? Can
there be any greater illustrations of "anti-entropy" than manna from heaven,
water struck from a rock, oil continually provided out of what had seemed to
be an empty barrel, the myriad spiritual healings of the most horrendously

advanced deteriorative diseases, the feeding of the multitude, the walking on water, the cleansing of leprosy in the river Jordan—to mention but a few of the Biblical miracles?

And what is the meaning of the Resurrection if not the triumph over entropy? Was Jesus so enamored of this finite material world that he wished all mankind (except himself) to accept its fatalistic premises and limits? "In the world ye have tribulation," he said, "but be of good cheer, I have overcome the world."

The central theme of Biblical prophecy is this "overcoming" and the bringing of order, healing, harmony, and peace of God to bear on individual human lives. "We shall overcome" is not merely a civil-rights spiritual, but the paradigm of Christian salvation summed up so gloriously by St. Paul in his first Epistle to the Corinthians:

> Now if Christ be preached that he rose from the dead, how say some among you [entropicists?] that there is no resurrection of the dead?
>
> But if there be no resurrection of the dead, then is Christ not risen:
>
> And if Christ be not risen, your faith is also vain. . . .
>
> For as in Adam [entropy] all die, even so in Christ [spiritual anti-entropy] shall all be made alive.

The growing number of Christian theologians who now embrace the limits-of-growth view, are apparently prepared to reject spiritual reality and its potential for "overcoming" and, instead, are lending their religious authority to a movement and a viewpoint whose purpose Rifkin smugly spells out: "By radically redefining humanity's relationship to the rest of God's creation, contemporary Christian scholars are thrusting a theological dagger directly into the heart of the expansionist epoch"—and, in so doing, condemning the poor of the world to permanent despair.

They are also of necessity giving up on the Church's basic mission to purify and reform mankind of sin. If there is no ultimate tomorrow, then why strive for perfection today? If there is no immortality, then mortality and sin become the models for human behavior, the market does indeed become a jungle, and the only alternative is totalitarian government to distribute the resulting impoverishment "equitably."

It is no accident that precisely in proportion as the established liberal Church has abandoned its prophetic purifying role in favor of "political solutions," the national moral fabric has tattered and poverty has grown, while the production of wealth has languished. Since, as this book has attempted to elucidate, wealth is at its root metaphysical (the product of ideas and the promotion of useful qualities and values), purification and spiritualization of thought are not merely Christian ideals, they are at once the keys to human prosperity and economic progress, and the disciplines that make human freedom possible and capitalism compassionate.

In other words, goodness and purity of thought are not merely the stuff of Pollyanna religion or of positive thinking, they are substantial economic assets, the most fundamental components of our real GNP; and they will grow even more important as this nation moves progressively into an economy based on the components of mind more than on the elements of matter. It seems ironic that at the very moment in human history when mankind appears poised for a leap away from a things-based economy to the cybernetic realm of ideas and logic (from the physical to the metaphysical sense of wealth)—that is, to follow Buckminster Fuller's challenge to "dare to spread our wings of intellect and fly by the generalized principles governing the universe"—the Church establishment should seem to be moving so determinedly in the opposite direction, from prophecy back to politics.

Ultimately this new economy depends on the creative inspiration that comes to enlightened thought; and it is the prophet's primary role to uplift and enlighten, to "shepherd" this creative upreach. In this sense, the Church, indeed all religious expression, is central to the economic well-being of the nation and the genuine relief of human poverty. Although simple human prosperity can never be the primary goal of moral and spiritual teaching, it is the inevitable result. Without this teaching, mankind is doomed to moral and economic decline, no matter what system of government or economics it chooses.

As Alexis de Tocqueville suggested, the greatness of our economy can continue only as a reflection of the goodness of our people.

Notes and Sources

Preface

Martin Feldstein, Introduction, *The American Economy in Transition* (Chicago: University of Chicago Press, 1980).

Chapter 1—THE UNLIMITED ECONOMY IN MIND

R. Buckminster Fuller, *Operating Manual for Spaceship Earth* (Carbondale, Ill.: Southern Illinois University Press, 1969; New York: Pocket Books, 1970).

The exchange between Adams and Jefferson is covered in Fawn Brodie, *Thomas Jefferson: An Intimate History* (New York: Norton, 1974), pp. 443–54.

The quotation from House Speaker Thomas P. O'Neill, Jr., appeared in a report of that speech in *The Boston Globe*, 22 May 1979.

The Robert Lekachman quotation from his book *Reaganomics: Greed Is Not Enough* (New York: Pantheon, 1981) was quoted in a speech by Congressman Jack Kemp to a Conference on Supply-Side Economics, Federal Reserve Bank of Atlanta, 17 March 1982.

Henry Fairlie's conversation was reported by Roscoe Drummond, *The Christian Science Monitor*, 19 November 1980, p. 22.

All of the quotations from George Gilder are from his book *Wealth and Poverty* (New York: Basic Books, 1981).

Quotations from St. Paul: II Corinthians 5:7 and Hebrews 8:14.

The Marx quotation is from *Capital [Das Kapital]* (Chicago: Kerr, 1867–83).

John W. Kendrick's analysis appeared in the November 1980 issue of the American Enterprise Institute's *Economist*, and in his essay "International Comparisons of Recent Productivity Trends," contained in the 1981-82 edition of *Essays in Contemporary Economic Problems: Demand, Productivity and Population* (Washington, D.C.: American Enterprise Institute, 1981). This essay also contains an analysis of Edward F. Denison's work on productivity, and in particular "How Japan's Economy Grew So Fast" (Washington, D.C.: Brookings Institution, 1976).

The quotation from F. A. Hayek appeared in his book *The Road to Serfdom* (Chicago: University of Chicago Press, paperback edition, 1976).

The various quotations from Professor Julian Simon come from both published and unpublished writings, including "Resources, Population and Environment: An Oversupply of Bad News," *Science*, 27 June 1980; "Global Confusion 1980: A Hard Look at the Global 2000 Report," *The Public Interest*, January 1981; "The False Religion of Farmland Conservation," a privately circulated monograph; "The Case for More People," *American Demographer*; November/December 1979. Simon's views are analyzed in "Simon Says," *Time*, 9 March 1981. Simon's most recent book is *The Ultimate Resource* (Princeton, N.J.: Princeton Universty Press, 1981).

The Goeller and Weinberg quotation appears in Simon's *Ultimate Resource* (mentioned above) and can be found in full context in "The Age of Substitutability," *Science*, Vol. 191 (1978), pp. 683–89.

Global 2000, a study published in 1980 at the request of President Jimmy Carter, was produced by a commission chaired by the Council on Environmental Quality and the Department of State and with which eleven other federal agencies "cooperated." It has been published commercially by both Penguin Books and Pergamon Press of New York as well as issued by the U.S. Government Printing Office.

Herman Kahn and Ernest Schneider, "Globaloney 2000," *Policy Review* (published by the Heritage Foundation, Washington, D.C.), Spring 1981.

The 1981 National Agricultural Lands (NALS) study is rebutted in a private monograph by Julian Simon drawing on extensive work by H. Thomas Frey of the U.S. Department of Agriculture's Economic Research Service—specifically his ERS study #291, "Cropland for Today and Tomorrow," which completely undercuts the NALS contention that we are losing 3 million acres of farmland per year.

Governor Thompson's executive order for preserving farmland was rebutted by Dale McLaren (of the Greater Wabash Regional Planning Commission) and Julian Simon, "Are We Losing Ground?", *Illinois Business Review*, April 1980, pp. 1-6 (and further, in that journal, December 1980, pp. 3-4), and they also exposed the debate in "Assuring the Future of U.S. Farmland," *The Wall Street Journal*, 10 November 1980, whereupon the Department of Agriculture "readjusted" its figures to attempt to refute its own prior data (which showed that cropland was actually increasing in Illinois). Even so, the new "adjusted" figures show that total Illinois cropland did in fact rise from 24,399,558 acres in 1974 to 25,366,407 acres in 1978.

All quotations from Jeremy Rifkin are from his book *Entropy* (New York: Viking Press, 1980).

Chapter 2—THE INDIVIDUAL AS CAPITAL

The Julian Simon quotation is from *The Ultimate Resource* (Princeton, N.J.: Princeton University Press, 1981).

For full information on the University of Illinois SIE analysis, see Julian Simon, "What Immigrants Take from and Give to the Public Coffers," a report to the Select Commission on Immigration and Refugee Policy, 15 September 1980.

Simon Kuznets, *Economic Growth of Nations* (Princeton, N.J.: Princeton University Press, 1971) is the source of this analysis of population growth versus economic output.

William Fellner explores the input of population growth and immigration on technological change and productivity growth in "Trends in Activities Generating Technological Progress," *American Economic Review*, Vol. 60 (1970), pp. 1–29.

Analysis of "A Tale of Two Cities," which I based on U.S. Census Bureau data, 1940–70, appeared in the *Boston Herald American*, 11 December 1977.

Julian Simon is quoted from his article "The Case for More People," *American Demographer*, November/December 1979, and from his testimony before the House Select Committee on Population, U.S. House of Representatives, 2 June 1978.

R. Buckminster Fuller, *Operating Manual for Spaceship Earth* (Carbondale, Ill.: Southern Illinois University Press, 1969; New York: Pocket Books, 1970).

Chapter 3—WHAT IS PROGRESSIVE ABOUT TAXATION?

In his Democratic National Convention speech, 19 August 1980, attacking Ronald Reagan, Senator Edward M. Kennedy quoted from a Reagan speech of 1964 entitled "Losing Our Freedom Inch by Inch." A rebuttal, including the correct sourcing of the Karl Marx-Friedrich Engels quotation on the graduated income tax, appeared in a column by James J. Kilpatrick, Washington Star Syndicate, September 1980.

George McGovern's "demogrant" program is described in Jack Kemp's book *An American Renaissance* (New York: Harper & Row, 1980), pp. 47–48.

For a full discussion of the Laffer Curve, see Jude Wanniski, *The Way the World Works* (New York: Basic Books, 1978), Chapter 6. For its origins, see Andrew W. Mellon, *Taxation: The*

People's Business (New York: Macmillan, 1924), especially pp. 216–27. See also John Mueller, "The Classical Economic Case for Cutting Marginal Income Tax Rates" prepared for the House Republican Conference (Washington, D.C., 20 February 1981).

The Keynes quotation on "Lafferism" is from his March 1933 essay "The Means to Prosperity," *The Collected Writings of John Maynard Keynes,* Volume 9, *Essays in Persuasion* (New York: St. Martins Press, 1972), p. 338.

The data on the Mellon tax cuts comes from the Tax Foundation analysis of IRS data for 1921–25.

The New York Times editorial, "Relieving the Rich," appeared in the issue of 23 December 1923.

The John F. Kennedy speech of 19 December 1962 was reported in detail in the New York *Commerce and Finance Chronicle,* 20 December 1962.

For discussion of Walter Heller's testimony, see John Mueller, "The Classical Economic Case . . ." (cited above), in which Mueller trapped Professor Heller's own economic "revisionism"—that is, his attempt to recant this testimony and suggest that it had been given over a decade before.

The unexpected rise in revenues was reported in "After Tax Cuts—More Prosperity, Higher Revenue," *U.S. News and World Report,* 13 June 1966, p. 117.

The startling increase in taxes paid by top income groups under the JFK tax cut was presented by Michael Evans in *The Wall Street Journal,* 7 August 1978.

For a full discussion of the tax-wedge theory, see Jude Wanniski, *The Way the World Works* (New York: Basic Books, 1978), pp. 97–115 and 212.

Milton Friedman, more than anyone else, has argued the case for the flat-rate income tax, and nowhere more cogently than in *Free to Choose* (New York: Harcourt Brace, 1979), pp. 293–94.

The tax distribution analysis is taken from Alan Blinder's lengthy essay in National Bureau of Economic Research, *The American Economy in Transition* (Chicago: University of Chicago Press, 1980), pp. 415–79.

Peter Gutmann made these comments in a *Wall Street Journal* editorial page essay in February 1977, elaborated on in "Statistical Illusions, Mistaken Policies," *Challenge,* November/December 1979, pp. 14–17, where he discussed the impact of the underground economy on tax avoidance.

Senator Abraham Ribicoff made these remarks to co-panelists Barber Conable, Paul Mac-Avoy, and Wilbur J. Cohen in an AEI Public Policy Forum, moderated by Robert Bork, that ran in the New Hampshire television market (Channel 9) in the fall of 1976. A reprint is available from the American Enterprise Institute (1976/RT/41, pp. 2087-89).

Professor Jerry Hausman of MIT has been a leading researcher into the econometric aspects of what he calls a "progressive linear" income tax, which is economese for the flat-rate system with a generous basic personal exemption. His work is summarized in National Bureau of Economic Research Working Paper #610 (Cambridge, Mass., 1980).

In applying Hausman's analysis, I used a tax-incidence study, Edgar Browning and William Johnson, *The Distribution of the Tax Burden* (Washington D.C.: American Enterprise Institute, 1979). (Study #246.)

Chapter 4—INFLATION AND THE CRISIS IN CONFIDENCE

All of the quotations from S. Herbert Frankel are from *Money and Liberty* (Washington, D.C.: American Enterprise Institute, 1980). (Study #293.)

"Macro-economics" (the government management of aggregate demand) owes most of its underpinnings to John Maynard Keynes, *The General Theory of Employment, Interest and Money* originally published in 1936 (New York: Harcourt Brace, 1964).

In a paper to be found in the English scholarly publication *Economica,* New Series, Vol. 25, November 1958, pp. 283–99, A. W. Phillips first charted, in a curve form, the "trade-off" that seems to exist between wage rates and unemployment. Its current relevance and lack of it are skillfully analyzed by Stephen McNees, "The Phillips Curve: Forward or Backward Looking?" in the *New England Economic Review* (Federal Reserve), July–August 1979, pp. 46–53.

Samuelson and Solow's thesis is spelled out in Jack Kemp, *An American Renaissance* (New York: Harper & Row, 1980).

The full text of the Klein-Simon "debate" can be found in the *Boston Herald American*, 10 October 1976, Section 2, p. 21.

Hobart Rowen's interview with W. Mitchael Blumenthal appeared in *The Washington Post*, 31 October 1979.

For an analysis of the floating exchange-rate system as a conduit for inflation, see Arthur B. Laffer, "The International Monetary Outlook," the H. C. Wainwright Co. (Boston, Mass.) investment letter of 22 November 1977. Laffer draws on the work of his doctoral student Moon H. Lee, whose Ph.D. dissertation *Excess Inflation and Currency Depreciation* was prepared at the University of Chicago Graduate School of Business Administration, 1974, and has been updated by H. C. Wainwright Co.

My column "Are We Headed for a Crash?" appeared in the *Boston Herald American*, 31 March 1978, op-ed page.

Samuelson was interviewed by Gwen Dilliard on WCVB-TV, Boston, Channel 5, over the Labor Day weekend, September 1979.

For a thorough account of the events leading up to the abandonment of the Bretton Woods agreement and the subsequent hyperinflation, see Jude Wanniski, *The Way the World Works* (New York: Basic Books, 1978), pp. 211–16.

Roy W. Jastram has written several analyses of the gold-oil connection in *The Wall Street Journal* and elsewhere. This one appeared 12 December 1979.

While David Stockman took deserved heat for the interview in *Atlantic Monthly*, November 1981, he cannot be faulted for his and Jack Kemp's extraordinarily prescient look at the terrible credit-market disorders facing President Reagan, in their unpublished monograph "Avoiding an Economic Dunkirk" (1981), which accurately warned, among other things, that Federal Reserve Chairman Paul Volcker "had been substantially overshooting [his] 1980 money-supply growth goals ever since midsummer" and that he would have to pursue "a zero money growth rate for the remainder of the year." Unfortunately, that's just what happened, and the country plunged into deep recession by July.

Stockman's "budget scam–money laundry" remarks were contained in an interview with Dennis Farney and Robert Merry, *The Wall Street Journal*, 12 December 1980, cover of second section.

For a lucid discussion of the gold standard's case today, see Lewis Lehrman, "Real Money," *Harper's*, August 1980. See also the transcript of Eugene Birnbaum, "Supply-Side Economics and the Gold Standard," a speech presented to the National Economists Club, Washington, D.C., 4 December 1980.

The employee contract referred to is mentioned in a speech given by Congressman Jack Kemp to the Conference on Supply-Side Economics, held in Atlanta, 17 March 1982, and sponsored by the Federal Reserve Bank of Atlanta.

The most comprehensive brief for an international gold standard revival is contained in Lewis Lehrman, *Monetary Policy, Federal Reserve System, and Gold*, monograph (New York: Morgan Stanley, 25 January 1980).

Chapter 5—IDEAS VS. THE BABEL OF BUREAUCRACY

The Kristol quotation is from his speech to the Associated Industries of Massachusetts (AIM) annual meeting, 22 April 1981.

The MIT study referred to is David Birch, "The Job Generation Process," an unpublished paper done for the Program on Neighborhood and Regional Change, 1979, and covered in Peter Ferrara, "Enterprise Zones," a paper for H. C. Wainwright Co. cited in Stuart M. Butler, *Enterprise Zones* (New York: Universe Books, 1981), pp. 66–67.

See also U.S. House of Representatives Report, *The Future of Small Business in America*, 7 November 1978, and *The State of Small Business*, Report of the President to Congress, March 1982.

F. A. Hayek's full conversation can be found in *A Conversation with Friedrich A. von Hayek: Science and Socialism* (Washington, D. C.: American Enterprise Institute, 1979).

John F. Bibby, Thomas E. Mann, and Norman J. Ornstein, *Vital Statistics on Congress, 1980* (Washington, D.C.: American Enterprise Institute, 1980). (Study #295.)

Tower of Babel: Genesis 11:1–9.

Murray Lincoln, *Vice-President in Charge of Revolution* (New York: McGraw-Hill, 1960).

John Gardner, *Self-Renewal* (New York: Harper–Colophon Books, 1965), pp. 54–64.

Martin Feldstein, in the Introduction to National Bureau of Economic Research, *The American Economy in Transition* (Chicago: University of Chicago Press, 1980).

Alexis de Tocqueville, *Democracy in America*, Part II, Book IV, Chapter VI.

Barney Frank, "The Sorry States—Federalism as a Protection Racket," *The New Republic*, 29 December 1979, pp. 7–10.

Chapter 6—THE ECOLOGY OF THE FREE MARKET

The quote from Ronald Coase is from his paper "The Market for Goods and the Market for Ideas," *American Economic Review*, 1974, pp. 384–85, as quoted in Bernard H. Siegan, *Economic Liberties and the Constitution* (Chicago: University of Chicago Press, 1981), from which other quotations in this chapter are also drawn.

The story of Mary K. Bruch first came to my attention in the *National Review*, 23 January 1981.

See also William Tucker, "The Wreck of the Auto Industry," *Harper's*, November 1980.

The Santa Monica rent-control fiasco was covered by James Ring Adams in *The Wall Street Journal*, 1 July 1981.

See P. H. Hendershott and S. C. Hu, *Inflation and the Benefits from Owner-Occupied Housing*, National Bureau of Economic Research Working Paper #383, August 1979, and the other references cited therein.

See *The Effects of Rent Control and Rent Stabilization in New York City*, The Fifteenth Interim Report of the Temporary Commission on City Finances, New York, June 1977.

The Kevin White interview is in "No Last Hurrah," *Barron's*, 21 November 1977.

See *Report of the Mayor's Committee on Rent Control*, submitted to Kevin H. White, Mayor, City of Boston (Boston, September 1977).

See *Phillips Petroleum v. Wisconsin*, U.S. Supreme Court, 4 June 1954.

Lester Thurow, *Zero-Sum Society* (New York: Basic Books, 1980), is cited several times.

For a complete look at the natural-gas potential, see Bryan Hodgson, "Natural Gas: The Search Goes On," *National Geographic*, November 1978.

The now famous Energy Research and Development Administration–Market Oriented Program Planning Study was ordered to be destroyed by President Carter in 1978, but copies of its three versions (original and two revisions) should be available by inquiring at the U.S. Department of Energy. The existence of the ERDA–MOPPS study was revealed in *The Wall Street Journal*, 27 April 1977, editorial page.

See Ernest J. Oppenheimer, *Natural Gas: The New Energy Leader*, available from the author, 40 Central Park South, 9D, New York, N.Y. 10019.

See William Tucker, "The Energy Crisis Is Over!" *Harper's*, November 1981, and Fred J. Cook, "The Natural Gas Boom," *The Nation*, 12 July 1980.

W. Mark Crain, *Vehicle Inspection Systems: How Effective?* (Washington, D.C.: American Enterprise Institute, 1980). (Study #258.)

Elizabeth Whelan, "Chemicals, Cancerphobia and Communication," *Imprimis* (Hillsdale, Mich.: Hillsdale College), April 1980.

The Wall Street Journal editorial appeared on 11 February 1977, p. 8.

See Milton Friedman, *Capitalism and Freedom* (Chicago: University of Chicago Press, 1962).

Chapter 7—SOCIAL SPENDING, SUBSIDIES, AND THE PURSUIT OF POVERTY

One of the polls referred to is by V. Lance Tarrance Associates, Houston, Texas, 2–8 April 1981, for the National Federation of Independent Businesses. This sample of 1,500 covered both retirement income financing and attitudes toward social spending programs.

The analysis on p. 160 was drawn from the following table used in a column by the author on 8 April 1980:

THE DECLINING "EFFICIENCY" OF SOCIAL SPENDING
(in constant 1972 dollars)

	Total social spending (in thousands)	Persons living below poverty line	Annual incremental cost for each person lifted out of poverty
1950	$ 43,810,590	45,833,570	————
1955	64,283,371	42,976,100	$7,165
1960	76,161,351	40,108,962	$4,143
1966	108,910,890	28,894,320	$2,920
1970	159,697,890	25,814,620	$16,491
1977	269,865,910	25,158,080	$167,939

SOURCE: U.S. Social Security Administration.

George Gilder, *Wealth and Poverty* (New York: Basic Books, 1981), pp. 133–34.

Martin Kilson, "Black Social Classes and Intergenerational Poverty," *The Public Interest,* Summer 1981.

Morton Paglin, "Poverty in the U.S.: A Re-evaluation," Heritage *Policy Review*, Spring 1979.

For more statistical backup for the impact of welfare on black and white poverty populations, the following table from the author's 13 June 1980 column is offered:

POVERTY POPULATION ON AFDC, 1978

	Whites	Blacks
Percentage of total poverty population on AFDC	32.4%	64.9%
Percentage of poverty population under 45 on AFDC	46.6%	82.0%

SOURCES: U.S. Bureau of the Census; U.S. Department of Health and Human Services.

The National Bureau of Economic Research published a "Summary Report of Youth Employ-ment" (Cambridge, Mass., 1980), by Richard B. Freeman and David A. Wise, which provided the following detailed table as a backup:

EMPLOYMENT AND UNEMPLOYMENT RATES

MEN	WHITES				BLACKS AND OTHERS			
	1954	1964	1969	1977	1954	1964	1969	1977
Percentage employed by age								
16-17	40.6	36.5	42.7	44.3	40.4	27.6	28.4	18.9
18-19	61.3	57.7	61.8	65.2	66.5	51.8	51.1	36.9
20-24	77.9	79.3	78.8	80.5	75.9	78.1	77.3	61.2
Percentage of labor force unemployed by age								
16-17	14.0	16.1	12.5	17.6	13.4	25.9	24.7	38.7
18-19	13.0	13.4	7.9	13.0	14.7	23.1	19.0	36.1
20-24	9.8	7.4	4.6	9.3	16.9	12.6	8.4	21.7
WOMEN								
Percentage employed by age								
16-17	25.8	25.3	30.3	37.5	19.8	12.5	16.9	12.5
18-19	47.2	43.0	49.2	54.3	29.9	32.9	33.9	28.0
20-24	41.6	45.3	53.3	61.4	43.1	43.7	51.5	45.4
Percentage of labor force unemployed by age								
16-17	12.0	17.1	13.8	18.2	19.1	36.5	31.2	44.7
18-19	9.4	13.2	10.0	14.2	21.6	29.2	25.7	37.4
20-24	6.4	7.1	5.5	9.3	13.2	18.3	12.0	23.6

SOURCE: National Bureau of Economic Research, *Summary Report on Youth Employment*, 1980.

See the 1981 Massachusetts Budget—analysis by Mark Ferber, staff director for the Senate Ways and Means Committee, as presented in Senate #2200, 15 May 1980, pages 18–5 through 18–12.

The analysis of welfare benefits and state economic growth appeared in my column "Welfare and Unemployment: There is a Connection," *Boston Herald American*, 13 June 1980, and in a follow-up column, 28 March 1982.

General Accounting Office (GAO) study HRD–81–48, dated 3 March 1981, shows the following trends and claim:

	Number of disabled workers receiving benefits	Annual benefits (in millions)	Average monthly benefits
1965	988,074	$ 1,159	$ 98
1970	1,492,948	2,352	$131
1975	2,488,774	6,747	$226
1981	2,869,000	16,978	$410
1985	2,991,000	24,000	$655

"As a result of SSA's [previous] . . . poor management . . . as many as 584,000 beneficiaries who do not currently meet SSA's eligibility criteria may be receiving disability benefits. These beneficiaries represent over $2 billion annually in trust fund costs. . . . substantial savings could be achieved if SSA focused on this problem."

For further discussion of the Social Security disability programs, see *Financing Social Security*, an American Enterprise Symposium (#78-H) chaired and edited by Colin D. Campbell (Washington, D.C.: American Enterprise Institute, 1978).

See Michael Novak, *The American Vision: An Essay on the Future of Democratic Capitalism* (Washington, D.C.: American Enterprise Institute, 1978).

For a discussion of the need for "disinvestment," see Lester Thurow, *Zero-Sum Society* (New York: Basic Books, 1980), pp. 76–102.

See Paul W. McCracken, "A United States Industrial Policy," *The Wall Street Journal*, 12 January 1981, editorial page, p. 20.

Chapter 8—MASSACHUSETTS ON THE LAFFER CURVE

Clayton Jones, "A Surprise Called High-Tech," *The Christian Science Monitor*, 10 March 1981, 20-page pullout section, p. B-1.

A. B. Laffer Associates, *An Analysis of Fiscal Policy and Economic Growth in Massachusetts*, a study for the Massachusetts Business Roundtable (Boston, 16 April 1981).

David Hume, *Essay: Of Taxes* (1756) in *Gateway to Great Books* (Chicago: Encyclopaedia Britannica, 1963), Vol. 7, pp. 85–88.

Warren Brookes, "A Tale of Two States," *Boston Sunday Advertiser (Herald American)*, 11 January 1976, Section Five, p. A-2.

David Wendell in *David L. Babson Company Weekly Staff Letter*, 26 February 1976.

Colin D. and Rosemary G. Campbell, *Comparative Study of the Fiscal Systems of New Hampshire and Vermont, 1940–74* (Hampton, N.H.: The Wheelabrator Foundation, July 1976). See also Colin D. Campbell and Edward G. Gagnon, *Rising Tax Burdens in Massachusetts, New Hampshire, and Vermont, 1957–1976* (Maynard, Mass.: Data General Corporation, 1978).

For backup detail see Warren Brookes, "What Massachusetts Welfare State Is Doing to Us," *Boston Herald American*, 4 March 1977.

Analysis by Alan Reynolds, chief economist for the First National Bank of Chicago, contained in the bank's *Monthly Letter*, June 1977.

Changing Patterns of Federal Aid to State and Local Governments (Washington, D.C.: General Accounting Office, PAD-78-15, 20 December 1977).

For further detail on the rising calls for tax cuts, see my columns in the *Boston Herald American*, 9, 14, and 15 March 1978.

For the origin of the Proposition 2½ referendum idea, see my front-page column, "It Might Well Bring Us Economic Revival," *Boston Herald American*, 8 June 1978.

For a detailed look at the primary election analysis, see my column, *Boston Herald American*, 28 September 1978.

Robert J. Genetski and Young D. Chin, *The Impact of State and Local Taxes on Economic Growth*, a study for the Harris Economic Research Office Service, a division of the Harris Bank and Trust Company of Chicago, 3 November 1978.

James Ring Adams, "Taxachusetts Turns Around," *The Wall Street Journal*, 5 February 1980, editorial page.

The regression analysis referred to by David Ranson (a former partner of A. B. Laffer) may be found in the previously cited Laffer report to the Massachusetts Business Roundtable, p. 8.

The 1983 Fiscal Budget for the Commonwealth of Massachusetts (Governor Edward King), H-1, Vol. 1, Economy Section, pp 1–3.

Joint Economic Committee of Congress, Hearing on the New Federalism, 24 February 1982.

Chapter 9—GOODNESS AND THE GNP

Walter Lippmann, *The Good Society* (Boston: Little, Brown, 1943).

William Barrett, in *Capitalism, Socialism and Democracy*, a symposium that first appeared in *Commentary*, April 1978, and was reprinted by the American Enterprise Institute, Washington, D. C., 1979.

Research and Forecasts, Inc., New York City, *Report on American Values in the 80's: The Impact of Belief* (Hartford: Connecticut Mutual Life Insurance Company, April 1981).

David Broder made his comment on a PBS telecast, "Washington Week in Review," 12 September 1980.

Alexis de Tocqueville, *Democracy in America*.

Michael Novak (ed.), *Capitalism and Socialism: A Theological Inquiry* (Washington, D.C.: American Enterprise Institute, 1979). Contains papers by Irving Kristol, Seymour Martin Lipset, Peter Berger, Muhammad Abdul-Rauf, Ben J. Wattenberg, and Penn Kemble. See also Irving Kristol, *Two Cheers for Capitalism* (New York: Basic Books, 1978).

For further background, see my four-part series, "Capitalism and Christianity: Can They Coexist?" *Boston Herald American*, 18, 20, 21, and 25 December 1979.

Norman Podhoretz, "The New Defenders of Capitalism," *Harvard Business Review*, March-April 1981.

St. Paul: Hebrews 11:12.

Luke 6:38.

Gallup Poll on religious belief, 1975. A new Gallup study for the Center of Applied Research in the Apostolate (CARA), Washington, D.C., includes over 15,000 interviews in Europe and over 2,000 in the United States. Assembled for public release in September 1982, its preliminary findings show consistency with the Connecticut Mutual Life poll cited above.

Peter Berger's paper appeared in Novak (ed.), *Capitalism and Socialism*, cited above.

Corliss Lamont, *The Philosophy of Humanism*, 6th edition (New York: Ungar, 1982).

Matthew 26:31–33.

Luke 17:20.

Ralph Waldo Emerson, *Progress and Culture*, a Phi Beta Kappa address, 18 July 1876.

Michael Novak, "The Myth of Compassion," *National Review*, 7 December 1979, p. 1564.

Karl Menninger, *Whatever Became of Sin?* (New York: Hawthorne, 1973).

John 10:10.

John 12:3–8.

Luke 10:40–42.

Matthew 25:14–30.

Leonard E. Read, "Statism and Goodness," *Notes from FEE* (Foundation for Economic Education, Irvington-on-Hudson, N.Y.), March 1981.

Juan A. Tamay, UPI story on Pope John Paul's visit to Mexico City and Puebla, 28 January 1979. See also "A Church for the Poor," *Newsweek*, 26 February, 1979.

II Corinthians 3:17.

Proverbs 29:18.

Jeremy Rifkin, *Entropy* (New York: Viking Press, 1980).

John 16:33.

I Corinthians 15:12, 13, 17, 22.

Index

Adams, James Ring, 15, 135, 183, 196
age of limits, 13, 22, 24
aggregate demand, 8, 21
Agriculture, U.S. Census of, 32
Agriculture, U.S. Department of: Economic
    Research Service, 32; farmland loss, 32–33;
    farm subsidies, 174–75
Aid to Families with Dependent Children
    (AFDC), 38, 162, 166–68
American Economic Review, 30
American Economy in Transition, 119
American Enterprise Institute (AEI), 25, 112,
    145, 207
American Humanist Association, 212–13
American Renaissance, An, 84
"American Values in the 80's, Report on," 204
Atlanta, Ga., 43–45
Atlanta Constitution, 43
Atlantic Monthly, 181
Australia, 38
auto industry, 133–35, 177–79
auto inspections, 145–46

baby boom, 46, 166
bailout, 172–76
Bakke case, 42
balanced budget, 54–55
banks, 80
Bible, 35, 77, 114, 206, 212
Birmingham, Ala., 43–45
black family, 162–64
blacks, 43–45
Blumenthal, W. Michael, 88, 92
Boston, Mass., 135, 138–39, 164, 190–91, 198
Boston Globe, 162, 186, 192, 195
Boston Herald-American, 8, 15, 183, 195
Bretton Woods Agreement, 84, 94, 97–98
Brookings Institution, 26
bureaucrats, 18, 36, 48, 77, 108, 110, 114–15,
    120–21
Butz, Earl, 174

California, 181, 193, 197
Cambridge, Mass., 27
Campbell, Colin, 15, 188–89
Campbell, Rosemary, 188
Canada, 38; economic growth and population,
    40; inflation, 91; price decontrols, 143
capital, human, 45–46
capital dilution, theory of, 40
capital formation, 7, 8, 28, 48, 61
capital-gains tax, 53, 59–63

capitalism, democratic, 214, 220, 223
Carter, Jimmy, 14–15, 62, 76, 83, 83–85, 111;
    civil rights and, 43; inflation and, 88–89,
    91–92; natural gas and, 141–43; natural
    resources and, 22, 31; pessimism of, 23; price
    supports, 175; taxes and, 66–67, 71–73
*Catalogue of Research Issues for Understanding
    National Economic Planning*, 128
CBS–*New York Times* polls, 23
charity, 217
CETA. *See* Comprehensive Employment and
    Training Act
Christianity, 208–13, 220, 224
Christian Science Monitor, 28–29, 180
Chrysler Corporation, 102, 134–35, 172–73, 176
Citizens for Limited Taxation (CLT), 194
Civil Aeronautics Board (CAB), 152
civil liberties, 19, 24
civil rights, 43–45, 152–53
Commerce, U.S. Department of, 108–9, 193
Communist Manifesto, 52
compassion, 14–15, 157, 211, 215
competition, 123–24, 132
Comprehensive Employment and Training Act
    (CETA), 158, 198
Congress, U.S., 48, 55, 58, 73; House of
    Representatives, 132; Joint Economic
    Committee (JEC), 200; regulations, 112–13
Constitution, U.S., 123–24, 153
consumer advocates, 129–30
Consumer Price Index (CPI), 82, 84, 91, 98,
    113, 151
Consumer Reports, 131
corporate tax cuts, 57, 63
COLA (Cost-of-Living Adjustment), 84
credit, 99–102, 135
crime, 162
Cryovac, 222
Cuba, 51, 77
Cuban refugees, 37–38

debt, federal, 105
decontrol, 134, 141, 143–45
deficits, 48, 79
demand elasticity, 53
demand-side economics, 12, 18–20, 22, 25
Democracy in America, 205
Denison, Edward F., 25, 41
dependence, 116–17, 158
Depression, Great, 15, 159
deregulation, 124–26, 153
Detroit, Mich., 133–35, 164

devaluation, 89–90
Dewey, Bradley, Sr., 222
disability, 170–71
Dukakis, Michael, 181–82, 183, 192, 194–95

easy money, 85–88
economic freedom, 12, 16, 18–19, 77
economic growth, 7–8, 13, 18–19, 20; limits to,
    29; population and, 40–41; through
    technology, 26–27, 36
Economic Liberties and the Constitution, 153
economic planning, centralized, 128
Economic Research Service, 32
economic rights, 154–55
Economist, 25
ecosystem, 126
education, public, 40, 120–21
Education, U.S. Office of, 122
Efron, Edith, 151–52
Einstein, Albert, 33, 34
election of 1980, 19, 23
employees, government, 108, 115, 118
Energy, U.S. Department of, 135, 140
energy crisis, 20, 21, 28–29, 36, 140–41
"Energy Crisis," 28
Energy Research and Development Administra-
    tion (ERDA)–MOPPS study, 141–43
entropy, 12, 23, 28, 34–35, 224–25
envy, politics of, 15, 18, 49, 69, 82
equity capital market, 60–61
exchange rates, floating, 91
exports, 27, 177–78, 179

failures, corporate, 172–76
faith, 23; and capitalist production, 24; triumph
    of metaphysical over physical, 25, 36
federal aid, 191–92
Federal Financing Bank (FFB), 101–2
Federal Power Commission, 139
Federal Register, 110, 113
Federal Reserve, 64, 80–81, 83; crackdowns, 86,
    91, 101; Gold Window, 95, 98–99
Federal Trade Commission (FTC), 132
Feldstein, Martin, 11, 15, 119–20, 166
female-headed households, 163–64
Finance Committee, U.S. Senate, 72–73
Florida, 38, 195
Food and Drug Administration (FDA), 130
Ford, Gerald, 15
Ford Motor Company, 63
France, 91, 152
Frankel, S. Herbert, 79–81, 105
Freeman, Richard, 166–67
free trade, 178
Frey, H. Thomas, 32
Friedman, Milton, 15; on bailouts, 173; on flat-
    rate tax, 68, 75; on government mismanage-
    ment, 151; on liberty, 155; on price
    regulation, 139
Frostbelt, 124
Fuller, R. Buckminster, 15, 17, 25, 29, 226; on
    living standard, 30; on productivity, 33; on
    synergy, 35–36; on wealth, 34, 48–49

Galbraith, John Kenneth, 7, 89, 181
gasoline, 133–34
General Accounting Office (GAO): study on
    federal aid, 170–71, 191–92
General Motors Corporation, 132, 134
Germany, 25, 40, 87; DM (Deutschmark),
    91–92; exports, 177, 179; high technology,
    110–11; inflation rate, 90, 94; oil prices,
    96–97; tight money policies, 89

Gilder, George, 16, 31; faith and capitalism, 24;
    statistics on family life, 163–64
Global 2000, 31–32
gold panic of 1979, 93–94
gold standard, 84, 94–95, 104–5
"golden-oil" standard, 95–99
Great Society, 59, 68, 158–59, 161, 165, 166
Gross National Product (GNP), 7, 48, 58, 66;
    goodness and, 205–6, 226; in Cuba, 51; in
    Japan, 28; in U.S., 83, 118–20, 151

Harper's, 103, 145
Harvard Business Review, 208
Hausman, Jerry, 74–75
Hayek, F. A., 28, 109, 152, 155
Health, Education & Welfare, U.S. Department
    of (HEW), 168
high technology, 13, 50; in Massachusetts, 8, 26,
    180–81, 201; in the U.S., 27–28, 111
home ownership, 136–37
Howell, James, 192–93
Hudson Institute, 31
humanism, 212–13
humanitarianism, 212
Humphrey-Hawkins Bill, 128

IBM, 109
immigrants: Cuban, 37–38; economic growth
    and, 38–40; Pilgrims, 37; University of
    Illinois study, 39
Immigration and Refugee Policy, Select Commis-
    sion on, 39
Income and Education, U.S. Census Survey of
    (1976), 39
Industry, 193
inflation, 11, 14, 15, 19–21, 27, 64, 68, 95–98,
    100–102; diminishing faith and, 80; housing
    values and, 137; money supply and, 81,
    90–91; as a moral issue, 105–6
innovation, 12, 25–28, 33, 38, 132
interest rates, 19, 86–88
Internal Revenue Service (IRS), 75
Italy, 40, 91

Japan, 25, 41; culture, 207; exports, 177, 179;
    high technology, 26, 110–11; inflation rates,
    94; life expectancy, 148; oil prices, 96–97;
    productivity, 28; tax rates, 125; tight money
    policies, 89
Jastram, Roy, 15, 95, 99
Jefferson, Thomas, 17, 19
Jews, orthodox, 209
jobs, 84; blacks and, 44, 166–67; in high
    technology, 46; immigrants and, 38; labor
    shortages, 47–48; small businesses and, 108–9
Johnson, Lyndon B., 158, 160. See also Great
    Society
Joint Economic Committee, 58
Jones, Paul Hastings, 140–41
Judaism, 210, 212–13, 220

Kemp, Jack, 15, 84
Kemp-Roth tax cut (1981), 59, 76
Kendrick, John W., 25, 26, 41
Kennedy, Edward M., 52, 60–61, 89, 125,
    152–53, 181, 200
Kennedy, John F., 51, 56–57, 58, 61, 66, 68,
    160–61
Keynes, John Maynard, 54–55, 59, 79, 83, 84,
    103
Keynesian economics, 11, 20, 80–81, 84; danger
    of, 79; demand and economy, 19, 21; failure
    of, 83; "macro-machine," 108

King, Edward J., 140, 182, 195–97, 199–201
Klein, Lawrence, 85–86
Knudsen, Christian, 142–43
Khomeini, Ayatollah, 208
Kristol, Irving, 15, 108, 207, 209, 213, 215
Kuznets, Simon, 40–41

labor, 46–47, 48–49
Labor, U.S. Department of: study of urban family
    budgets (1978), 191
Laffer, Arthur, 15, 59, 184; devaluation, 90;
    Laffer curve, 53, 61, 66, 180–81, 183,
    196–97; tax wedge, 64
lawyers, 110–12
Lee, Moon H., 89–90
Lehrman, Lewis, 15, 103–4
Liberty City (Miami, Fla.), 164
life expectancy, 148–49
limits to growth, 22–23
Limits to Growth, 40
Lincoln, Murray, 114–15
loan guarantees, federal, 102

McCracken, Paul, 178
McCulloch v. Maryland, 50
McGill, Ralph, 43–44
McGovern, George, 52, 183
Mahler, Ernst, 223–24
Malthus, Thomas, 12–14, 25, 40, 49
Management and Budget, U.S. Office of (OMB),
    109, 171
Marx, Karl, 24; Communist Manifesto, 52;
    Marxism, 18, 69, 220; on private property,
    155; on wealth limits, 12, 14, 25, 49
Massachusetts, 14, 38, 125, 185, 216; AFDC,
    167–68; auto inspections, 167–68; Carter
    primary, 71; federal aid, 191–92; gross state
    product, 51; growth and, 8, 26, 123, 180; high
    technology and, 8, 26, 180–81, 193, 201–2;
    Proposition 2½, 8, 162, 182, 195, 197–200;
    tax cuts, 181–82, 192–93, 196; tax burden,
    183, 186, 190; wages, 188
Massachusetts Business Roundtable, 183
Mellon, Andrew, 53–55, 57, 59
mercantilism, 19
microeconomics, 12
misery index, 67
mixed economy, 152
monetarism, 64, 80–81
money supply growth, 64–65, 99
Mundell, Robert, 15, 64, 95

Nader, Ralph, 132–33
National Bureau of Economic Research (NBER),
    15, 74, 136, 166–67
National Commission on Materials Policy, 29
National Commission on Supplies and Shortages,
    29
National Geographic, 140, 144
National Highway Traffic Safety Administration,
    146
National Science Foundation, 109
natural gas, 139–45, 176
Natural Gas Deregulation Act of 1978, 144
Natural Gas: The New Energy Leader, 144
natural resources, 7, 12–13, 22, 25, 28–31
Nebbia v. New York, 154
New Deal, 113, 117
"new federalism," 124
New Hampshire, 122, 123, 190; growth and, 187;
    low taxes, 186, 189; population gains, 185;
    primary, 184
New Jersey, 125

New Republic, 124–25
New Social Gospel, 210
New State Ice Co. v. Liebman, 154
New York City, 14, 102, 114, 125; bailout of,
    176; fiscal crisis, 123–24; rent control,
    137–38
New York Times, 55
Nixon, Richard M., 91, 95, 98–99
no-fault policies, 215–16
Northeast, 124; decline of, 23; gas dependency,
    140
Novak, Michael, 172, 211, 214, 223

Occupational Safety and Health Administration
    (OSHA), 146–48
oil, 7; decontrol of, 15, 90, 141; embargo on,
    134; prices, 96–99, 139, 142, 178;
    production decline, 21, 28; technology, 33
O'Neill, Thomas P., 22, 181
OPEC (Organization of Petroleum Exporting
    Countries), 20, 94, 96–99, 134, 139, 142,
    145, 178
Ornstein, Norman, 110
OSHA. See Occupational Safety and Health
    Administration

Paul, St., 24, 25, 210, 224
Pennsylvania, 125
Phillips Curve, 83–86
Phillips Petroleum v. Wisconsin, 139
Podhoretz, Norman, 204, 208
Poland, 77
pollution, 27, 31
price controls, 134–35, 143
prime interest rate, 87
Procter and Gamble, 131
productivity, 12, 20–21, 25; agricultural, 32;
    decline of, 24, 61, 67, 107–8; progress, 51;
    technological knowledge and, 26; wealth
    and, 33
Professional Employees Federation (New York),
    103
profit motive, 221–22
Proposition 2½, 8, 162, 182, 195, 197–200
Proposition 13, 181, 193, 197
protectionism, 177–79
Public Interest, 15, 143, 164

Ranson, David, 15, 197
Raushenbush, Walter, 210
real wages, 20
Reagan, Ronald, 22, 48, 57, 124; budget cuts,
    162, 168; food stamp cuts, 157–58; "new
    federalism," 124; price supports, 175;
    revolution, 18; Social Security cuts, 169; tax
    plan, 66, 76
recession, 64, 66–67, 74–75, 84
redistribution, 11, 12, 14, 18, 21, 49; demand-
    side economics, 25; through taxation, 69–70
regulation, 14, 18, 19–20, 36, 107, 110–13,
    132–33; safety, 145–51
reindustrialization, 8, 13, 36, 152
religion: and commitment, 204; debate on view
    of universe, 23
Rely, 131
rent control, 135–39
research, basic, 110
Rifkin, Jeremy, 32, 33, 34; entropy law, 35, 224
Roosevelt, Franklin D., 107

safety regulations, 145–51
Samuelson, Paul, 84, 94, 128
Santa Monica, Calif., 135

SAT scores, 121–22
savings and investment, 19, 20, 21, 26, 63
Say, Jean-Baptiste: Say's Law, 19, 210; wealth, 12
Schultz, Charles, 85
Science, 29
Section "8," 137, 176
segregation, 42–45
Selma, Ala., 44
semi-conductor industry, 7
shipbuilding industry, 173
shortages: in labor, 46–48; in natural gas, 140, 143; in rental housing, 135
Siegan, Bernard, 153–54
Simon, Julian, 15, 29, 32; on decline in prices of raw materials, 30; on people as resource, 37, 46
Simon, William E., 73, 85–86
sin, 208–9
Singapore, 42
small businesses, 108–9
Smith, Adam, 12, 19, 24
socialism: "lemon socialism," 175–76; and religion, 211
social programs, 117, 157–58
Social Security, 21, 40, 72, 118, 170–71; COLA's, 84; Reagan cuts, 169
social spending, 12, 18, 69, 124, 157–62
Solow, Robert, 41, 84
South Bronx (N.Y.), 164
South Carolina, 44
South Korea, 27
Soviet Union, 31, 77
Spain, 27
spending, government, 117
"stagflation," 21, 64, 67, 84
Steiger, William, 61
Steiger Amendment, 62
Stockman, David, 101–2, 181
subsidies, 136–38, 172–74, 175–76
Sunbelt, 23, 43, 48, 124–25, 179, 188, 190, 193
supply-side economics, 7–9, 18–20, 22, 55, 81, 103; growth and, 25; sum of individual efforts, 108; tax wedge, 64–65; "trickle down," 76–77
Supreme Court, U.S.: *Bakke* case, 42; *McCulloch v. Maryland*, 50; *Nebbia v. New York*, 154; *New State Ice Co. v. Liebman*, 154; *Phillips Petroleum v. Wisconsin*, 139
Sweden, 117
synergy, 35–36

Taiwan, 27
tariffs, 177
taxation, 14–15, 21, 60–62, 72; bracket-creep, 59, 68, 71; capital-gains, 53, 59–63; cut proposals, 18, 73; flat-rate tax, 68–69, 75–76; graduated income tax, 50–51, 56, 68–69, 71, 74; in Massachusetts, 180–202; loopholes, 52, 68, 72–73; marginal rates, 51, 53, 56,

58–60, 63, 71, 74–76, 118, 137, 162; progressive, 50–53, 55, 68, 75; Reagan plan (1981), 63, 66, 76; tax wedge, 63–67
Taxation: The People's Business, 53, 58
"taxflation," 20, 52, 70
Texas, 169, 191
Thatcher, Margaret, 80
Theresa, Mother, 214
thermodynamics, first law of, 34; second law of, 11, 25, 34, 114
Third World, 25, 42, 69, 148
Thomson, Meldrim, 186–87
Thurow, Lester, 139, 173, 175, 176, 177, 181
tight money, 20, 86–87, 89
Tocqueville, Alexis de, 113, 115, 205–6, 226
Treasury, U.S. Department of the, 66, 73, 101
"trickle down," 18, 57, 59, 76–78, 214
TRIS, 129–30

Ultimate Resource, 29
underground economy, 52
unemployment, 14, 19; in auto industry, 133; in the 1970s, 83, 85; in World War II, 13; of teens and blacks, 48, 162, 165–67
unions, 47, 84, 188
United Kingdom, 19; devaluations, 89; easy money, 87; the dole, 77; high tax rates, 63, 125; inflation, 80; productivity, 26; social programs, 117

Vermont, 189–90
Vietnam war, 68, 205
Vital Statistics on Congress, 112
Volcker, Paul, 80

Wall Street, 81
Wall Street Journal, 15, 99, 102, 143, 144, 150, 196
Wanniski, Jude, 15, 64, 95
War on Poverty, 158, 160, 165
Washington, D.C., 44, 114, 136
Washington Post, 103, 113, 130, 143
wealth, nature of, 12, 19, 24–25, 179; limitless, 34; of ideas, 30; potential of, 70–71
Wealth and Poverty, 9, 16, 24, 163
Wealth of Nations, 19, 24
Weinberg, A. M., 30–31
welfare, 40, 69, 120, 162–63, 164–69
Wendell, David, 187–88
Whelan, Elizabeth, 149–50
White, Kevin, 138–39, 183
Wise, John, 166–67
World War II: and U.S. economy, 13; progressive tax rates, 56; synthetic rubber, 222

Zaire, 28
zero population growth, 46, 48
zero-sum economy, 12, 18, 23
Zero-Sum Society, 175